ETHICS IN SOCIAL MARKETING

ALAN R. ANDREASEN, EDITOR

GEORGETOWN UNIVERSITY PRESS
WASHINGTON, D.C.

Georgetown University Press, Washington, D.C.

Printed in the United States of America

10 9 8 7 6 5 4 3 2 1 2001

This volume is printed on acid-free offset book paper.

Library of Congress Cataloging-in-Publication Data

Andreasen, Alan R., 1934–
Ethics in social marketing / by Alan R. Andreasen.
p. cm.
Includes index.
ISBN 0-87840-819-3 (cloth : alk. paper) —
ISBN 0-87840-820-7 (pbk. : alk. paper)
1. Social marketing—Moral and ethical aspects. I. Title.

HF5414 .A53 2001
174′.4—dc21 00-061750

Contents

Preface

This edited volume grew out of a seminar series on social marketing ethics conducted at Georgetown University's McDonough School of Business in the Spring of 1999. The seminar series, partly funded by the Connelly Program in Business Ethics, represented a recognition of two important forces.

First, the field of social marketing has grown dramatically. From its early beginnings in international family planning work and in the domestic National High Blood Pressure Education Program, social marketing has expanded and broadened its reach and impact. It is now routinely employed by agencies as diverse as the Centers for Disease Control and Prevention; the World Bank; and New Zealand's Children, Young Persons and Their Families Service. Social marketing has moved beyond its central focus on health care to attack problems of crime, consumer debt, long term insurance, environmental protection, and the treatment of animals.

A raft of consulting agencies has sprung to life. Social marketing job titles are common. There is an annual conference now in its sixth year. Texts and readings books have come to market, a journal has emerged, and social marketing centers and institutes have sprung up in such diverse locations as Strathclyde, Scotland; Washington, D.C., and Tampa, Florida. Corporations have found social marketing attractive for their own social programs and as an outlet for executives seeking to apply their marketing skills in areas beyond the commercial world.

The second important force is the growing recognition on the part of social marketers that, if the field is to grow significantly as a respected profession, it must pay careful attention to the ethical standards and practices of its practitioners. Because social marketing concepts and tools are becoming more widely adopted, they can—and will—come under increasing scrutiny. Two examples in early 2000 indicate the kinds of issues that can be raised.

On January 9, 2000, the CBS program *60 Minutes* presented a segment called "Adopt Me." This program portrayed a number of innovative methods to bring adoptable children to the attention of possible future parents. Among the approaches described was a series of picnics sponsored by adoption agencies at which adoptable kids could play and talk with potential parents in a natural setting. The belief of the marketers was that this would provide more data to the adults and create interpersonal chemistry higher than is possible with more conventional "catalogues" and web pages. However, many critics argued that this approach was cruel to the children, exposing them to rejection of a very personal nature. The interviewer, Morley Safer, likened the approach to the same way one markets automobiles. Critics said that children are not cars and should not be treated as such.

Also, in early January 2000, *Salon* magazine reported on a controversial element of the anti-drug program of the U.S. Office of National Drug Control Policy (ONDCP). ONDCP employs a significant amount of paid advertising in its various campaigns and it requires television networks and other media to donate a specific amount of time or space to anti-drug ads. ONDCP also recognizes the power of popular television programs to influence attitudes and behavior. It had adopted a well-tested social marketing approach that for decades introduced family planning and child health themes into radio and television soap operas in developing countries. ONDCP encouraged writers and producers to include anti-drug messages in their program scripts and, as an incentive, agreed that ONDCP would "give back" some of the advertising time networks were required to donate—thus allowing them to sell this time for further profit. What *Salon* magazine and many other critics found troubling was ONDCP's requirement that the networks clear the program ideas with them *before* the programs were aired—ostensibly to insure that they met ONDCP's guidelines for credit. To many critics, this smacked of prior influence on programming, possible censorship and, if extended, unacceptable intrusion of government into what we see and hear over powerful media channels.

The specter of Big Brother was clearly in the minds of many of these critics.

As these examples suggest, social marketing presents us with some extremely powerful tools that can have important effects. However, those who use them will come under high public scrutiny to ensure that they are used wisely. And, many would argue that this *should* be the case. There is a minority view that social marketers can afford to have lower ethical standards than does the commercial sector when it comes to the strategies and tactics they use because they are seeking noble goals. For example, it should be acceptable, this position holds, to withhold information from target audiences that, if divulged, might discourage desirable behaviors. They would also say that it is acceptable to exaggerate risks or distort facts if this will motivate people to do something they really "need" to do! The justification here is that the higher social goal that is being pursued justifies what in commercial contexts would be seen as shoddy and sinister practice.

There are others who argue that social marketers should be held to higher standards than the private sector for the very same reason, namely that they are pursuing noble goals. At one level, as Kirby and Andreasen note in this volume, it is hard to argue that one is on a noble quest if one is using ignoble means. Added to this argument is the fact that most social marketing programs are funded by government agencies using the public's tax dollars or nonprofit organizations funded by private charitable contributions. These sources of funds bestow a public trust on social marketers who therefore must be held to the highest ethical standards in their uses of this funding.

Objectives and Organization of the Book

This volume offers a series of papers designed to achieve several objectives. First, they seek to introduce the reader to some of the major ethical problems that social marketers face in the field. The intended reader here is both the student seeking to learn about the many dimensions of social marketing, and the practitioner who may not be aware of the many issues that ought to be addressed by themselves and the organizations in which they operate. Several of the chapters provide such examples, often drawn directly or indirectly from personal experience. Other chapters focus on specific contexts in which many ethical issues arise. For example, the chapter by Andreasen and Drumwright discusses a range of problems that can occur when social marketers form alliances with others, particularly corporations in the private sector. Brenkert discusses a range of issues in international contexts whereas Davidson and Novelli consider the use of social marketing approaches by corporate, rather than government or nonprofit, marketers.

A second objective is to offer readers a sense of the complexity of the ethical dilemmas that social marketers face. In the lead chapter, William Smith of the Academy for Educational Development describes a number of ethical challenges and makes clear that the question of what is ethical and what is not is very much contingent on who the actor is, the context in which the action takes place, and who is impacted by the action.

A third objective is to provide frameworks within which individuals and organizations can make ethical decisions. Rothschild, for example, raises the "meta-issue" of whether and under what circumstances one should use social marketing solutions to a social behavior challenge as opposed to using simple education or more draconian legal solutions. For those using social marketing, Bill Smith proposes that in each ethical dilemma, managers consider seven factors: the actor, action, context, intended audience, unintended audience(s), and the consequences for both.

Several chapters introduce philosophical rules to guide decision makers. Michael Basil distinguishes between ontological and deontological rules for making ethical judgments. Craig Smith introduces social contract theory as an alternative way to assess ethical problems. Kirby and Andreasen offer a specific practical format, the Social Marketing Ethical Assessment Matrix, for assessing the consequences of marketing programs and program elements.

The final objective of this volume is to increase the likelihood that social marketers will, in fact, pay increasing attention to maintaining high ethical standards. Kirby and Andreasen propose a strategy for marketing ethical practice to social marketers through the kind of segmentation approach the field typically uses. Basil emphasizes the teaching of ethics and considers when and how this should be done. Andreasen and Drumwright also consider the issue of how to develop and maintain ethical standards, proposing industry-wide codes of conduct, among other approaches.

The Bottom Line

In the latter discussions, authors recognize that improving a profession's ethical practice has two major components. First, individuals and organizations in the profession need to make ethical judgments more often. This requires that they be alert to the *need* for such judgments. It also requires that they or their organizations have some formal or informal procedure for detecting occasions for ethical analysis. The second requirement for improved ethical standards is that the field more often "take the high road." This means that executives should question or forego strategies that raise ethical questions. It means that organizations should spend the extra money to research a tactic's or strategy's unfortunate side effects. It means they should be more transparent in their actions, and in controversial situations, they should explain their well-reasoned positions rather than hoping no one will notice.

Finally, we must remind the reader that the ultimate guide to ethical behavior is the individual's own conscience. It is hoped that the publication of this book will increase the frequency with which individuals invoke their conscience. It will be a sign of significant improvement in social marketing ethical practice when the field abounds with stories of whistle-blowing on questionable behavior, stories of brave managers making tough ethical calls in the face of pressures to "just get the job done," and, finally, the occasional story of the singular hero who chooses to quit a job or a firm because it did not live up to his or her high ethical standards.

Acknowledgments

I would like to thank the Connelly Program in Business Ethics at Georgetown University's McDonough School of Business and its director, George Brenkert, for the support that made this volume possible. Professor Brenkert was the first to propose the idea of a seven-week seminar on ethical issues in social marketing in the spring of 1999. The Connelly program then provided funding to bring several of the present writers to Washington, D.C., to make seminar presentations and discuss their papers.

I also wish to thank the participants in the seminar. These included faculty and students from Georgetown's MBA program and its graduate program in public policy, as well as many visitors from Washington's social marketing community. Their provocative questions and refreshing insights materially strengthened the seminar and the papers that resulted from it.

Alan R. Andreasen
Washington, D.C.

CHAPTER ONE

Ethics and the Social Marketer: A Framework for Practitioners

William A. Smith

Thoughtful social marketing practitioners are faced all too frequently with ethical dilemmas—some minor, others major. We live in an age of situational ethics that exaggerates and obscures many of those dilemmas. We often find ourselves in situations, looking for ethical guidance. For example, we discover that in order to effectively promote a remedy for a disease like infant diarrhea, we must capitalize on the widely held belief that there exists in every child a bag of worms that causes diarrhea.

We know this belief is untrue, but we also know that if we ignore or attack that belief in our program we will lose the confidence of our audience. Experiments show that accepting the bag of worms explanation is the best way to get this critical new medication accepted. Do we use the untrue belief to promote a highly effective drug or not? We would all agree that lying or misleading is unethical. But so is withholding proper treatment because we refuse to use a powerful existing belief that happens to be untrue and is not apparently harmful in itself.

This problem is compounded by the fact that there is a lack of dialogue about ethics in social marketing. This book is intended to begin to solve that problem and raise the level of conversation about the issue. Today, few programs have a statement of their ethical principles. As a community of professionals we have adopted no standards of ethics and it is probable that most of our community has not read or analyzed the guidelines set up for either commercial advertising or commercial marketing.

For the purposes of discussing ethics, this chapter presents a practical framework—a set of variables with a few suggested criteria—that will be discussed in the context of specific samples of social marketing and advertising decisions. The chapter provides a starting point for what we need to "argue about" in creating an approach to ethics in social marketing.

Let us begin with a word of caution. This chapter will describe the work of several people, professionals whose motives it does not pretend to know. The goal is to encourage discussion about ethics and social marketing, not to judge the work of other professionals. We do need to judge each other's work, but a fair assessment requires more information than will be given here.

Ethics Is about Making Decisions

Ethics is typically defined as the study of standards of conduct and moral judgment. It is particularly useful to us when it helps us resolve conflicting standards or moral judgments. It is not as simple as deciding what is right and what is wrong. The toughest ethical dilemmas arise when two seemingly "right" principles are in conflict. There are many examples of such conflicts in the world today. The debate over pro-life versus pro-choice is a classic conflict of two values—life versus choice—in the setting of a woman's option to abort a fetus. But there are many more. This chapter will argue that ethics are contingent upon various factors, not a single factor. A controversial (or perhaps unethical) tactic used by one social marketing organization might be ethically acceptable if used by another organization. For example, if an African American organization uses the N—— word in an advertisement addressed to African Americans, is that its ethical prerogative? If a white organization used the same word, most people would find the word morally offensive. How do morals and ethics interact? What's the difference between morally offensive and politically incorrect acts?

In social marketing, we often deal with products and services that are controversial or not well understood, and often involve sensitive behaviors such as blood donation in the era of AIDS or child abuse in an era of tabloid journalism. Marketing these social "products" is particularly prone to ethical dilemmas because, unlike most consumer products, they deal with some of our most deeply held beliefs and moral judgments.

Selling Coca-Cola is not the same as selling sexual abstinence. Life and death, pain and suffering, reproduction and sexuality are at the cutting edge of what society makes moral judgment about and they are often the centerpieces of social marketing. In the use of mass media, for example, it is possible for Coke to target a specific audience and not worry about how its program affects unintended audiences. After all, what does it matter if confirmed Pepsi drinkers are upset by Coke's claims that *Coke tastes best*? But when targeting a mass audience for a media message about the nastiness of smoking behavior, such a campaign may imply that all smokers are nasty or unfit parents. These unintended consequences are only part of our dilemma. Indeed, commercial marketing may have things to learn from us. Many commercial products are now promoting social causes as part of their marketing programs (cf. Davidson and Novelli, this volume). In this case, their campaigns may offend unintended audiences and this may have important negative social consequences. Recent Calvin Klein advertising appears to exploit preteens.

The standards that most regularly present both social and commercial marketers with ethical dilemmas are:

Be Truthful. Is what we say truthful, accurate, complete, or exaggerated?

Protect Privacy. Are we invading the privacy of an individual or group, or revealing facts about people that others don't need to know?

Don't Model Inappropriate Behavior. Are we, directly or unintentionally, modeling antisocial behavior, actually teaching or even inciting people to practice a negative behavior? At one point, a recent anti-smoking program aimed at teenagers was to be branded, "RAGE." This moniker was eventually changed to "Truth" by the teen leaders of the campaign themselves. But, would RAGE have been a desirable concept to promote to teenagers?

Don't Be Offensive. Are we showing or promoting behavior that society deems offensive? In showing teens how to use a condom, are we using unacceptably sexually explicit photographs of young teens?

Be Fair and Balanced. Are we being fair to everyone in our programs? For example, does demonizing a behavior like overeating in order to create breakthrough advertising for an anti-obesity campaign treat the obese person with fairness, accuracy, or respect?

Avoid Stereotyping. Are we projecting inaccurate and harmful images of groups based on historical stereotypes?

Protect the Children. Are we exposing children to programs that are inappropriate for their age? There is general societal agreement that a target audience's age should be considered in determining content. Sexual explicitness, for example, in mainstream U.S. society is not considered appropriate for young children. Parental approval is considered essential when doing research on children. This is not true of older, mature audiences. U.S. society at the end of twentieth century will accept sexually explicit commercial advertising (see any teen magazine), but will find a government-sponsored program of sexual disease prevention totally unacceptable because children might be exposed to such a campaign.

Unfortunately, these standards cannot be used as a checklist or scorecard. We can't give each issue equal weight, and then ask program directors to score their programs as if a standardized minimum score will mean that everything is fine. Ethical dilemmas are precisely those moments when two valid concerns—privacy and justice, or truth and confidentially, or truth and moral offensiveness, for example—come in conflict.

On the other hand, many ethicists agree that a rational framework for recognizing and analyzing ethics is our best protection against bad ethics. The following framework is suggested as a starting point.

In Figure 1-1, you will notice that there is an *actor,* someone who is producing or sponsoring a product. The *product* or offering can be an object, a service, or a behavior. A *motive* guides the actor, the *act* of offering the product, and the *context* in which that act occurs. The act affects

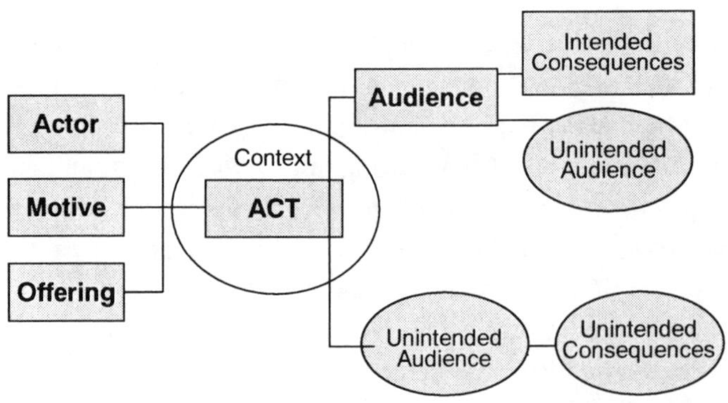

Figure 1-1. An Ethical Framework for the Practice of Social Marketing

audiences, both an *intended audience* and an *unintended audience.* And finally, *consequences* affect both the intended and unintended audiences. This set of elements constitutes a framework for questions we should ask ourselves to help us determine, from a social marketing perspective, the ethical parameters of the act or program. Let's discuss each element of the framework with a few examples.

Actors

The actor in a social marketing program is typically an institution. It may be for profit, nonprofit, or a government agency. It is not the same thing for a government to promote AIDS testing as an insurance company, or a gay activist organization. The actor is perceived to have motives. Often these perceptions may be false, but they are critical in judging the role of the actor. One possible basis for judging the ethicality of an actor's motives is to assess the actor's similarity to the target audience, in social, economic, political, or cultural position. An AIDS activist organization is often much more like the gay male at high risk who is the frequent target for AIDS campaigns, than is an account manager for an insurance program. How much like the audience is the actor?

The greater the similarity of the actor to its audience, the greater the perceived level of truth and accuracy of the program or act.

Product

The product influences the nature of the ethical dilemma. If the product is an object such as silicone breast implants, safety and costs may be important issues. If the product is a service such as childhood immunization, equal access to that service may be the critical issue. Assume for a moment that a social advertising campaign motivates thousands of mothers to go to clinics where vaccines are not available. This is not only a tactical issue of consumer disappointment, it causes poor families to invest scarce resources and travel time to go to centers without vaccines. This is unethical because it is misleading and untruthful. If the product is a behavior such as "choose to have fewer sexual partners," factors such as conflicting community norms may be important. Government programs have asked gay men to give up having multiple partners to prevent the spread of AIDS. But for some gay men, multiple sexual partners help define who they are as sexual beings. In the United States, the predominant culture broadly supports, although it does not practice, monogamy. But what about African society where polygamy is a well-established cultural characteristic?

These examples show how various factors in the framework interact to make ethical discussion more complete and clear. It provides us with no simple answers, but rather helps ensure we are looking at a more complete picture.

Motive

Motive is usually discussed along a continuum ranging from total self-interest to absolute altruism. Is the actor doing this exclusively for self-interest, or is this act a mixture of self-interest and altruism? Take for example the tobacco industry's funding of programs to reduce family violence. Many observers would see this exclusively as an act of financial self-interest. But what if the Catholic church were sponsoring the same domestic violence prevention programs? Fewer questions would be asked about the motivation. Is one program more ethical than the other if both have positive outcomes? What if a company has mixed motives? It wants to increase sales by being—or perhaps appearing to be—socially conscious. Is the key distinction here the desire to appear in a certain positive light, rather than an honest desire to be socially responsible?

In joint ventures, we might also want to ask to what degree is the actor's motive shared by the partner? If a social marketing partner, say a small struggling women's group, believes that smoking is bad for women but takes tobacco money in order to fund a program on domestic violence, is that more or less ethical than if the women's organization had no stand on tobacco, or believed the tobacco industry to be falsely accused?

If there are multiple motives, does it matter which one dominates? Finally, how do we know what the motivation is: by what the actor tells us, by independent investigation, or by reasoned attribution? How many times have we heard people say, "I know why they *really* did that," thereby asserting that the public motivation masked a different, private one?

The Act

Typically, the act is judged using multiple criteria. If it involves communication, one asks: is it truthful and accurate? Does it deliver what it promises? In advertising, we have come to distinguish between truth that is "all the truth . . . the whole truth . . . and nothing but the truth" versus "half-truth . . . some of the truth . . . and exaggerated truth." We also have to ask, does the *act* stereotype groups of people, projecting images that pander to popular and often harmful misconceptions?

One example is the information being given young people about the dangers of smoking. Is it ethical to withhold the information that much of the physiological damage done by smoking during the first ten to even twenty years will be repaired by the body? While this information is not being hidden (it does appear on the Centers for Disease Control web site), no one I know in tobacco prevention has ever mentioned it in any of the anti-smoking messages in the media. We are, in fact, giving only part of the truth. Is that ethical . . . and if so, why?

Context

Context deals with issues of when and where a program is implemented. Promoting condoms in school has different ethical implications for some people than putting condoms in a gas station or brothel. They argue that schools are an inappropriate place to put condoms because the very presence of condoms in schools will lead to increased sexual activity among teens, which they consider morally wrong outside of marriage. The cultural context is also critical. As we have already noted, promoting sexual monogamy in a polygamous society is different from doing so in a monogamous society. Context is also influenced by the choice of media for a social marketing program. What may be appropriate for a counseling session may be morally wrong broadcast via mass media. Timing of a product's presentation is also critical. Placing condoms ads on Saturday morning TV is seen by most people as inappropriate.

As we examine each of these factors, it becomes clear that the distinction between "offensive to some," "morally offensive to many," and "unethical" is a spectrum of judgment. It is a spectrum of judgment that changes over time and in relation to context. To break through the clutter of prejudice against gay culture, many gay activists have deliberately used images that offend some, perhaps most, Americans. Photographs of two men kissing were highly offensive in the popular press only ten years ago. But in gay magazines it has been acceptable for years. Exposure to male-to-male love is now acceptable in many more venues, but not in all. The distinction between offensive and unethical is difficult to discern for those of us in social marketing because our actions change society's reactions.

Audiences

There are often two types of audience that need to be considered in our ethical assessments: intended audiences and, particularly in the case of mass media, unintended audiences. There are a number of issues to raise about each of these audiences.

1. Does our intended audience have the ability to understand and accept the advice or the product? For example, do illiterate women in underdeveloped countries have the ability to understand the complexities of the use of oral rehydration solution to treat their children's diarrhea without causing the children to suffer negative consequences? To advise a woman to bottle-feed almost always means she will stop breast feeding, yet promoting breast feeding in some parts of the world where women are highly infected with HIV presents a medical risk to their child. Do we have the resources to help women understand the tradeoffs, or should we just promote what we feel is in the best interest of public health? Age, gender, education level, socioeconomic condition, literacy, and level of empowerment are a few of the characteristics that influence our understanding of a particular audience's ethical role.

2. The potential effects on unintended audiences present even more complex issues. Typically, we have much less information about these groups' values or beliefs because we have been targeting our resources at understanding our intended audience. Take, for example, a program designed to reduce adolescent pregnancy. Imagine that our research shows that young women resent the loss of their freedom when they have a child. We develop a campaign with a picture of a teen trapped at home alone taking care of an infant child—with a bold tag line that says something like, "Don't Let Your Child Become a Trap," and a subtext saying, "Plan

Your Family, Plan Your Life." This may be a good message for family planning, but what does it do for the problem of child abuse. Is it possible that teens already pregnant, seeing that society apparently agrees with them that children can be a trap, take the message to condone child abuse. Perhaps not, but do we have an obligation to find out?

Consequences

Finally, there are *consequences,* both intended and unintended, that affect audiences. Key issues include benefits, relative benefits, and harm that may result from the act. Again, it is clear that each factor of the framework interacts. In the teen pregnancy example given above, if we discover that no teens react to the promotion in the negative way—that is, that the consequences of this program are not negative, and that it has wonderful impact on teenage pregnancy—we would not call it unethical . . . or should we? If consequences are the only measure of ethics, then we are in an "ends justifies the means" world. But suppose our *means* are questionable. Does a desirable set of consequences justify our actions? Self-righteousness is tempting, particularly when fighting tobacco companies, polluters, drug dealers, and pimps. But does anything go? Where do we draw the lines and how do we agree on a conversational format that will lead to resolution, rather than conflict among social marketers?

All the elements of this framework interact to influence each other. The same *actor* with the same *motive* may be viewed as ethically different if the consequences of the act change due to the situation. For example, let us examine a company whose motive is to generate a good corporate image and do some altruistic good at the same time. To do so, it decides to promote a childhood immunization program. It funds a local organization to carry out the program. In Situation A, the immunizations are delivered well and children benefit. In Situation B, the immunizations are poorly stored and several children suffer negative side effects. In Situation A, the company's motive would not be questioned publicly. In Situation B, the campaign might become a cause celebre. While the company's actions were identical in both cases, the public evaluation of its ethics may be quite different.

Guidelines for Making Ethical Judgments: Weighing Actions Against Consequences

Generally, we are concerned with *motive* and *consequences* when we make snap ethical judgments. Our tendency is to say a program was unethical because it was motivated by "self-interest" or because "somebody got hurt" as a result. If the motive is wrong and the results are positive, or if the motive was right but the results were negative, we cannot simply say that the actor is ethical or unethical. Often we do, but it is hoped this framework will give us a slightly more comprehensive way of analyzing ethical situations, particularly those that arise in the context of social marketing.

Many of our ethical problems in social marketing are inherent in our profession. We know what it takes to convince people to change brands and adopt new products. We apply many of these techniques from the commercial sector to promote socially beneficial behavior. For example, we all know that we need to:

"Do unto others as we would have others do unto us." This classic admonition still has great value in our search for ethical guidelines. It assumes that we don't want anything bad to happen to us, so we shouldn't do anything that hurts others. It is a kinder, gentler version of "the ends justifies the means." This approach may put consequences to the individual above consequences for the population, however, and for those of us filled with the righteousness of our causes, this too is a dilemma. Take the example of an anti-tobacco organization and the tobacco industry. Imagine that a tactic the anti-tobacco folks think might work is to publicly embarrass corporate executives by revealing details about their personal lives, details that have little to do with their tobacco decisions. Imagine that the argument is, "they have to be stopped and nothing else seems to be working." Compare this to gay activists who want to "out" closeted public officials and closeted leaders. How would we assess these acts against a "do unto others" guideline. Obviously there are laws that govern some of this behavior, but much outing behavior could actually be accomplished legally. Should we, as social marketers adopt a "do unto others" guideline in all cases?

"Build on the values of our audience." We must persuade by understanding and tying into the audience's values. Persuade, don't preach. This is a simpler principle to apply when selling bath soap than selling safe sex. After all, in social marketing we often try to change some of the most fundamental values people hold. For many gay men, multiple sexual partners are a basic part of being a gay man. To ask these men to be monogamous as the only alternative to protect themselves from disease conflicts with a community value. In addition, we must recognize the dilemmas that surround "using the values of our audience" if that audience has a lot of harmful stereotypes about other people. To decrease female circumcisions, how do you build on the values of traditional families in some parts of Africa where female circumcision is commonly practiced?

"Break through the clutter." We know as professionals that unless we attract attention to our message, the quality of the message itself is irrelevant. But, to break through the clutter in markets as crowded and competitive as those in Canada and the U.S. often means competing against sophisticated commercial marketers. To break through the clutter of messages about the elegance of furs, animal rights activists splatter blood on women wearing furs. To break through the clutter of social messages on abortion, anti-abortion activists wave a fetus in front of a crowded street. To break through the clutter of messages we depict impossible situations: a young man is shown to be pregnant to dramatize the consequences of pregnancy that only women have to bear. Which of these goes too far, if any?

"Be competitive." Many of our social marketing topics compete. Campaigns to promote the environment may compete with campaigns to promote jobs, homeless issues compete with tax issues, condoms versus morality. Is it ethical to attack the competition? Are some competitive tactics permissible and some not? For Pepsi to attack Coca-Cola is one thing, but for one set of moral values to attack another is different. Or, is it? Those who argue that the end justifies the means might also argue that social debates are all the more important to win. After all, if you believe that population growth in developing countries is dramatically more important than radon testing in the United States, is it not ethical to try to move money away from radon into family planning?

What happens when the competition represents a compatible value? We saw during the 1980s and early 1990s in the United States that fear of AIDS drove dollars and support away from other health programs. Today we see tobacco and drug prevention spending in amounts unimaginable a few years ago. To mobilize a social marketing campaign on the environment, for example, may mean calling attention away from abortion, or cancer, or smoking.

In social marketing we are not choosing between two brands of soup. To what degree does our competitive drive lead to apathy and backlash among an embattled public?

"Be single-minded." We know from the practice of commercial marketing that to communicate effectively we should not teach or preach about everything. We must find a key benefit, present it creatively, repeat it often, and hope it works. But to reduce complex social issues like abortion, or AIDS, or environmental protection to a single simple slogan is another question. Single-mindedness may work as a tactic, but what impact does it have on our responsibility to educate and inform the public about decision making?

The techniques of targeting, segmentation, single-mindedness, audience-centeredness, competition and break-through messaging work. They certainly work better than those didactic pamphlets proposed by opponents of marketing. It is, after all, not an ethical improvement to promote accurate messages that no one understands, believes, or listens to. Herein lies the real dilemma. How do we balance the ethical needs of social marketing with the power and obligation of our profession to reach and persuade?

I heard a National Public Radio report on a study of California's new Channel 1, the current affairs channel for schools. The study showed that the kids didn't learn any current events from the channel but they did remember the commercials. If the message (in this case the classroom studies) doesn't get through, its ethical quality is irrelevant.

Some Examples

Let's look at a few examples. But if you think I'm going to tell you what is or is not ethical in these examples, dissuade yourself from that belief right away. I'm just like you . . . trying to figure these out for myself.

Example 1

In Britain, two ads by the English Collective of Prostitutes read: "What Do You Call Men Who Take Money from Prostitutes? Magistrates and

Pimps." and "No One Screws More Prostitutes than the Government."

Using the proposed framework, we see that the actor sponsoring this communication was a private, nonprofit equal rights group. Its motive was to call attention to what they believed to be discriminatory practices. The product was legal reform. The context was public viewing of the ad. The intended direct audience was the public, the indirect audience was the government. And the direct consequences are unknown. The campaign was never evaluated. The indirect consequences could be significant in that these ads could be offensive to many. Is the topic worth offending a few people? A tricky moral call. Note the actor: the government? No, it was a private group of activists in Britain. Does that change the ethical score for you? If we changed the context, for example specifying that the ad appeared in gay bars, would that make the campaigns more ethical (and less effective)?

Example 2

A recent ad for women's clothing shows a young man with his head buried under the dress and in the lap of a young woman who appears to be in sexual ecstasy. Her dress is up, and it seems clear that he is performing oral sex on her.

This message was not placed in a porno magazine, but rather in a mainstream magazine available at any Borders or Barnes & Noble magazine counter. This is an ad for clothes, not the *Kama Sutra*. Its actor is a commercial company. The motive is to break through the mold of traditional advertising and appeal to young singles. No one created an uproar about this ad. But, suppose the ad had been for safe sex—a demonstration that dental dams are effective during oral sex, then what would have happened? Would the public have been offended? Does this make it an ethical issue, a social issue, or a political issue? What if the actor had been the government? Or the Catholic Church? Or a dental association?

Example 3

In Southern California, a print ad shows a dramatic picture of two Ku Klux Klan hooded individuals. One individual carries a flaming torch. In bold letters it says, "Nothing I Like Better than Seeing a N——er Smoke."

The "N" word was spelled out. It is so offensive to me that I don't want to write it down even to illustrate a point. Is this ad ethical? The actor is an African American ad agency. The motive is to dramatize the racism involved in white tobacco companies targeting African American audiences. The approach was chosen to break through the advertising clutter and reach minority audiences. Perhaps to some people the use of the "N" word is justified. But what if the actor were the government, or what if it were the Klan itself? Again we can see that changes in one or another of the framework's factors influence our decision about ethics.

Example 4

A computer-altered photographic image of Ronald Reagan shows the president with Kaposi sarcoma, a primary symptom of AIDS. The text below the picture is an ironic message about how slowly Reagan moved to respond to the AIDS epidemic.

The actor here was *Colors* magazine, a publication sponsored by Benetton. What if the same image was sponsored by the Democratic National Party, by an AIDS Action Committee, or by the government? It would certainly have changed the careers of the people who had done such a thing within those organizations—but what about the ethics? What makes it ethical for *Colors* magazine to run such an ad but not the government? The framework argues that the factors interact. Actor, context, and audience all influence our evaluation of a single product.

Example 5

An ad paid for by the Children's Defense Fund shows hungry children in an African country. The tag line below reads: ". . . and what about hunger in America?"

Here, the actor is a major U.S. nonprofit. The motive is to focus attention on Hunger in America. There is an implied "Why give to them but not to us?" Many readers may see this as an attack on foreign aid. The context is advertising to the general public through a major newspaper. If the result is to increase assistance to hungry children in America without eroding America's support for hungry children in Africa, we might all agree that the ethics are not critical. But if the ad has an unintended but serious effect on America's willingness to support African children, too, then we might suggest that this is unethical. What if the motive changed? What if the motive was to transfer support from African to American children?

Again we see the interaction of factors that imply ethical judgments.

Conclusion

There is no easy answer to the question of how to balance ethics and effectiveness, between doing good and being powerful. To do a good job it sometimes seems that we must skirt some pretty tricky waters. The framework presented in this chapter suggests that it is not enough in our tracking research to ask about what we expected to happen to the intended audience as a result of our campaign, we also have to look for unintended consequences. It is not only what we intend to communicate, but what we actually do communicate, that matters.

When we do look at unintended consequences we may be surprised. Work by Susan Middlestadt and others have documented the unintended effects of messages. Follow-up research on a program in the Philippines revealed that messages meant to calm the general public about the spread of AIDS had the unintended effect of lowering public empathy for those suffering from AIDS (Middlestadt 1991). Another study showed that in the United States, messages on national media addressed to gay men unintentionally communicated to nongay populations that they were not at risk of AIDS (Middlestadt 1990).

We also need to be cautious in the selection of the social products we promote. We must take care to substantiate health claims before we become too deeply involved in promoting them. It is one thing for a shampoo to produce a little less luster than promised, but quite another for a breast self-exam to give a woman a false sense of security about her risk of breast cancer.

Summary

Ultimately, our only real protection against acting in an unethical manner is to become self-critical while at the same time remaining committed to our ultimate goal. The framework in Figure 1-1 is proposed as one way to begin the process of becoming self-critical. It is clear from the examples reviewed here that many ethical judgments are contingent upon the relationships among several factors. No one factor provides the key to ethical solutions. This framework shows the way in which the factors interact and yields a checklist of factors to monitor, discuss, and interpret.

References

Middlestadt, S. E. 1990. "Limitations of social marketing: An illustration from the National AIDS Information and Education Program." Paper presented on a review panel discussion on Applied Advertising Research, American Association of Advertising, Orlando, FL (April).

———. 1991. "Formative evaluation of public information campaign: Unintended effects and effects on unintended audiences." Paper presented on a peer review panel discussion, *Can We Make American Respond to AIDS?* International Communication Association, Chicago, IL (May).

CHAPTER TWO

Ethical Considerations in the Use of Marketing for the Management of Public Health and Social Issues

Michael L. Rothschild

Most societies attempt to manage at least some of the behaviors of at least some of their citizens at least some of the time. Currently there does not seem to be a strong discussion over whether the state has the ethical right to manage some behaviors. Indeed, citizens accept such management on a daily basis when they observe speed limits, pay taxes, recycle, adjust their diets, exercise, and matriculate at public universities.

If it is acceptable for societies to manage some behaviors, then the question to be considered in this chapter should not be "Is social marketing ethical?" The proper questions should concern "What is the ethicality of marketing when compared to education and law as alternative tools of behavior management?" and " Under what conditions will education, marketing and law be most appropriate and most ethical?" If there are three major sets of tools for managing behavior, then marketing needs to be considered along with education and force of law in considering how to manage. This chapter is not concerned with the moral questions of whether a society has the right to manage the behavior of its citizens, or of whether any specific tactic is ethical. The focus will be on the ethicality of social marketing as a management philosophy and tool kit in comparison with the available alternatives of education and law.

This chapter considers the ethicality of using social marketing in the management of behavior. The discussion begins by considering a taxonomy of ethical issues related to behavior management, continues with a context within which marketing and behavior management occur, and then looks at marketing in comparison with the tools of education and law. The chapter continues with a brief introduction to some of the dominant ethical theories of Western culture, and their potential in the consideration of the ethicality of marketing. The chapter concludes with some thoughts on the development of a code of ethics for social marketing.

A Taxonomy of Ethical Issues

A discussion of the ethics of managing choice behavior can take place on three levels. The broadest level considers the ethicality of the policy or goal itself in the absence of any consideration of its implementation. The middle level compares the ethicality of the underlying philosophies of the major strategic tools that may be employed. The narrowest level compares the ethicality of the tactics available within any area of strategic philosophy. This chapter will focus on the middle level, that is, the ethicality of the philosophy of marketing in comparison with that of education and of law. In this section, all three levels are considered.

The broadest level considers the ethicality of the behavior management policy. For example, is it ethical to manage the reproductive behaviors of citizens when some of these citizens will pass along genetically based disabilities to their offspring. Such a policy might be seen by some as ethical on the basis of the economic savings for the overall society; it might be seen as unethical by others on the basis of religious principles and the sanctity of life.

A second level for discussion considers the ethicality of the use of broad classes of strategic tools such as education, marketing, and force of law. *Education* refers to messages that attempt to inform and/or persuade a target to voluntarily behave in a particular manner. These messages do not, on their own, provide direct and/or immediate reward or punishment ("Quitting Isn't Easy—Keep Trying"; "Just don't do it"; "Eat five fruits and vegetables per day"). While messages such as these are often used to inform and/or persuade as an aid to the marketing of a product or service in an exchange, or as an aid in the enforcement of law, these supporting tactics are not included under the heading of education in this chapter. Messages that support in these ways are important to the overall integrated behavior management process, but are different from messages that stand in isolation. The former are included under marketing and law; the latter are education.

Marketing refers to attempts to manage behavior by offering positive reinforcing incentives and/or consequences in the environment. The choice environment is made favorable for appropriate behavior through the development of alternatives with comparative advantage (products and services), favorable cost-benefit relationships (pricing), and time and place utility enhancement (channels of distribution). Positive reinforcement is given when a transaction is completed.

Law refers to the use of coercion to force desired behavior (e.g., military conscription), or to threaten the use of punishment to discourage inappropriate behavior (e.g., penalties for littering). Law also can facilitate marketing solutions by increasing (via price subsidies) or decreasing (via taxes) the probability of various transactions occurring.

If, at the broadest level, the society and its policy makers have concluded that it is ethical to control reproduction to manage genetic disabilities, then the second level of ethical decision making examines whether education, marketing and law can ethically be used as instruments of control. With *education,* the government could inform and persuade citizens with respect to the value for the individual and the society of genetic testing, and, for individuals with relevant genetic markers, could provide education on the value of voluntarily choosing not to have children. Education does not restrict the free choice of citizens and therefore its use implies the acceptance of externality costs (costs imposed on some by the behavior of others) that result if citizens make socially undesirable choices.

Through the use of *marketing,* the government could encourage voluntary genetic testing by providing test sites in shopping malls and, in exchange, could offer counseling on genetics, family planning, and disabilities based on the test results and other issues of concern to the family. For those with relevant genetic disability markers, voluntarily choosing not to have children might be compensated for with a priority status for adoption. Marketing also does not constrain free choice, but attempts to reduce externality costs by offering benefits in exchange for behaviors with fewer externality effects.

Through *law,* the government could require genetic testing of all children as they approach the age of reproduction, and could require involuntary sterilization of those who carry genes that might lead to disabilities. Failure to comply could be harshly punished. Law restricts free choice by punishing socially undesirable choices, but reduces externality costs more than education or marketing approaches.

These options are presented to show the differences between, and the opportunities and limitations of, the three major classes of behavior management tools. In reality, issues such as genetic testing probably would be managed through a combination of the three classes of tools both over time and across different targets. The relative weighting of the tools would be a function of individual and societal values, as well as macro public policy considerations.

The third and most narrow level for ethical discussion considers the ethicality of using specific tactics within a particular class of strategic tools. For example, once the ethicality of reproduction control and the use of marketing have been agreed upon, then the ethicality of particular tactics such as segmentation can be considered.

Segmentation can be considered by first asking whether it is ethical; that is, is it ethical to offer rewards to, or impose costs on, only one part of society? Some would say that it is unethical to limit genetic testing; the state should offer testing to all. Others will say that the resources don't exist to test all, so the state should pursue those most likely to be at risk.

If a tactic such as segmentation is ethical at the conceptual level, then one must ask if a specific execution of segmentation is ethical. Is it permissible to primarily target African Americans for genetic testing because they are more likely to be carriers of the sickle cell trait, a genetically transmitted abnormality that can lead to sickle cell anemia, a disease that occurs almost exclusively in this community? Is it permissible to target African Americans for genetic testing because they have historically achieved lower levels of educational achievement?

Creating a Context

The chapter continues by considering several contexts necessary for evaluating the ethicality of social marketing. The context for considering marketing as a tool of behavior management needs to be broad enough to look both at ethical issues and at the value of marketing in comparison with education and law.

Several Sets of Tools of Behavior Management

The focus of this paper is on marketing, but marketing is just one of the major sets of tools available for behavior management. Marketing needs to be considered as a behavior management option relative to education and force of law. In this context, the question is not whether it is ethical to use marketing, but, given that attempts at behavior management will take place, how does marketing compare to the alternative choices? This contextual issue was introduced above and will be expanded upon later in the chapter.

Time and Place

This chapter limits its consideration to contemporary democratic societies, primarily the United States. In democratic societies, markets rather than law are the main means by which individuals tend to their own needs. Merit is rewarded in democratic economies, but not equally for all or according to need.

Individual and Community

Individual self-interested choices with accompanying externalities will likely lead to conflict between these choices and the interests of the community. The conflict between individual and community tends to increase as the society becomes more multicultural and its members become more geographically and economically mobile. As a result, the individual's roots in the community become more shallow (Walzer 1990).

Ouchi (1980) considers related issues with respect to the transactions costs of clans, markets and bureaucracies. He posits that clan members share common values and beliefs, and their information needs are focused on tradition; markets have reciprocity as an underlying requirement and focus on pricing information; bureaucracies are based on legitimate authority, which leads to a focus on rules. One can infer from Ouchi that members of a closely knit community are more prone to behave as per the group values and may respond well to education. The most disparate groups in the society will need laws to induce action for some common good. A middle ground consists of groups who respond well to satisfactory exchange offers. As society becomes increasing mobile and diverse, the balance shifts away from clan-like communities, so that the concept of the "good of society" may come to have a different meaning than it may have had in the past. Under these conditions there is a greater need for market and bureaucratic solutions.

Power and Competition

In a free society there is competition for the acceptance of ideas and behaviors: to binge drink or drink in moderation, to eat fresh produce or junk food, to exercise or watch more television. Because there is competition in the choice set, citizens have the power to reject the policy advocated by the greater society. Because the society values free choice, the use of law is minimized. In addition, behavior management goals may be difficult to achieve through education due to the appeal of competitive offerings. Marketing and the development of exchanges may be most appropriate in a competitive environment where citizens have the power to choose freely.

Rights and Responsibilities; Free Choice and Externalities; Efficiency and Effectiveness

Important functions of government are to allocate rights and responsibilities, to balance free choice and externalities, and to achieve efficient and effective management. If it is the responsibility of the manager to implement policies set by others, then it also is the responsibility of the manager to be efficient and effective in this execution. This means that the manager must accomplish policy goals at the lowest possible cost (efficiency) and the greatest level of impact (effectiveness). The manager must do this while considering the rights and responsibilities of the society to its citizens, the rights and responsibilities of the target market, and the rights and responsibilities of those other citizens who are impacted upon by the actions of the target and the society. The manager needs to consider the tradeoffs of externalities caused by the society's own actions against the actions of the target, as well as the tradeoffs of the target's rights to free choice against the societal externality costs of those free choices. Education, marketing and law are considered within these sets of tradeoffs.

In selecting tools for behavior management, there must be a consideration of a balance with efficiency and effectiveness. If citizens have (at least implicitly) relinquished some power to the state to manage some behaviors, then, one might argue, the state has the ethical responsibility of managing for the benefit of these citizens. This means that managers are called upon to be efficient in their use of scarce resources and effective in meeting policy goals. Indeed, it may be unethical to abrogate the responsibilities of efficiency and effectiveness, if poor management leads to lost lives or higher taxes.

Balancing ethicality, effectiveness and efficiency raises a number of issues. Does a noble societal goal justify tactics that are considered unacceptable in the commercial sector, or do noble goals require more noble tactics? The answer to this question may lie in finding a balance; by trading effectiveness for a noble manner of execution, the manager may be behaving concurrently in an unethical manner towards the funders of the program (taxpayers, donors) by failing to accomplish program goals.

Policy Making Versus Execution

A marketer generally does not make public policy, but manages its execution, much as a contractor builds from the plans made by the architect. Policy reflects the goal setting of the organization or the society, while marketing is one set of tools to be used in implementing policy and meeting goals. As such, this chapter does not focus on the ethicality of a policy, but on the ethicality of the manner in which it is being implemented.

The Philosophy, Strategies, and Tactics of Marketing

Ethicality also can be examined within the context of marketing's own philosophy, strategies, and tactics—that is, with the ethicality of a philosophy of achieving the long-run goals of the society by meeting the needs and accommodating the self-interest of a target market through the development of exchanges and transactions. If this philosophy of marketing is considered just and is followed, then the strategies and tactics that emerge also should be just. Unfortunately there is ample evidence that this chain of logic does not always exist. Our focus here is on the underlying philosophy of marketing, and whether it is consistent and compatible with several basic moral and political philosophies.

If we are to consider the ethicality of social marketing, it should be within the several contexts described above. The next section of this chapter considers the first contextual issue introduced above, that is, the several sets of tools available for behavior management.

Review of a Behavior Management Framework[1]

Prior levels of motivation, opportunity, and ability (M, O, A) in the target will determine behavior (MacInnis, Moorman, and Jaworski 1991) and will lead to a target's being prone, resistant, or unable to behave (Figure 2-1). Motivation to behave considers goal-directed arousal, which occurs when individuals can see that their self-interest will be served. Opportunity to behave considers the presence of environmental mechanisms in situations where the individual would like to act. Ability to behave considers individual skill or proficiency at solving problems, and may include breaking a well-formed or addictive habit, or countering the arguments of one's peers.

As seen in Figure 2-1, when M, O, and A are all high, the target will be prone to behave appropriately, and education generally will be sufficient to achieve the desired end. When motivation is low, but opportunity and ability are present, then the target will be resistant to respond appropriately, and law generally will be necessary to achieve the desired goal. Between these two extreme points, there are various combinations of levels of high and low M, O, and A, where the target is unable to respond due to various circumstances. In these situations, some combination of marketing, education, and law will be needed to effect change.

Education will most likely provide a sufficient set of tools when it is easy for the target to see that the desired behavior is in its self-interest, when the intensity of competition for the behavior is minimal, and/or when the target is asked to continue behaving as it has in the past. Law will be more likely to be needed to affect behavior when the target is unable to see the self-interest in behaving as desired, when the intensity of competition for the behavior is great, and/or when the target is asked to

MOTIVATION	yes		no	
OPPORTUNITY	yes	no	yes	no
ABILITY yes	① prone to behave *education*	② unable to behave *marketing*	③ resistant to behave *law*	④ resistant to behave *marketing, law*
no	⑤ unable to behave *education, marketing*	⑥ unable to behave *education, marketing*	⑦ resistant to behave *education, marketing, law*	⑧ resistant to behave *education, marketing, law*

Figure 2-1. Applications marketing, education, and law.

behave differently from the past. Marketing will be most appropriate at the middle ranges of these issues.

A more macro policy view of education, marketing and law can be considered in addition to the micro managerial view from the previous paragraph. Here the concern is with the rights and responsibilities of the government and of the target when the individual has free choice, but when some individual choices lead to externalities for the society or for other individuals. In comparing the three sets of tools, education clearly offers free choice, but may do little to mitigate resulting externalities; education would be the choice of the libertarian. Force of law would minimize externalities, but also restrict freedom; law would be the choice of the paternalist. Marketing may offer a favorable compromise position; it offers freedom by giving the target a choice of alternatives in the environment, yet it also can manage externalities through exchanges which offer something in the self-interest of the target and ask for behavior which minimizes externalities in return.

A commonly used example is the management of motorcycle helmet use. By advocating the use of helmets through an educational campaign, the state allows the rider to freely choose whether or not to wear a helmet, and is silent with respect to who will absorb the medical costs in case of an accident. An alternative is to pass a law that requires the wearing of helmets; such a law lowers medical costs for the society when accidents occur, but also constrains the free choice of the rider. A middle ground would use a marketing paradigm of exchange. Here each rider would have the choice of wearing or not wearing a helmet, but, in return, would agree that in case an accident occurred when a helmet was not worn, the individual would be personally responsible for all medical costs. This compromise position would give free choice to all riders and lessen the costs imposed on the other members of the community.

Education would be most appropriate in situations when the target already is prone to behave as desired, when the predicted level of resulting externalities would be low, and/or when the rights of the targeted individual are felt to dominate over those of the society or other individuals. Law would be most appropriate in situations when the target is resistant to behave as desired (wearing seat belts), when the predicted level of resulting externalities would be high (excessive speed), and/or when the rights of the society or other individuals are felt to dominate over those of the targeted individual (drug laws).

In democratic states, individuals typically have the right to free choice and to not be imposed upon by other individuals, and, in return, have the responsibility to minimize the costs that their actions impose on others. The society and its managers have the responsibility to maintain the general welfare, to manage behaviors that cause harm to others, and to preserve the freedoms of its citizens. The difficulties lie in creating a balance between allowing free choice and minimizing externalities, and in creating a balance between the rights of the individual and the society. Striking a balance is at the heart of the debate on many policy issues in democratic societies. In the United States, some advocate free choice in personal issues (e.g., abortion, obscenity), and management of economic issues (e.g., minimum wages, labor standards, welfare). Others advocate free choice in economic issues, and management of personal issues.

A Brief Review of Several Paradigms of Moral and Political Philosophy

Of the many ethical paradigms that exist, four dominant ones (Utilitarianism, Liberalism, Contextualism, and Deontology) will be introduced next, and will be considered with respect to the ethicality of using social marketing as a tool to manage behavior within the contexts and framework introduced above.[2]

Utilitarianism (Mill [1859] 1991) is one "member" of a set of moral philosophies known as *Teleology* (Frankena 1963) or *Consequentialism*, and is based on the idea that a behavior is moral if it leads to the greatest good (or lessens the harm) for the greatest number. These frameworks focus on the end results (greatest good) and on the individual's responsibility to the good of the community. They provide a basis for welfare economics by advocating a social cost/benefit analysis that allows for an assessment of the efficiency and effectiveness of an act. This, then, combines with the economist's free market model which posits that the unrestricted market allocates resources in a more beneficial manner to society than does a tightly controlled market system.

With Utilitarianism, for example, segmentation would be an ethical practice when it leads to the greatest good for the most people. While calling for the greatest good for the greatest number, it does not require that all share equally in the good or that an attempt must be made to serve all. A program that provides a mediocre result for all might be less preferable to one that serves many well, but serves some poorly. By focusing on providing the greatest good, or greatest utility, to the greatest number, ends justify the means. "Good" and "utility" can be defined on many dimensions including monetary, happiness, freedom, welfare, justice, social acceptance, or rights dimensions.

Liberalism (Mill [1859] 1991; Feinberg 1984) (using the classic definition related to libertarianism, not the current political usage) also calls for the greatest good for the greatest number, with the additional conditions that all persons have an equal right to free choice without coercion, and that freely chosen behaviors do not impede on any other person's ability to equally pursue free choice. By including freedom from coercion, the means of achieving the greatest common good are important in gaining end results. By focusing on individual rights and freedom from coercion, contracts, with free choices made in self-interest, become important.

The liberal view advocates the most freedom for the most people. Each person has the right to life, but has no right to expect that another person will provide the means. Laws that prevent potential harm to others are acceptable, but laws that ensure assistance to others are not acceptable. Libertarians feel that each individual is entitled to what can be acquired fairly. Such a philosophy opposes taxation or redistribution of wealth, but permits user fees where revenues are needed. One goal is to eliminate free riders (who impose on the rights of others). The result is free market laissez faire capitalism.

Liberalism seeks to protect the private sphere from government intervention. Relevant issues become more difficult to resolve, however, when private behaviors have public externalities. For example, is the choice to smoke a private matter when the health care costs of the society and other individuals are increased (due to higher taxes or insurance premiums) by illnesses that are more likely to occur as a result of smoking?

While Utilitarianism seeks the end that could benefit the most people, Liberalism allows this end to occur by allowing each individual to get whatever each can. Utilitarianism is neutral on questions relating to the distribution of wealth. Thus, when the gain of one person is greater than the loss of all others, it is considered a utilitarian improvement.

In *Contextualism* (Morone 1997), ethics are bound by time and place. While Contextualism is often presented as a postmodern interpretivist view, it also is similar to one presented by the Sophists of ancient Greece who felt that right and ethicality were defined by the power elite of society (Plato 1892). In Contextualism, we see a moral-, bounded-, or cultural-relativism where ethical standards are dictated by the society and those in power, judged by the customs, rules, and norms of the society, and grounded in the history of the community. Postmodern writers doubt that a unitary ethical theory is possible. For some, an act is morally right if it is part of the traditional moral code of the society (Robin and Reidenbach 1993). Integrative social contract theory (Donaldson and Dunfee 1994) is one such theory that takes social norms as the foundation for rules of behavior.

Thompson presents the view that ethics reflect judgments made through a socially constructed contextual lens, and are constantly being negotiated through a dialogue between the parties in power (1995). In Contextualism, what is ethical or moral is seen as being the result of negotiations among those in power. Such a view is especially relevant in considering marketing since the field is so contextually based in its explication.

Contextualism, wherein nothing is absolute, may be seen as the opposite of *Deontology* (Kant 1964), wherein there are absolute ethical standards that hold universally and categorically. Kant's Categorical Imperative states that one ought never to act unless one is willing to have the maxim on which one acts become a universal law. An example of such an absolute would be a fundamental principle not to lie or deceive.

In a contemporary example, public health workers may overstate the risk of certain behaviors (or lack of behaviors) because they feel the target might not respond appropriately if the true risk of the behavior were known. Is this an acceptable lie? Would the community be better off (Utilitarianism) if people knew the true riskiness of a behavior (which might lead to no behavior change), or if people behaved in the most health conscious manner even though that behavior might not always be necessary (Sherrard 1998)? Current ethical thought often arrives at a neo-Kantian perspective, which is more subjective and contextual, and separates the inherent moral propriety of an action from the consequences that may follow (Thompson 1995).

Both the extreme of Contextualism and the extreme of Deontology generally fail in democratic pluralistic societies (Thompson 1995) in favor of a balancing of Utilitarianism and Liberalism. Contextualism raises important issues with respect to policy making and application issues relevant to Utilitarianism and Liberalism. With respect to Utilitarianism, Contextualism requires definitions for terms like "greatest good," or "community"; as many societies become more multicultural, the definitions of "community" and "greatest good" become more difficult. With respect to Liberalism, Contextualism requires specification of the limits of freedom and of relevant externalities. How will a society decide on the tradeoffs of private liberty versus public cost? What does it mean to cause "harm to others"; must the harm be physical, or can it be emotional or economic? In trading personal freedoms against societally imposed costs, what public services deserve cost sharing (e.g., roads, national defense, compulsory education, and universal health care)?

On issues of application relevant to this chapter, Contextualism provides input into the question of whether behavior management should be a neutral force, provide information, persuade, motivate, provide incentives, or coerce. For example, when there is a drug abuse problem in a community, how will the community be defined; a narrow definition of community might be defined based on ethnicity and might lead to a neglect of the problem by those in power or to a coercive legal solution; a broader definition of the community including all who reside in a metropolitan area, for example, might lead to a greater use of education or marketing. Defining the greatest good, the community, respect for individual rights, and an acceptable level of externalities are issues that need to be considered along with the choice of behavior management tools in judging the ethicality of the tools.

Several Views of the Tradeoffs of Individual Versus Community Good

An examination of the history of democratic states shows the juxtaposition of individualism and community, and of Liberalism and Utilitarianism. Individual effort is rewarded, but the liberties offered also foster geographic and economic mobility (Walzer 1990). Children grow up, go away to college, settle elsewhere, and become geographically and economically different from their parents. This, in turn, leads to weaker community bonds since the members haven't grown up in the place they now live. When geographic and economic mobility are coupled with increasing ethnic multiculturalism, the result can be a loss of sense of community, and a reduction of voluntary cooperation for the betterment of others.

Ouchi has pointed out that "cooperative action necessarily involves interdependence between individuals" (1980); with shallow roots and increasing distrust, individuals are less prone to act for the good of the larger community and more likely to seek a self-interested return on any investment that they make. The continuing change in the forces of individualism and community are reflected in the ever-changing balance of political forces leaning towards Utilitarian or Liberal perspectives.

Several contemporary philosophers have written about the issues raised in this chapter, although none have specifically addressed social marketing. Their views will help to inform a consideration of the ethicality of social marketing. These are presented next, with the more Liberal first followed by the more Utilitarian; each philosopher has a significant following.

Nozick (1974), a Liberal Deontologist, favors the absolute right to life, liberty and legitimately acquired property. He feels that government has no right to impose upon the citizenry or to take wealth for redistribution, and that individuals have no responsibility to help others. Economic arrangements are just if there is free consent among the parties and no fraud. While charity is acceptable as a voluntary form of wealth redistribution, taxes are not acceptable. Nozick's view would favor education and marketing as tools of behavior management.

Mead (1986) writes that citizenship gives full membership in a community and grants both rights and responsibilities equally to all. Individual success is a responsibility; welfare is not a right. From this perspective, social marketing can be seen as an exchange of rights and responsibilities between the individual and the society, and as more acceptable than assistance provided via the force of law.

Feinberg (1984) argues that liberty is not absolute, but can only be constrained to minimize harm or offense to others or to one's self. He has developed a continuum of justifications for constraint. For Feinberg the key question concerns "When is it ethically proper to constrain or manage an individual's actions?" Given free choice or coercion, Feinberg advocates free choice.

For Feinberg, behavior may be required, permitted, or prohibited. Requiring or prohibiting behaviors is coercive, but permitting behavior allows choice. Liberty should be the norm, and coercion should require justification. Feinberg presents ten Liberty-Limiting Principles that represent different levels of justification for placing limits on behavior. The choice from among education, marketing, and law would be based on the intensity of the prevailing situation and the need for control.

Liberty may be limited due to potential private harm to others (e.g., murder, theft) or public harm to others (e.g., pollution, tax evasion), but curtailing liberty becomes more difficult to justify in considering the public harm (e.g., health care costs) resulting, for example, from the private behavior of eating fatty foods. Some other liberty-limiting principles pertain to behaviors leading to harm to self (e.g., smoking), or behaviors that may inflict moral harm to others (e.g., selling pornography) or on self (e.g., viewing pornography).

Rawls (1971), a Utilitarian, presents a middle ground with his Theory of Justice. Society should provide maximum liberty for all, as long as the welfare of the least advantaged is not diminished. His Theory of Justice can be seen as supporting socialism and welfare capitalism. Here policy makers must make decisions as if they were cloaked in a "veil of ignorance." This veil does not allow them to see what their own status would be after the policy is set; with the veil, each policy maker is required to set policy which is most beneficial to the general community.

In this Contractualist view, self-interest has limits; Rawls' social contract encourages maximum liberty for all, but any forced change in the distribution of wealth must favor the least advantaged. This strategy seeks to maximize the minimum welfare of the lowest level of society, although it may harm the wealthier in order to do so. This Utilitarian view sacrifices some welfare of some citizens for the greater welfare of the community. Rawls' view would favor marketing and law as the preferred tools of behavior management; as clannish communities become less prevalent, marketing and law become better ways to explicate this perspective.

For Dworkin (1988), individual rights dominate. His view is similar to Kant's perspective that respect for the individual is the fundamental principle of ethics. In addition, Dworkin argues that concern, respect, and assistance for others should be given as needed. This means that while individual rights are important, the state may need to intervene in order to assist in the protection of these rights, rather than leave the individual to survive alone.

Walzer's work (1990) seems to justify the rightness of social marketing as a set of tools to be used in the context of democracies with their continual search for balance between Utilitarian and Liberal positions. In his view of the Liberal perspective, it is difficult to get a social consensus because the individual is most important. As liberalism fosters mobility (discussed above), it also lessens community ties and voluntary cooperation, making education less impactful as a behavior management tool. This, in turn, would call for a greater use of marketing and law, but the liberal view would not be supportive of an increase in the use of law. Marketing remains as a set of tools that reward individual effort yet can meet community needs, as exchange incentives motivate the individual to be part of the community.

The most Utilitarian of the contemporary philosophers is Etzioni (1993), who proposes Communitarianism. Here self-interest is strongly tempered by community contributions. When individuals are likely to follow norms that lead to a communal good, then education may be the preferred tool of behavior management.

Each of the above philosophers addresses whether it is acceptable for a society to ever manage the behaviors of its citizens, when it is acceptable, and which management may be accomplished best. If there are conditions under which management is acceptable, then we must consider if marketing is the set of tools with which to do so.

Support for the Ethicality of Social Marketing

This chapter has focused on macro issues relating to the ethicality of social marketing. As Robin and Reidenbach (1993) point out, without first considering the macro ethical questions, micro level tactical concerns can always be criticized from a macro perspective. For example, once the ethicality of segmentation has been established at a macro level via an understanding of Utilitarianism, specific micro instances of segmentation can be considered. While segmentation may be difficult to condone if, for example, racial or gender criteria underlie the tactical decisions, it can be supported in a more general sense as an ethical component of marketing strategy.

Judging the ethicality of social marketing must be done in the context of the choices available for behavior management. If an agency is to manage the behavior of a target, is social marketing a reasonable way to proceed? This chapter has attempted to create a framework for answering this question based on the political philosophies of Utilitarianism, Liberalism, Contextualism, and Deontology, as well as a consideration of the efficiency and effectiveness of the available tools. Such a blend is consistent with the underlying political makeup of most democratic states (Robin and Reidenbach 1987).

In contemporary democratic states, most citizens have agreed to relinquish some level of freedom to the state. If we accept this premise, then the ethicality of some level and type of behavior management is not in question. If the policy being executed is deemed to be valid and ethical, then the most appropriate set, or mixture, of tools needs to be selected to implement the policy.

Returning to MacInnis, Moorman, and Jaworski's model of motivation, opportunity and ability (M, O, A) in Figure 2-1, education, marketing and law each can be impactful, depending on the state of the target and its environment. That is, education, marketing and law each have the potential to be efficient and effective. Education, marketing and law each provide a different tradeoff of free choice and externalities. The manager needs to consider which tradeoff is most appropriate for the case at hand.

Informing and persuading through education are acceptable if the externalities related to the behavior are low, but may be seen as unethical by reason of ineffectiveness if the resultant externalities are high; more forceful management may be called for in the latter case. If we assume that most people are rational and act in their own self-interest with respect to most issues most of the time, then it may be difficult to change most existing behaviors, since these existing behaviors reflect earlier rational self-interested choices. As a result, education may not be effective enough to lead to significant change; behavior management may need to depend more on marketing and law.

Coercion, through law, is acceptable if externality effects are sufficiently high, but it may be considered unethical to take away freedoms and rights if only low levels of externalities could result from the behavior in question. If free choice is embraced with a minimum of coercion, then we should resist the use of law since it restricts freedom. As a result, behavior management will depend more on marketing and education.

Under many conditions, marketing provides the best combination of effectiveness, efficiency, and ethicality. Marketing accommodates Utilitarianism. According to economists, the greatest good results when all choose in their own self-interest in a free market based on exchanges. The sum of self-interested decisions can yield the greatest good. Marketing can create an environment of choice that accommodates both the self-interest of the individual and the goals of the agency.

Marketing accommodates Liberalism. Marketing does not constrain free choice. In a market environment, choices are made based on an evaluation of the available options. The agency representing society chooses to present its options in a way that accommodates the needs of the target and the goals of the society and its policy; the individual chooses the best of the available options offered in the relevant competitive set.

Marketing accommodates the rights and responsibilities of both the individual and the society. In addition, the competition of alternative choices and the power of the individual to choose from amongst the alternatives force the manager to be both efficient and effective if the agency's goals are to be met.

Moving Toward a Code of Ethics for Social Marketing

One of the goals of the 1999 Georgetown University Seminar Series on the ethics of social marketing was to move toward a code of ethics for social marketing. The following are proposed as some desirable characteristics for such a code. These proposals focus on the ethicality of marketing as a tool of behavior management to be considered along with education and law; they do not consider either the ethicality of a particular policy or the ethicality of the specific tactics that may follow.

Do more good than harm. Utilitarianism supports the choice of strategies that fix more problems in the community than they cause. Seeking the greatest good for the greatest number acknowledges that we may not be able to develop strategies that always help everybody, but that we need to focus our efforts.

Favor free choice. Liberalism supports the choice of strategies that allow targets to make their own choices rather than have limited options thrust upon them. If a strategy that allows free choice can achieve the goals of the policy, then, other things being equal, it should be chosen. Given the values of most contemporary democratic states, allowing free choice provides an ethical advantage. A basic underpinning of a marketing transaction is that it must be entered into freely by both sides.

Evaluate marketing within a broader context of behavior management. Education, marketing, and law are each appropriate in different settings. It is premature and potentially unethical to select any strategy in the absence of a thorough analysis of the situation. Law may offer the most ethically appropriate mechanism when the target is resistant to behaving as policy makers desire, or when externalities are high; while law allows the individual less personal freedom, it may be more effective at managing externalities. Education may be most ethical when the target is prone to behave as the policy makers desire, or when externalities are low; while education allows the individual greater personal freedom, it may be less impactful at managing externalities. Marketing may be the best combination of ethicality and effectiveness when the use of law is overly coercive and restrictive of freedom, and when education will be inefficient and/or ineffective.

Select tactics that are effective and efficient. If marketing is seen as a set of tools of ethical merit, and if managers have the right to use marketing, then managers also have the moral responsibility to use marketing well. In a competitive, free choice society where the citizenry has a high level of power, managers must strive for efficiency and effectiveness. It is unethical to select a set of strategic tools that are not felt to be the most efficient and effective for the task at hand.

Select marketing tactics that fit marketing philosophy. If managers truly attempt to meet needs and develop exchanges that provide benefit to the target, then the resulting tactics generally will be ethical. The tactics that are found to be reprehensible in both commercial and social settings generally do not attempt to accommodate the needs of the target, but, rather, attempt to manipulate the behavior of the target for the self-interest of the organization.

Evaluate the ethicality of a policy before agreeing to develop strategy. Education, marketing, and law are neutral sets of tools; in the abstract none are ethical or unethical. The ethicality of their use depends in part on the ethicality of the policy that is being implemented. If the policy reflects societal values and is felt to be ethical, then resulting strategies also may be ethical; if the policy is not ethical, then it is questionable whether the chosen strategies can be ethical. Marketers need to separate the ethics of a policy from the ethicality of the tactics used to explicate the policy. If a policy is felt to be ethical and favors the management of a specific behavior, then the question of concern deals with the best way to implement the policy. Managers are obligated to assess the ethicality of a policy before agreeing to attempt to manage behavior on its behalf. For many issues (e.g., abortion), there may be more than one "ethically right" perspective being contested. Marketers need to make value judgments about the ends that they are choosing to promote.

The use of social marketing occurs in an extremely complex environment where there are many competing goals and values. This chapter has attempted to raise issues that allow the manager to work through some of these competing pulls, and to arrive at a position that balances ethicality, effectiveness, and efficiency.

Notes

Michael L. Rothschild is a professor in the School of Business, University of Wisconsin. This chapter is an expanded version of "Some Ethical Considerations in Support of the Marketing of Public Health Issues," which appeared in the *American Journal of Health Behavior* (January 2000). The author thanks Shauna Fugelstad for her assistance in the early stages of the development of this chapter, and Alan Andreasen, Laura Hartman, and Rodney Stevenson for their helpful comments.

1. This section summarizes many of the key ideas found in Rothschild (1999).
2. This section benefited considerably from Goldberg (1995).

References

Donaldson, T., and T. Dunfee. 1994. "Toward a Unified Conception of Business Ethics: Integrative Social Contracts Theory." *Academy of Management Review* 19: 252–264.

Dworkin, G. 1988. *The Theory and Practice of Autonomy*. Cambridge: Cambridge University Press.

Etizioni, A. 1993. *The Spirit of Community.* New York: Crown.

Feinberg, Joel. 1984. *The Moral Limits of the Criminal Law: Harm to Others.* Vol. 1. New York: Oxford University Press.

Fost, Norman. 1996. "What's Wrong with Genetic Engineering? Nothing New Under the Sun." *American Journal of Ethics and Medicine* 14 (Spring): 14–17.

Frankena, William. 1963. *Ethics*. Englewood Cliffs, NJ: Prentice-Hall.

Goldberg, D. T. 1995. *Ethical Theory and Social Issues: Historical Texts and Contemporary Readings*. Second Edition. Orlando, Fl: Harcourt Brace.

Kant, Immanuel. 1964. *Groundwork of the Metaphysics of Morals.* Transl. by H. J. Paton. New York: Harper and Row.

MacInnis, Deborah J., Christine Moorman, and Bernard J. Jaworski. 1991. "Enhancing and Measuring Consumers' Motivation, Opportunity, and Ability to Process Brand Information from Ads." *Journal of Marketing* 55 (October): 32–53.

Mead, Lawrence M. 1986. *Beyond Entitlement: The Social Obligations of Citizenship*. New York: The Free Press.

Mill, John Stuart. 1859/1991. *On Liberty and Other Essays.* Oxford: Oxford University Press.

Morone, James A. 1997. "Enemies of the People: The Moral Dimension to Public Health." *Journal of Health Politics, Policy and Law* 22: 993–1019.

Nozick, R. 1974. *Anarchy, State, and Utopia.* New York: Basic Books.

Ouchi, William G. 1980. "Markets, Bureaucracies, and Clans." *Administrative Science Quarterly* 25 (March): 129–141.

Plato. 1892. From *The Republic.* Trans. by Benjamin Jowett. *The Dialogues of Plato*. Oxford: Oxford University Press.

Rawls, John. 1971. *A Theory of Justice.* Cambridge: Harvard University Press.

Robin, Donald P., and R. Eric Reidenbach. 1987. "Social Responsibility, Ethics, and Marketing Strategy: Closing the Gap Between Concept and Application." *Journal of Marketing* 51 (January): 44–58.

———. 1993. "Searching for a Place to Stand: Toward a Workable Ethical Philosophy for Marketing." *Journal of Public Marketing* 12 (spring): 97–105.

Rothschild, Michael L. 1999. "Carrots, Sticks, and Promises: A Conceptual Framework for the Management of Public Health and Social Issue Behaviors." *Journal of Marketing* 63 (October): 24–37.

Sherrard, Michael. 1998. Personal correspondence.

Thompson, Craig J. 1995. "A Contextualist Proposal for the Conceptualization and Study of Marketing Ethics." *Journal of Public Policy and Marketing* 14 (fall): 177–191.

Walzer, Michael. 1990. *Political Theory* 18 (1): 6–23.

CHAPTER THREE

The Ethics of International Social Marketing

George G. Brenkert

Challenging Social Problems

Both developed and developing societies face a number of important problems, some of which have proven remarkably intractable. Among these difficult problems are the following: preventing the abuse of drugs, encouraging family planning, increasing the percentage of children immunized, decreasing the number of people smoking, and reducing pollution (Rangan et al. 1996). In addition, other such problems have included reducing the population explosion through sterilization campaigns and the use of condoms; eliminating leprosy; modifying purdah customs which harm women; encouraging families to use oral rehydration salts to protect children with diarrhea; reducing the abuse of women; increasing the number of women receiving an elementary education; preventing AIDS; encouraging the use of mass transit; and increasing the consumption of micronutrient-rich food by vulnerable individuals and communities.

Various attempts to solve these problems using education programs, government regulation, and voluntary groups, have had mixed success. Often these efforts are uncoordinated, poorly researched, and designed for those who seek to correct these problems rather than those for whom the social problems exist.

Social marketers believe that they have "a better idea" when it comes to resolving these problems both at home and abroad. And indeed a number of social marketing campaigns have been rather successful. In Sri

Lanka a social marketing campaign to eliminate leprosy has achieved its aim.[1] Other campaigns have also demonstrated considerable success.

My concern in this paper, however, is not to evaluate such successes or other purported failures of social marketing. Rather, it is to consider the ethics of social marketing, independently of any particular projects in which social marketers have engaged. In particular, I wish to focus, as much as possible, on the moral issues that specially arise with regard to international social marketing. It might well be expected that particularly interesting, important and difficult ethical issues arise when social marketing efforts are undertaken in other countries than the home country of the social marketer. It is these issues I want to explore.

With regard to the ethics of social marketing more generally, a number of ethical issues have been raised. Among these issues are those of coercion, justice, freedom, and privacy. Those issues also arise on the international level. However, I do not wish to proceed by announcing at the outset the ethical problems that arise regarding international social marketing. Further, I do not wish to raise ethical issues of social marketing in a manner in which they might arise with any form of marketing. Instead, I wish to look to international social marketing and to allow the ethical issues social marketers must face to arise out of an examination of the activities in which they are particularly engaged. In this manner, I believe, the ethics of social marketing will be more securely rooted in the phenomenon itself.

After having said a few things about what I take to be the nature of social marketing, I will contend that social marketers must be concerned with what I will call the problem of access, the problem of ends and the problem of means.

In each of these problem areas we may identify criteria by which to measure the morality of the activities social marketers undertake. As such, the point is to set up a structure within which to ask various questions, rather than to answer specific questions. I will, however, suggest various moral guidelines as I proceed, which will be more directed hopefully at the specific problems that international social marketers face. However, to begin we must fix our ideas as to the nature of social marketing.

What Is Social Marketing?

Social marketing is defined in a twofold manner, both by its aim and the method it adopts to achieve that aim.[2] Andreasen says that (A) "Social marketing is the application of commercial marketing technologies to the analysis, planning, execution, and evaluation of programs designed to influence the voluntary behavior of target audiences (B) in order to improve their personal welfare and that of their society" (Andreasen 1995). Neglect of either one of these defining characteristics runs the risk of assimilating social marketing to some other activity.

The aim of social marketing is to resolve certain social problems. Social marketing is identified by the non-commercial end it seeks to achieve. By this I mean problems that are not susceptible to, or have resisted, a market resolution, i.e., there are not particular products or services that marketers can sell for profit to the individuals said to have the problem.[3] As such, social marketing differs from commercial marketing in at least two important ways.

First, the aim of social marketing is individual or social good (welfare), not simply individual satisfaction. That is, the social problems social marketers attack are not simply a matter of individual wants or desires, but a matter of some deficiency or problem of individual or social well-being. In short, individuals may be able to satisfy their present wants, while their welfare and/or that of their society remains deficient. The two are not the same. Smokers may be content to smoke, husbands may desire that their wives be repeatedly pregnant, or drug abusers may want another fix. Nevertheless, there may be good reasons to hold that both individually and socially the welfare of those involved would be enhanced by reduced (or eliminated) smoking, reduced pregnancy rates and the absence of drug abuse. Accordingly, those situations calling for social marketing (i.e., those situations involving social problems) are identified based upon values and norms which may or may not be held by those people whom the social marketer addresses.

Second, the end to be achieved through social marketing is something which those experiencing the social problem need not themselves have identified as a social problem, e.g., improved education for women or the end of leprosy. Social marketers do research regarding what immediate "products"[4] would get those addressed to change their behaviors so as to foster various ends. The investigation of the responses of these groups relates to their acceptance of instrumental and immediate products, rather than the ends behind them.

The preceding is a first, necessary characteristic of social marketing. Obviously questions may arise over those who engage in commercial marketing while also addressing social problems. There are no sharp lines to be drawn in such cases. It is a question of emphasis and direction, not all of which may be obvious to external audiences. However, we might consider guidelines such as the following:

- If a marketer (M) aims at fostering both commercial exchanges (CE) and solving social problems (SP), and would claim success if CE were achieved, even if SP were not, then M is not a social marketer.
- If M aims at CE and SP and would not claim success if CE went great, but SP did not, but still would not reduce CE to achieve more SP, then M is not a social marketer.
- If M aims at CE and SP, but M's activities are measured by M's success in CE, but not SP, then M is not a social marketer.

However, the remainder of the answer to the nature of social marketing also depends upon the methods used to resolve social problems.

Methodologically, it is important to emphasize that social marketing is not simply the same as education, advertising, or propaganda, even though it may include some (or all) of these. Politicians, educators, church leaders and volunteers have tried to follow these different means of social change with varying success. Social marketers claim that they have a better, more comprehensive and more reliable approach to eliminate or reduce social problems.

This approach, as a form of marketing, involves market research; the design or identification of a "product" to fit needs of "customers"; the determination of a price the customer can pay; the location of a place where the customer can get the product; and the promotion of the product through advertising, incentives, etc. In short, as with commercial marketing, social marketing seeks to foster exchanges following the lines of the 4 Ps: Product, Place, Price, Promotion (cf. Andreasen 1994, 112).

Thus social marketing is a complex process involving interviewing target audiences, persuading them to engage in the exchanges social marketers (and others) seek to promote, setting up distribution networks, etc.

It involves infrastructural work, as well as attempts to maintain the effects of the exchange or to encourage ongoing exchanges in the future so as to eliminate the social problem addressed. In this way it is a form of marketing, as its very name implies.

There are two important implications that follow from the preceding. First, social marketing is not to be identified with any of its parts. Social marketing does not occur when a lone advertisement with social content appears. Accordingly, if Benetton runs an ad on behalf of racial harmony, it does not follow, without additional information, that this is an instance of social marketing. The efforts of such for-profit and nonprofits—when limited to such advertisements—may better be identified as a form of cause-related marketing, but not social marketing.[5]

Second, as a form of marketing, social marketing involves various values. Neither it nor commercial marketing are value-neutral disciplines. They both involve various values regarding the exchanges they examine and seek to promote. Among such values are: (a) the value of voluntary action, (b) the view that problems can and should be solved by human intervention, (c) the view that behaviors of one type may be justifiably exchanged for behaviors of another type; (d) the sense of self-efficacy; and (e) the importance of providing people with information about the products and/or themselves.

Finally, we should distinguish three concepts: (a) the techniques of (social) marketing, (b) social marketing, and (c) social marketers. The techniques of social marketing (e.g., focus groups, surveys, etc.) may be value neutral in ways in which the other two items are not, and cannot be, value neutral. Social marketing itself is some set of these techniques together with various values which guide their application. Sometimes social marketers distinguish only two of these three. Distinguishing all three can help to address various moral issues that confront social marketing.

With this view of social marketing in mind, we can now ask what ethical issues particularly arise when social marketing goes global.

International Social Marketing

We may begin by recalling some of the projects social marketers have undertaken internationally. These include efforts to eliminate leprosy (e.g., in Sri Lanka), to increase the level of education of girls in developing countries (e.g., in Bangladesh), to reduce the physical abuse of women by husbands, to increase the use condoms to prevent unwanted pregnancies and exposure to the AIDS virus, to increase the use of oral rehydration salts to combat the effects of diarrhea in children and to decrease the practice of female genital mutilation.

In all these cases, social marketers have sought to remedy a public or social problem through marketing efforts designed to change the behavior of those involved.

It is obvious that the nature of these projects differs considerably:

A. Locus of benefit. Some projects involve a change in behavior that solely benefits the individual, while other behavior changes directly benefit others. In yet other cases, all those involved may benefit.

B. Targeted parties. In some cases, the behavior change is required by an individual; in other cases, the changed behavior is required by that individual as well as others.

C. Values changes. In some cases, requiring change of behavior will not require any change in values or norms, while in other cases it will require just such changes.

D. Moral changes. Some changes in values and norms will involve moral changes, others will not. To persuade a husband or community to cease the practice of female genital mutilation may require changes in the moral values and/or principles held by that community. On the other hand, efforts to get men to use condoms to prevent pregnancies they do not want may not involve moral changes, but changes in values or norms related to questions of pleasure, convenience, or customary forms of sex.

And in all these cases, I am supposing that those playing a prominent role in fostering such changes are social marketers who are not members of the society in which the changes are sought.[6]

In examining the ethics of international social marketing it is important also to recall, as I noted above, that various ethical questions regarding fairness, manipulation, wastefulness, intrusiveness, etc. (Laczniak and Murphy 1993, 245) have been raised both about marketing and social marketing. However, the questions we consider should not look simply at these generic ethical problems which arise for marketers, but at the ethical problems which arise for social marketers in an international context.

In this spirit, I suggest that social marketers who work internationally may encounter ethical questions in three general areas:

First, questions may arise when social marketers from one country undertake these projects in another country. On what grounds or bases do such outsiders undertake these projects in a country other than their own? (The Problem of Access)

Second, ethical problems may arise over the value ends these projects involve (implicitly or explicitly). These are projects with ends regarding which the values of the society may conflict or members of the society may disagree. Do social marketers place themselves in the position of imposing their values on those targeted? Are they modern missionaries engaged in moral colonization? (The Problem of Ends)

Third, ethical issues may arise over the means used to achieve the preceding ends. The very methods that marketers use imply certain values and norms. Hence, even if a native or citizen of the country used these methods (he/she had learned them from books or studying where they were developed), questions might be raised about importing an alien methodology to this particular setting and imposing it on the individuals involved. This would be a question not about undertaking these projects as such, but about the methods with which these projects were undertaken. (The Problem of Means)

The Problem of Access

Consider first the *Problem of Access* and the conditions under which social marketers from one country may have access to address such (moral) issues in another country.

There are several unique features characterizing social marketers operating internationally that raise ethical concerns. Four of these features are the following:

First, ex hypothesis the social marketers are not members or citizens of the country in which they are undertaking a social marketing project.[7] Because they are not members of that society, they do not have the same responsibilities or rights of citizens of that society. In short, they do not have a stake in that society similar to that of members of the society. The implication is that they might leave or abandon the country and their projects in ways in which those who are members of that society might not (or could not). This reminds us that global social marketers are "guests" or "visitors" in the countries in which they work. They arrive only with permission, and may leave without the same implications as citizens of that country. This raises special ethical problems.

Second, as guests or visitors, social marketers may be of a different race, ethnicity, and/or religion from those they seek to change. Certainly, they will have been shaped by a different cultural heritage and history. Individuals who are not from the society they work in may well lack certain common background knowledge, assumptions, world views and values which may, as a consequence, lead them to undervalue or disregard certain implications of their work more readily apparent to others. These formative influences may raise questions of bias, indifference, lack of understanding, lack of sympathy, etc., toward those they seek to change. Hence, they must take special precautions against these consequences.

Third, social marketers generally will have greater powers and resources than those they seek to change. These powers may be due to their country of origin, prestige that derives from that origin, resources that they have, and other factors. In short, global social marketers are involved in projects in which there may well be power imbalances between themselves and those they seek to help, as well as those in the country with whom they work.

Fourth, for outside social marketers to undertake such projects may imply or suggest that local agencies or talent are inadequate or incompetent. It might be said that an invitation to foreign social marketers to work on social problems in another country already suggests mutual dependence, cooperation, and community with others. Although there may be some truth to this, this response does not refute the previous suggestion that the fact that outside social marketers are required may imply some sort of inadequacy on the part of local talent and/or resources.

These features of international social marketing raise various moral questions which social marketers must address prior to undertaking the particular projects they are engaged to resolve. In particular, they suggest that we must ask about the conditions social marketers must fulfill in order to have morally justified access to a targeted population in another country. I wish to suggest six moral guidelines, apart from any conditions regarding the moral justifiability of the projects themselves.

First, it is important to remember that typically social marketers do not have a moral obligation to correct the social problems they address, particularly when these occur in other countries. These are problems they may choose to help resolve, but which they are not morally required to help resolve.

There are situations, of course, under which we could imagine that they do have a moral obligation to address these problems. Such situations would be characterized by the following facts: the social marketers in question have the ability to correct the problems, they are proximate (in some manner) to the problems, no others are more capable of solving those problems, and there is an urgency which requires that they exercise their abilities to do so rather than waiting for some other group to develop those abilities.[8] But generally, this won't be the case.

Second, assuming the moral legitimacy of national boundaries and national authorities, social marketeers seeking to operate in other countries are obligated to seek permission not only to enter those countries, but also to address the social problems they seek to resolve. Even in such cases—which I call normal social marketing—social marketers must be aware that the authorities themselves may not have thought through all the implications of such activities. Permission to enter a country and to address a social problem does not absolve social marketers from responsibility for their actions regarding this problem. Further, the authorities may have various "off-purpose" aims behind allowing social marketers access. Perhaps they are trying to gain favor with other international groups or to add to their luster by inviting foreign social marketers to address local problems. In any case, social marketers must be concerned about these "off-purpose" uses of their efforts. Though a social marketer need not demand that there be no "off-purpose" effects of their activities, they must ascertain that these do not, or will not, undermine the justification for the project that they undertake.

Third, it is mistaken, however, to hold that the moral permission to address social problems in a country could only come from the permission or the acquiescence of the national (and local) authorities. The reason is that these individuals and/or institutions may be corrupt or illegitimate. In short, it is possible to imagine radical social marketing where the authorities do not agree or are not legitimate, and yet the social problems themselves are dire, requiring social marketing from a distance or undercover.[9] I won't discuss this kind of case, though it is important as a limiting case and an indication of the boundaries within which normal social marketing operates. In radical social marketing, social marketers might be sought by international agencies or agencies of other nations to engage in activities from a distance or undercover so as to correct various social problems. It has been suggested that such a project would involve working to change the social systems involved (Laczniak and Murphy 1993, 242). The point here is that the moral authorization comes from the nature of those social problems within the particular society, rather than any approval by the de facto authorities. Such considerations, as just noted, can override the authorities. Indeed, the greater the problem that the members of a society face, the more easily could a lack of authorization by its authorities be morally overridden. This is not to say that it can be more practically overridden. Ethicists must worry not only about what should be done, but also about what can be done.

Fourth, because international social marketers come from different countries they must take special steps to ensure that they adequately understand the culture, its values, norms, expectations, possibilities, and limitations before undertaking social projects and proposing solutions. The same techniques used in different societies may carry very different implications and associations. Part of the moral justifiability of their access to groups in different societies is that their understanding of the context in which they propose to operate is adequate to the task.

Fifth, because social marketers seek to introduce behavioral (and possibly value) changes which may in turn have important direct, as well as indirect and unforeseen consequences and implications, social marketers must take steps to ensure that there will be responsible parties who can be held accountable for the changes produced. Because social marketers are, ex hypothesis, from another society and culture, they do not (as such) have comparable stakes in the present society. Hence, the importance of there being a responsible party to be accountable for unwitting changes.

Sixth, in proposing solutions in one country, social marketers must seek to eliminate (or make transparent) conflicting interests that they may have with commitments in other countries. If a solution for social problems in one country is driven by interests the social marketers have in another country, these conflicting interests must either be open (and accepted by those authorizing the social marketers' activities) or eliminated.[10]

It is in light of these guidelines, I suggest, that social marketers could be said to have morally justified access to attempt to resolve the social problems of another country. Of course, these conditions themselves are not sufficient for those efforts to be finally justified. For this, both the general ends social marketers seek (and in terms of which various situations are identified as social problems) and the means they use to solve problems must be justified. These items are discussed with special reference to the international setting in the next two parts below.

Social Marketing and the Ends of Social Problems

The second issue (the *Problem of Ends*) concerns the ends the particular projects implicitly or explicitly involve. Recall that the above examples of social marketing included the following: eliminating leprosy, increasing the number of young women educated, preventing the circumcision of young women, stopping the physical abuse males engage in against women, seeking to get children with diarrhea to be treated with oral rehydration salts, and increasing the number of children immunized.

In considering the ethics surrounding these projects, I suggest that we need to distinguish between proximate ends and general ends. The preceding examples list the particular, or proximate ends intended by these projects, e.g., increasing the number of women educated. However, these proximate ends imply more general ends (which may involve either goods and/or rights), such as those of physical health, sexual or physical integrity, greater equal opportunities for educational and individual development, and environmental sustainability.

These general ends are important in two ways:

First, it is only in light of such general ends that the situations addressed are seen as involving social "problems." A low number of women being educated is a social problem only if we value, or view as a right, not only education, but some sort of equality of education. A high number of children being born per family is only a "problem" if we hold not simply various empirical beliefs about resources, but also accept certain general ends about individual development and environmental sustainability. As such, the social projects undertaken by social marketers can be seen as means to, and/or constitutive of, various ends. These general ends give the rationale (or, at least part of it) for claiming that the individuals involved face social problems or that their individual and/or social welfare is deficient.

Second, it is only in light of such general ends that attempting to accomplish the above proximate ends is justified. Because we believe that young women should be educated in a manner comparable to young men, the fact that this does not occur in Bangladesh deserves redress. Because we believe that a healthy life does not involve diseases such as leprosy, we believe we should seek to eliminate leprosy. If, contrariwise, we believed that epilepsy was a sign of the spirits, we might not want to intervene to alter those who have been chosen by the spirits.

Now, regarding these general ends, (at least) two ethical issues arise: First, what view or interpretation of the general ends on which we operate is morally justified? Second, what is the order or priority of those ends (both proximate and general)?

Clearly I cannot resolve these important, difficult, and basic moral issues in this paper. What I can do is to point them out as problems with which social marketers wittingly (or unwittingly) will have to have a stance and to make some brief suggestions as to the directions in which more complete answers would or would not go in an international context.

What is clear, as I noted earlier, is that marketers cannot simply leave the determination of these questions to the national and/or local authorities because those authorities may or may not be legitimate. Further, they may arrive at mistaken interpretations or identifications of the problems that require resolution and the ends to be sought in resolving them. Social marketers must be convinced that the ends they seek to promote are themselves justified. They may not, simply as agents for a client, undertake projects that reason suggests are morally impermissible, wrong or harmful. Social marketers are not like lawyers, hired to ensure a legal process; rather they are engaged to achieve specific ends. They are not engaged in some competitive process which, if properly pursued with the proper adversaries, will reasonably lead to acceptable results. They must be reasonably convinced that the ends towards which they work are morally or rationally justified.

In short, social marketers must have a theory of general ends. They must determine whether the proximate ends they seek and the more general end embracing it (conceptually or instrumentally) are morally worthy of pursuit in any particular situation. Then, given justified access, they may (but generally are not obligated to) pursue those specific (and general) ends (using means which must themselves be morally justified). This requires a theory of general basic values and rights. Further, it requires an interpretation and hierarchical ordering of these for specific societies.

	Rights	Goods
Positive Ends	Equal educational opportunity; self-determination	Various physical and mental health conditions; beautification projects (planting trees)
Negative Ends	Physical security (lack of physical abuse); unpolluted environment	Absence of disease; reduction in smoking

Figure 3-1. General Ends

To open up this discussion, I would note the differences existing between the various general ends sought by social marketers. Some ends are positive in that they require that action be taken for oneself or others, while others are negative, requiring that various actions not be taken. Some ends involve rights, that is, various justified claims or entitlements which one can assert against others to demand certain forms of treatment. Other ends concern the nature of goods, that is various desirable conditions or states of being which comprise individual or social welfare. If we put the preceding distinctions together we get the following matrix (see Figure 3-1) which we may explore.

With this matrix in mind, I suggest (but cannot argue here) the following:

First, there is a set of general ends that hold for all humans. These include some of those noted above: physical and psychological health, freedom from harm, freedom of movement, etc. Some of these have been captured, in part, by the United Nations Declaration of Human Rights, though we might dispute the extent and significance of these rights rather than goods. In identifying these ends, two particularly important and difficult issues arise. One concerns the distinction between those ends required in some similar fashion for all people (rights), and those ends that are highly desirable, but which different societies might (or might not) adopt as part of their view of the good life.[11]

The other issue has to do with the interpretation or content of these ends. General ends such as the lack of physical harm, education, and mental health may be valued universally, but the particular forms may differ among societies. Hence, the issue arises as to how specifically we can identify the content of general ends to which social marketers must appeal. Unless we can specify some similarity of content for these general ends, they might seem to evaporate in an air of abstraction. That is, if everyone is for health, education, and physical security but nobody intends the same content for these terms, what are the general ends everyone really supposedly agrees upon and to which social marketers must appeal to justify their activities? On the other hand, if we insist that the nature of these ends is exactly the same for all societies, charges of moral imperialism might plausibly be brought against social marketers.

There are a number of directions in which we might look to address these questions. For example, the more the ends people seek involve behaviors that tend to physically harm other people, the greater the similarity of content that might justifiably be attributed to those ends. Hence, the general ends that social marketers invoke against torture to individuals might plausibly display greater similarity of content across different societies than other more positive general ends in the form of various goods (e.g., various housing or food requirements). In addition, the former will be regarded as rights to be protected (e.g., the right to live free of physical torture or coercion), rather than merely goods to be fulfilled. Finally, the more the background institutions of two societies are similar, the more reasonable may be our expectation that general ends of the same content or nature may be applied to both. In each of these cases, the concern is to find ways to specify some content to general ends that justify more particular ends and activities.

Second, given a justified set of general ends, the members of a country may decide to use their resources in one way rather than another to achieve those ends. That is, there may not be a single correct distribution of such resources. Reasonable people may attack some problems as more immediately important than others. Accordingly, there is no single sanctified hierarchy according to which all ends must be realized. Different societies and times might emphasize some ends more than others.

Nevertheless, some general guidelines are also possible here. Again, those general ends which involve negative ends will tend to be viewed as more pressing than those which involve positive ends. That is, all things being equal, the fulfillment of negative (moral) ends would take precedence over other positive ends. Further, those ends that involve rights are more important than various goods. The reasons here may be consequential, constitutive of our humanness, or linked to fundamental universal principles (i.e., deontological).

What follows, I suggest, is that social marketers operating in other countries must give particular attention (though not necessarily final acceptance) to the hierarchy of ends justifiably adopted by that country. Other things being equal, social marketers should operate in accordance with the hierarchy of the host country rather than any such hierarchy exported from their home country. In this sense, host hierarchies trump home hierarchies, at least among legitimately different hierarchies. In short, the burden of proof is on social marketers to demonstrate that hierarchies they bring from abroad may justifiably replace hierarchies established by the host society for itself.

Further, if social marketers determine that their efforts to achieve some general end will directly render the society's efforts to achieve some other more highly esteemed end less possible, then they have an obligation to inform those involved of this implication or consequence. For example, if birth control methods will endanger the health of the women involved, then marketers have an obligation to inform those involved that efforts to achieve one general end (pursuit of adequate resources through a manageable population size), may (or will) impact another general end (promoting the health of people in that society). The responsibility of the social marketer for these effects is direct, as is their obligation to inform other responsible or interested parties.

However, some consequences are indirect. For example, the education of women may produce additional indirect results in the society concerning the size of families, the nature of families, and changes in the social order of which the society should be made aware. Social marketers should also convey information regarding these results to those who employ them. The responsibility of the social marketer for these effects is diminished to the extent to which these results may be affected by other trends in society and may not occur for other reasons. So, too, the responsibility of the social marketer to inform relevant others as to the implications of their actions is reduced the less likely and the less significant such results become.

The general implication here seems to be that the more direct and the more significant the results of the social marketers' actions upon the realization of various ends in a hierarchy of ends, the greater the obligation of the social marketer to inform those involved of these consequences. Otherwise, marketers are (at the least) accomplices if, for example, they undertake projects that waste or misuse public funds or private funds to solve social problems. They cannot simply identify projects from which they would profit and seek to undertake these without engaging in thoughtful consideration of the consequences.

Third, the above general ends extend to all people equally and in a similar manner unless good reasons can be given to show that they must be restricted in their extension to a particular class of people (e.g., women; children; people of a certain race, ethnic group, or religion), or significantly modified (in a morally relevant fashion) in their realization by that group of people.

Such modifications or restrictions may be justifiably imposed only if they can be shown to promote those general ends. This is different from saying that they promote the general welfare. Instead, restrictions on how equality extends to certain persons must serve to promote equality; restrictions on how justice is administered to various people must serve to promote justice.

Within the preceding qualification, the traditions, history, and customs of the society play an important and justified role. In particular, social marketers must be able to show that no other specific end compatible with the general end would accomplish or fulfill the same end (and its priority) and do so with greater compatibility with the target group's other moral views, customs, traditions and history.

Fourth, some of these ends involve various objective, empirical elements which are subject to scientific examination, e.g., matters concerning physical and, to some extent, mental health. As such, a person may not be knowledgeable about what is in his or her own best welfare. The use of condoms does give greater protection against the AIDS virus than failure to use them. Vaccinations against smallpox, diphtheria, etc., do give greater protection against these diseases than reliance on prayer. In short, people may "get it wrong" concerning their own health and well-being.

Still, these scientific, or "objective," facts need not always be morally determinative. For example, the fact that a course of behavior leads to a person's death is not necessarily a overriding reason to prevent that person from engaging in such behavior. In the United States, for example, Jehovah's Witnesses are permitted to reject blood transfusions for themselves. The principle here is that when people hold a normative principle deeply and on a religious basis, and their holding it does not harm other people, then they may act on that principle even though their doing so may harm, or even indirectly kill, themselves.[12] There is no reason not to extend this principle to those in other countries in which social marketers seek to operate.

On the other hand, it also follows that it is less plausible to allow Jehovah's Witnesses to deny education to their children or to physically or mentally harm them in other ways that do not have the widely recognized and respected sanction of their religion. Again, cultural forms will play important roles here. Many western societies allow male circumcision, body piercing, and tattooing without moral condemnation or legal or moral prohibition.[13] Again, the principle that I assume we view as justified is that one ought not to deny certain basic formative activities and experiences to a human being without some terribly significant, overriding, and compelling reason. On the other hand, other life-defining effects may be imposed on children if those effects nevertheless leave a significantly open door to other activities they may later engage in. However, having achieved maturity, individuals may themselves make decisions that restrict their own activities and future possibilities.

What about groups restricting (scientific) information to their members about the lives and views of other people? They may view it as biased or invalid information, or even an attempt to undermine their identity or values. They might believe, for example, that the scientific information establishing the danger of not being vaccinated should not be known by their group. Other groups may wish to educate their children in ways that exclude, for example, information about evolution. In both cases, the groups involved may believe that such information may be damaging to their cultural identity and basic beliefs. Nevertheless, such information may also be play a crucial role in a proposed social marketing campaign.

In considering situations in which people act to exclude information in order to protect their own cultural values, it is important to distinguish three different concerns: (a) What is (we believe) morally required? (b) What morally justifies the use of state power (through laws and regulations) to correct such situations? And (c) What may social marketers feel morally justified in changing through the use of their influence, but not through use of physical, coercive power? This last case might even have two subcases: (1) when social marketers work at the acquiescence or with the permission of the government, or (2) when they become involved at the direct request of the government.

Surely it is justified to want one's children to be like oneself, at least in those aspects that are desirable and justified. It is also justified to try to defend one's own cultural identity. However, in both cases this tendency toward preservation of cultural or family identity should be limited to characteristics that are not morally undesirable and/or unjustifiable. Thus, it is morally troubling, I suggest, when some deaf people do not want to have their children's hearing repaired because it perceived as an attack on their cultural identity. Accordingly, I suggest that the values of a group may override the evidence of science when doing so does not harm others, when it only indirectly harms those who refuse the benefits of change, and when doing so does not close off opportunities for those who are unable (or too young) to choose for themselves.

Fifth, the manner in which people exercise their ends or purposes is important. Here again, we must address another set of questions: Does this group harm others or simply itself? Do those who follow these ends do so in an informed or uninformed manner? Do they understand the implications and consequences of their behavior (both individually and collectively)? If the general ends sought by social marketers do not involve the participation of those involved in the selection of proximate and general ends, but simply in the means to achieve those ends, then we should also be concerned about the paternalistic effects on those targeted and the implications for developing societies of a democratic nature. Giving voice to those affected, not simply with regard to the means, but also regarding general ends is surely a matter of treating those people with respect. If targeted individuals are permitted no say, and little awareness, regarding the general ends towards which they are being directed, they are treated more like incompetent individuals than adults.

Finally, we may feel compelled to promote certain other general ends, such as the importance of diversity. Still, diversity can be overdone; it can rupture social bonds. Societies need bonds that create unity within a society. And a society may take limited, but positive steps to ensure that that takes place. This is clearly true in the case of actions that cause physical harm to other people, that immorally appropriate their property, or which defame their good character. However, it may also be the case with other less obvious values and standards, such as those regarding actions held to be deeply offensive to the vast majority of the citizenry. Social marketers undertake to challenge such standards and values at great moral risk.

Only when a social marketer's actions to promote proximate and general ends meet these conditions do social marketers justifiably operate in another country. This is a second necessary—but still not a sufficient—condition for the justification of the actions of social marketers.

Social Marketers and the Means to Solve Social Problems

The realization of these proximate and general ends requires various means or methods which may themselves be ethically questioned. These means, methods, or techniques flow from marketing's achievements in commercial marketing. And, as in ordinary marketing, "influencing behavior is social marketing's fundamental objective" (Andreasen 1995, xi).

The means social marketers use to influence or alter behavior should sound familiar to commercial marketers. They include:

First: Researching consumer change profiles. Social marketers stress that their emphasis is on the customer. By this they mean that the characteristics of the customer determine the best means by which proximate ends may be achieved.

Second: Returning repeatedly to consumers to see what they can/will accept and what will motivate them. Social marketers draw on studies of their customers' motivational and cognitive development.

Third: Creating structures to handle the 4 Ps. Social marketing involves creating or identifying a product that those addressed will seek or adopt, a place where those individuals can get that product, a price they can afford, and the promotion of that product. Social marketing is an integrated effort to bring about desired behavioral change.

In short, social marketing seeks, through continued interaction with the customer, to modify or influence his/her behavior (and values, etc.) such that the problems to be resolved are reduced, if not eliminated. This process requires a close knowledge of those involved so that such influence over these customers may be effected.

What special ethical problems (if any) does the use of such means, even if so generally described, incur for social marketing when it is pursued internationally? There are two major sets of considerations involved.

First, though the solution to these social problems is said to involve behavior changes, some of the problems also require value (or attitudinal) changes on the part of some individuals. Further, some of the value changes involved may relate to basic values the individual(s) hold, while other value changes may not. Changes in behavior (without or without value changes) may involve acquisition of new information, new incentives (pulls) provided or new pressures (pushes) applied.

Second, some problems require behavioral changes that (a) benefit others directly (in the present or near future), (b) benefit oneself only indirectly (or in the future), or (c) benefit both (in the same manner). These categories and those of the preceding paragraph are captured in Figure 3-2. Clearly many of the items listed in one category might also be brought under one or more other categories. The means and aims of social marketers cannot be neatly isolated in separate boxes. Further, depending on which groups are involved and what their basic values and beliefs are, items in one box might occur more plausibly in other boxes. The items in Figure 3-2 would have to be determined for each group addressed.

Nevertheless, this categorization is helpful. How, using these categories, does international social marketing pose special ethical problems?

First, it is often suggested that the methods social marketers use are value free. Such methods include focus groups, surveys of groups to be addressed, analyses of consumer behavior and motivation, segmentation analyses, etc. Since these methods are supposed to be value free, one might conclude that few ethical or value issues could arise when social marketers apply such methods in their home country or in a foreign country. On the contrary, I suggest, the methods that social marketers use are not value free. The idea of value-free methods in the social and human sciences is very questionable. What values, then, do these social marketing methods involve?

I suggest that they involve such values (and value assumptions) as: (a) humans (and not God or fate) may solve various problems which afflict them; (b) the solution to problems that face people requires listening to (or gaining input from) those affected, such as by conducting surveys or focus groups; (c) the fulfillment of certain general ends for individual welfare or social welfare (as defined by non-local standards and in part by objective

	Benefits to Oneself	Benefits to Others	Benefits to Oneself and Others
Behavioral Change	Exercise programs	Reducing abuse of women	Immunizing children
Basic Value Change (BVC)	Elimination certain basic role stereotypes	Eliminating female circumcision	Allowing education of women family members
Peripheral Value Change (PVC)	Stopping smoking	Reducing polluting activities	Male use of condoms

Figure 3-2. Behavioral and Value Changes and Their Benefits

standards) is important and desirable; (d) knowledge of the problems facing a group is important for the solution of those problems; (e) we can and may control various aspects of our environment deemed undesirable by us or others; (f) individuals should be offered something in return for their changed behavior; (g) people must voluntarily make these changes and be rewarded for doing so if the behavioral change is to "stick"; (h) voluntary action is desirable; (i) problems can be solved; (j) behaviors of one type may be exchanged for behaviors of another type; (k) the sense of self-efficacy is important and desirable; and (l) granting people information about themselves and their problems is desirable (cf. Andreasen 1995, 264).

These values and value-laden assumptions may seem terribly obvious to us. However, the fact that they are obvious does not render them less important as values transmitted wittingly or unwittingly by social marketers to those they address. In short, the means that social marketers use imply various broad value and normative ends that may be at odds with the values and norms of a targeted group. Thus, some groups may view leprosy or other diseases as some form of punishment from some spiritual or religious being which afflicts humans. Similarly, the use of scientific medical means, rather than prayer, may be seen by Jehovah's witnesses, the Hmong, or some Christian Scientists, as an unjustifiable intervention into a religious realm. Asking women or certain castes of people about what they would like about certain topics may also be seen as a threat to values that a society lives by.

In this sense, social marketing may itself be seen as a Western, if not a North American creation. Hence, whoever employs it will be introducing values that may be "foreign" to the countries in which it is used. For example, if a Hmong were socialized in the United States and returned to Laos with social marketing techniques, though this person was native to Laos, he or she would still be bringing foreign values to bear.

Accordingly, social marketers must ask themselves if it is appropriate to foster these foreign values in those whose behavior they seek to change.[14] A decision to do so implies that the values (and behavior) of some individuals will be modified in ways that they may or may not fully comprehend. In doing so, one may be promoting (more or less) a very different way of life, and thereby contributing to the demise of the way of life it replaces. This may have implications that the social marketer will have difficulties determining, but for which they are nevertheless responsible.

What guidelines should social marketers follow when it comes to the question of introducing these values into the process whereby various means are identified to change people's behavior? I suggest one background condition and two general guidelines.

The background condition is that the use of these means and values is justified only when they are in the service of proximate and general ends that are justified for these people. Good or ethical means, in the service of ethically unjustified ends is a non-starter. In considering the present question of the values implicit in the means we must assume that these means are directed towards justified ends (cf. previous section).

The two general guideline principles are these. On the one hand, implementation of the above values through the means of social marketing will, ex hypothesis, speak to the values (either basic or peripheral) of those addressed. The general principle that should be invoked here is that the more basic the values of those addressed by social marketers and the greater discrepancy between those values and the values implicit in social marketing means, the greater the care that social marketers must take to accommodate their means to those values.

The other general guideline is that the more those basic values are incompatible with general ends and the more they involve other-destructive behavior, the greater the justification of social marketers, ceteris paribus, to use their value-laden methods to try to change that behavior and those values.

It is true that through their economic means, prestige, etc., they may bring certain forces and pressures to bear on others. They may, in short, be seen as seeking to impose their values on others. The upshot must be that not all attempts to impose values are equal; some are more justified than others.

Second, though these problems are designated as "social" problems, and hence we speak of social marketing, these problems frequently have political, religious, and economic dimensions. Children develop diarrhea because of dirty water; dirty water may result from inadequate sanitation facilities or industrial plants; these in turn may result from local or national political leaders who siphon funds away from sanitation projects to build nuclear bombs. The equal treatment of women (equal education opportunities, freedom from physical abuse and female circumcision) may raise political fears of the ruling male classes about unleashing forces in society they do not know how to handle or control. Certain political factions may find it attractive to target impoverished classes for family planning through the use of sterilization in an attempt to control their numbers, and thus their political power. On the other hand, family planning efforts may be aimed at middle classes because they offer the greatest receptivity to the social marketers' campaign. In this case, those groups or classes most in need may be left behind.

As such, attempting to resolve many of the immediate problems social marketers face may leave other important background problems and collateral effects in place. It may protect those with the power to change the underlying or background problem. Indeed, the use of foreign social marketers in developing countries might carry implications of prestige and legitimacy for the privileged classes, which could undermine social marketers' efforts to change relevant parts of the society.

Consequently, social marketers must consider not simply whether the means they suggest to resolve present problems, but also whether those means and resolutions may produce collateral effects that negatively affect surrounding problems either by preventing or inhibiting their solution, or by creating new problems. The more that such undesirable collateral effects may develop, the less justified such efforts are.

Accordingly, a means to change behavior is only morally acceptable if it will not create more social problems than it solves; if it does create additional problems, there are means readily available to solve those problems. However, this guideline leaves open the question of what we should say when the means adopted to change behaviors are not successful. Suppose that a means adopted to change behavior harmed people even more than if no help had been proffered at all. It would seem peculiar to say that this failed means was morally acceptable simply on the grounds that if it had been successful then the situation would have been improved.

Consequently, we must also say that a means to change behavior is only morally acceptable if, should it be unsuccessful, it either creates no additional harm, or if greater harm is created, measures will be undertaken to alleviate that harm.[15] Because social marketers, rather than commercial marketers, seek to promote social welfare, these considerations are ones to which they must be specially attuned so as to avoid any charges of self-defeating actions, i.e., actions which undercut or undo the very end which the actor seeks to accomplish.

Third, though social marketers speak of placing the customer first, they do so only in a limited manner. As noted above, they tend to ask those they address about what means they will most readily accept, rather than the proximate or general ends they seek to realize. The questions put to Bangladeshi fathers do not concern the proximate end of educating their daughters, but the circumstances under which they could accept it or be led to accept it. In short, the social marketing approach to correcting social problems does not give those addressed a say in defining the social problems to be addressed, only in the means used to solve those problems. Further, the criteria defining a solution are also designated by others. It leaves those addressed to accept or reject what is proposed to them on the basis of surveys, focus groups, etc.

Is there anything problematic with this? They can, after all, reject the proposals or solutions offered. But social marketers will also seek to bring social and peer pressures to bear on these individuals to accept such proposals. Suppose, however, that the ends are justified (or believed to be justified) by the social marketers. Still, the process by which those ends are selected is not, as such, addressed. Accordingly, such individuals are not given a voice in the ends to which they are being persuaded. To the extent that such individuals are denied a voice in identifying the ends as well as means, this method of correcting social problems may undercut basic democratic values.

This approach to social problems and its undesireable effect is encouraged, I believe, by labeling those individuals "targeted" by social marketers as "customers."[16] Customers, in a market society, do not have a political voice in the firms that "serve" them; they cannot vote, other than by using their money to buy or not buy its goods and services, to boycott or to petition the businesses involved. But these means are not a "vote" in a traditional political sense. On the contrary, in a traditional democratic political system, each person has one vote. In a market economy, those with the most money have much more influence in their purchases or failure to purchase. Those without money have little or no influence. Similarly, the fathers of daughters with inadequate education are not properly "customers." Relationships involving customers are different from those involving "clients," "patients," "citizens," etc. These terms refer to different clusters of values, moral principles, and justified expectations. Modern philosophical and political thought has established the importance of the words we use and how we conceptualize the problems we face.

Suppose, then, that social marketers referred to those they sought to help as "citizens" or "clients" to better reflect the social nature of their task. These appellations would suggest that those they addressed would deserve some sort of voice in what was being proposed to them, and not simply the means to achieve that proximate end.

However, not everything must be collectively decided even in societies that are very democratic. The guideline here, I take it, is that the more important the proximate ends that social marketers are trying to persuade people to adopt, the more they are obliged to incorporate democratic means in the selection of those ends.

I would note that I have cast this point in terms of various democratic procedures in a society. I take it that those procedures are means whereby people in a society may exercise their own self-determination. As such, this point may bear interesting connections with the view, noted elsewhere by Craig Smith, that an ethical issue specific to social marketing is that individual autonomy of those addressed may be compromised by the program goal of serving the broader society.[17]

Fourth, it was noted above that social problems exist within a political, economic and historical context. Accordingly, gaining knowledge about social problems and how various groups or individuals respond to them may have far broader implications. As a consequence, in gaining knowledge about targeted groups, social marketers may learn important information about individuals in groups (e.g., information leaders), as well as about groups of people themselves, information that could be of use to political organizations seeking means or reasons to increase their influence over such groups or individuals. This information might be directly, or incidentally acquired in response to questions or surveys social marketers undertake. In any case, this information could expose various individuals and groups to possible harm if not treated confidentially.

For example, surveys gathered from certain groups regarding how to reduce their drug usage or their views of government programs might turn up information that government officials might use against members of that group. If social marketers focused on a social problem in a town run mainly by a large corporation, the officials of that corporation might misuse some of that information against the group the social marketers were seeking to help. It might be that individuals' views on such things as abortion or child planning might be used by officials in a group against those with "mistaken" views if such information became available to them.

This issue here is, obviously, related to other questions of privacy, confidentiality and trust. However, these questions may particularly arise in settings in which social problems are addressed, as well as in settings where those targeted are particularly open about their opinions, or trusting in those who influence or govern them. Social marketers must be very careful that the knowledge they gain is not captured and misused by political rulers or other groups who have their own parochial interests at heart, and not the well-being of those studied.

I suggest that several moral guidelines are implicit in this point. First, information that is private or that potentially places those surveyed at risk should be kept confidential. Such information should not be shared with others, and efforts should be undertaken to resist sharing it with others. Second, social marketers should not seek to acquire information from those addressed if it is not essential to their task. As such, they should resist pressure to acquire information of a sensitive nature, unrelated to the social problem in question. Third, social marketers should not acquire information in their efforts if they reasonably believe that such information will become known by others, and having become known, used to harm those surveyed.

Finally, what may we say more generally about the means social marketers may undertake when changing the values of those they address? Assuming that issues of access and general ends are resolved, there still remain moral questions about the means to effect these ends. These issues are difficult since there may be not only moral differences but differences over questions of fact, or the interpretation of facts. For example, a situation that some might consider harmful for a specific person, others might consider to be the action of God in favor of that person. The Hmong apparently see a child who falls down, in convulsions, choking and blue-lipped as someone whose soul had been scared away and who needs a shaman (a spiritual healer) to call it back home again. They refuse to use the medications and means offered by Western doctors to treat a clear case of epilepsy. Accordingly, while Westerners may find this shamanistic practice harmful for the child, the Hmong see quite differently. The Hmong believe they are doing everything they can to help their child; indeed the afflicted child is perceived as very special because her condition indicates that she may grow up to be a shaman, herself.

Social marketers might face this kind of situation were they to focus on the problem of epilepsy. In any case, they may face other, similarly difficult situations. Still, their situation is less difficult than that of physicians who are not only professionals sworn to do no harm, but who also have individual relationships with their patients. Social marketers should do no harm, despite the lack of a professional oath. Further, they do not have a similar doctor-patient relationship with those they address. Still, social marketers must ask what means they may use in light of the different values of others, and their different interpretations of the situations they face. Under what conditions may social marketers seek to change those interpretations and values?

First, they must realize that the values and interpretations attached to any particular case come within a complex of other values and interpretations. In Western eyes it may be wrong to allow parents to impose harm upon a child through inaction or misdirected action. However, these actions, or inactions, occur within a context such that to alter them is to alter an entire system of values. Accordingly, not everything that we believe to be morally wrong is something we believe that we should use any means to correct. Not everything is within our power, and those situations that are within our power may not be within that power at a cost that is acceptable to us (or anyone else). So the appropriate moral guideline here is that not everything that is morally wrong can be fixed. Social marketers must recognize the limits of moral action.[18]

Second, the means used should correspond to the ends sought. If social marketers seek health, justice, freedom, etc. for those they address, then the means that they use should correspond to these ends. Accordingly, deceptive approaches or means to resolve social problems are, prima face, at odds with the ends that social marketers seek.

Third, social marketers attempt to use persuasion to effect the change of behavior they seek in those they address. This approach implies that those they seek to persuade must be permitted some form of exit or noncompliance, if they so choose. Otherwise, social marketers are not engaged in persuasion, but rather coercion. Accordingly, the use of social and peer pressure to try to convince people to adopt different or new forms of behavior raises the issue of coercion. The stronger the social pressure, the more plausible the charge of coercion. This may particularly be the case amongst those who are poorer and in developing countries where people are more tradition directed and the decisions of opinion leaders such as village elders or local leaders, and the views of peers carry significant force and even the threat of exclusion. The moral algorithm here is, as before, that the more the behavior involved harms or violates the rights of others, the stronger the persuasive means that may be used to change it. However, this must be set within the context of the preceding moral guidelines.

Fourth, social marketers must seek to inform those whose behavior they wish to change about the nature of the change and the reasons for it. Obviously this will have to be handled differently with different audiences. Still, those addressed must know and understand what it is they are agreeing to. Andreasen makes a point about external versus intrinsic rewards for behavior (1995, 284–286). This moral point piggybacks on his motivational point. If people do not understand the behavior change they buy into, it is unlikely that the change will be long lasting. The other side of this point is that social marketers should also determine whether those whose behavior they seek to change have engaged in that behavior on the basis of a correct understanding of their own culture or values. It may be that they engage in the behavior that creates social problems for them and society on the basis of a mistaken view of their own culture.[19]

Finally, if these kinds of social marketing issues are to be resolved as well as possible, then social marketers must develop relationships of trust with those they wish to affect, in addition to following the above guidelines. The very reason these people's behaviors need, supposedly, to be changed is that they are at risk for one reason or another. The risk may be immediate, personal and physical, or it may be distant and psychological. In such cases, those whose behavior will be changed must trust those who would change them, and have confidence that social marketers will change them only under conditions such as those above.

Conclusion

The preceding does not claim to have addressed all the moral issues, let alone suggest all the moral guidelines, which social marketers must follow when engaged in international social marketing. However, I have attempted to identify the phenomenon of international social marketing and to propose a structure within which questions of ethics arise for social marketers. In addition, I have proposed a number of moral guidelines.

These guidelines must be used with care and sensitivity. They provide few, if any final and specific answers to particular situations. But, I have suggested, they must be used in arriving at those final and specific answers. Thus, I have not proposed specific solutions to such issues as education for Bangladeshi girls, or female circumcision.

Still, answers to these and other questions must come from following guidelines such as those above. I do not pretend here to have resolved all disputes. The answers can only come after a close examination of the particulars of the situations in conjunction with the preceding moral guidelines.

Notes

I am indebted to Alan Andreasen for helpful comments on an earlier version of this paper.

1. Penny Grewal Williams. 1999. "Social Marketing to Eliminate Leprosy in Sri Lanka." http://www.hc-sc.gc.ca/hppb/socialmarketing/smq-abstracts/abstract7.htm (January 4).

2. This twofold nature of social marketing can be seen in the definitions of "social marketing" given both by Kotler and Zaltman, as well as Andreasen. I will in-

dicate these two parts by "(A)" and "(B)" in the following quotations. Kotler and Zaltman say that (B) "Social marketing is the design, implementation, and control of programs calculated to influence the acceptability of social ideas and (A) involving considerations of product planning, pricing, communication, distribution, and marketing research" (Kotler and Zaltman 1971, 5).

3. Note that this allows that a problem may be a social marketing problem in one context, but a commercial marketing problem (or opportunity) in another. Middle-class and wealthy people who are overweight or have poor diets may be a commercial opportunity for some marketers. However, those poor people who are overweight or (more likely) have poor diets would not be a commercial opportunity, but a social problem to which social marketers might respond.

4. By "product" I do not necessarily refer to physical things which people exchange. Instead, I will use this term to include physical products (various medicines), as well as services (health screenings), and states of affairs (some desired situations people may want).

5. A recent article on Shell's current advertising program that features safe driving advice was dubbed "Cause Branding" (Sullivan 1999, B9).

6. It is quite possible, of course, that social marketers, native to the country involved, might engage in these activities. Nevertheless, they are using the techniques and skills of social marketing (with all its assumptions) which have been developed in other countries.

7. By "ex hypothesis" I mean, roughly, "according to the (present) supposition."

8. This is drawn from the Kew Gardens principle as described in Simon, Powers, and Gunnemann, 22–25.

9. This might be similar to the revolutionary social marketing which is included among the three types of social marketing Kotler distinguishes (cf. Laczniak and Murphy, 1993, 241–42).

10. I am implicitly distinguishing here between conflicting interests and conflicts of interest. The former may be acceptable if revealed; the latter remain problematic even if revealed since they refer to obstacles which may prevent an agent from properly performing an assigned task.

11. What would constitute proof of these claims? Ultimately this will require some form of reflective equilibrium, by which I mean a theory of justification in which we identify the basic intuitions of those involved, compare them with a range of moral principles and values, correct such intuitions, modify the principles, until we arrive at a point where we find ourselves in reflective equilibrium. I cannot lay out such a theory here. Others have discussed such a theory. I will direct my attention to what the social marketer must do, given such a view. I will assume that such a theory has a pragmatic character to it. Far from knowing everything about morality, or morality being fully encompassed by the Ten Commandments or the Golden Rule, I think that there is much we have to learn, both descriptively and normatively, about morality. Further, I assume that the forms of morality can, and do, change over time. Such a morality will also be contex-

tual. But the morality (and its contexts) will also be bounded—i.e., we are not looking at a thorough-going relativism. It will have a number of basic moral principles and values that apply to all people.

12. I say "indirectly kill themselves" because we do not think that they should be permitted to kill themselves, e.g., the Jones massacre or Heaven's Gate, where large numbers of people kill themselves for a religious reason.

13. Suppose we learned that male circumcision increased a child's chance of prostate cancer one hundred percent when that child had reached the age of 50. Supposing that parents were then considering circumcision for their infant: what would our reaction then be to male circumcision?

14. Of course, they must also ask about the ends (both proximate and general) as were discussed in the preceding part of this paper.

15. I take "harm" in such cases not simply to be a utilitarian notion, but also to range over the violation of people's rights. This too causes them harm.

16. Cf. Andreasen's comments on "customer" (Andreasen 1995, 8).

17. Cf. Chapter 6, this volume.

18. This is not intended to imply that therefore we should immorally fix what is immoral. Rather, some immoral things cannot be fixed, or only could be fixed at the cost of greater immorality. Our powers and actions are limited.

19. Cf. Baylis and Downie 1997.

References

Andreasen, Alan R. 1994. "Social Marketing: Its Definition and Domain." *Journal of Public Policy and Marketing* 13: 108–114.

———. 1995. *Marketing Social Change.* San Francisco: Jossey-Bass.

Baylis, Francois, and Jocelyn Downie. 1997. "Child Abuse and Neglect: Cross-Cultural Considerations." In *Feminism and Families.* Edited by Hilde Lindeman Nelson. New York: Routledge.

Kotler, Philip, and Gerald Zaltman. 1971. "Social Marketing: An Approach to Planned Social Change." *Journal of Marketing* 35: 3–12.

Laczniak, Gene R., and Patrick Murphy. 1993. *Ethical Marketing Decisions: The Higher Road.* Upper Saddle River, NJ: Prentice Hall.

Rangan, V. Kasturi, Sohel Karim, and Sheryl K. Sandburg. 1996. "Doing Better at Doing Good." *Harvard Business Review* (May–June): 42–54.

Simon, John G., Charles W. Powers, and Jon P. Gunnemann. 1972. *The Ethical Investor.* New Haven: Yale University Press.

Sullivan, Allanna. 1999. "Shell Gains by Giving Safe-Driving Advice." *Wall Street Journal* 18 February: B9.

Williams, Penny Grewal. 1999. "Social Marketing to Eliminate Leprosy from Sri Lanka." http://www.hc-sc.gc.ca/hppb/socialmarketing/smq-abstracts/abstract7.htm. January 4, 1999.

CHAPTER FOUR

Social Marketing as Business Strategy: The Ethical Dimension

D. Kirk Davidson and William D. Novelli

Introduction and Definitions

For almost thirty years there has been an increasing interest, among both academicians and managers, in the field of social marketing. That interest has been concentrated almost entirely on governmental and nonprofit organizations. Fine (1990) used as a subtitle for his book *Social Marketing,* "Promoting the Causes of Public and Nonprofit Agencies." The lengthening list of other books, articles, and papers on the subject limit their exploration, with only a few exceptions, to these two types of "actors."

The exceptions include an earlier work by Fine in which he includes for-profit organizations in a survey on the perceptions of social marketing and the tactics used (1981, 26, 47–51). A footnote in a forthcoming article by Rothschild includes "private sector managers" among social marketers along with nonprofit administrators and civil servants (1999). But these are indeed exceptions to the general rule that the literature of the social marketing field has focused on nonprofit and governmental examples.

The purposes of this paper are to further extend that focus to the for-profit world, to argue that the strategies and programs of some for-profit organizations fit within the broader definition of social marketing, to explain why it is important not to neglect or dismiss this element of the social marketing field, and to explore some of the ethical issues raised.

The phrase "social marketing" has had a variety of meanings in its brief history. In 1973 Lazer used the phrase "social marketing" to cover not only its current applications but a number of other areas including what we know today as marketing ethics and macromarketing. For the purposes of this paper, however, we will use Kotler and Zaltman's much more precise definition: "Social marketing is the design, implementation, and control of programs calculated to influence the acceptability of social ideas and involving considerations of product planning, pricing, communication, distribution, and marketing research" (1971).

Andreasen states, "In simplest terms, social marketing is the application of marketing technologies developed in the commercial sector to the solution of social problems where the bottom line is behavior change" (1995, 3). While his emphasis on "behavior change" makes his definition significantly different from that of Kotler and Zaltman, there is nothing in it that excludes the efforts of for-profit firms from the field of social marketing.

This matter of definitions has special importance for this paper because a number of scholars rule out including the activities of for-profit organizations within the boundaries of social marketing precisely because the orientation of those organizations is directed inward toward making a profit. They look to the motive, or in some cases the primary motive, of the organization in applying the social marketing definition. For example, in response to an Internet search for information, an Australian marketing professor responded that a program would not be considered social marketing if "the primary reason [for the marketing program] is to increase patronage/purchasing behavior from the consumer, which ultimately and primarily benefits the organisation" (Fry 1998).

We believe this is a mistake for two reasons. First, there is nothing in the above definitions that would prevent including the activities of for-profit firms. Indeed, the emphasis is on *what* is done, not on *who* does it. Second, the criterion of motive is a tricky one. Fine tells us that "the social marketer is more altruistic than his or her commercial counterpart" (1990, 21), and we would not necessarily disagree. But surely the actions and decisions of every governmental and nonprofit manager include *some* component of personal or organizational benefit. Their actions can never be 100 percent altruistic. The performance of an administrator at the Centers for Disease Control (CDC), who initiates a social marketing program designed to heighten public awareness of the need for inoculation against childhood diseases, will be judged in part by the effectiveness of that program. That administrator will have a personal stake in the program's outcome. If the Congress, in its wisdom, were to decide that the efforts of the CDC were either more or less effective, then funding for the CDC might be either increased or decreased. Not just the administrator, but the entire organization, has more than an altruistic stake in the decision to initiate such social marketing programs. Therefore, we would need to somehow measure the degree of altruism to determine what falls within the bounds of social marketing and what does not. This would seem to be a singularly needless and problematic activity. We conclude, therefore, that the programs of for-profit organizations, such as those described in this chapter, should be included within the definition of, and the study of, social marketing.

More importantly, we believe that both social marketing practitioners and scholars can benefit from studying the occasional uses of social marketing by for-profit firms: the former to broaden their search for effective strategies, the latter to explore and better understand the relationship between social marketing and philanthropy, sponsorship, and cause-related marketing. It has become increasingly common for firms to think of each of these activities as part of their overall marketing or business strategy, and it is accepted practice for firms to target their charitable giving to complement their strategic goals (e.g., Varadarajan and Menon 1988; Conference Board 1999). Much more thought must be given as to how all these activities fit into the all-encompassing concept of corporate social responsibility.

In this paper we will limit our study, for the most part, to the programs of for-profit firms acting by themselves or with other for-profit organizations. We acknowledge that quite often firms will act in concert with nonprofit, or sometimes even governmental, organizations, but we will leave that exploration to others.

In the following sections we will introduce a number of examples of for-profit firms pursuing social marketing programs and goals. Bear in mind our concern here is not to judge whether these programs are effective in accomplishing their purposes or whether they are a justifiable use of the firm's resources. We want to demonstrate that such programs and activities do indeed belong within the scope of the social marketing field of study. We will then go on to report on what the firms have told us about the motives and outcomes of their efforts. We will then propose several ways of categorizing these efforts and link them to the larger business strategies of the firms. Finally, we will explore ethical issues raised in the course of these marketing activities.

For-Profit Firms Engaged in Social Marketing

The following are our examples of for-profit organizations engaged in social marketing to pursue a variety of goals:

Benetton, a multi-billion dollar Italian apparel manufacturer with owned and franchised retail operations in Europe, North America, and Asia, has since 1985 been running a series of provocative and dramatic advertisements dealing with such subjects as race relations, the brutality of war, and HIV infection (see Klages 1994; Baron 1996). Some of the images have been so controversial (e.g., bloody, maimed bodies in the Yugoslav conflict, a priest and nun kissing) that they have sparked consumer boycotts in Germany, a fine imposed by the French government, a denouncement from the Vatican, and complaints from U.S. franchisees. There is no mention or display of the company's merchandise in these ads; there is no indication even of what business the company is in. This has puzzled much of the advertising community and has been the reason for the dismay of the company's franchisees. The company has maintained that it is simply trying to rivet the world's attention on serious issues in the hope of promoting a higher level of peaceful understanding among ethnic and racial groups.

Zero Casualties, a recently-formed apparel manufacturer in the United States, is promoting in its advertisements and on its hang-tags an end to violence in inner cities. One of its slogans is, "Be remembered as a hero to the community. Not a chalk outline," (Ho 1998). Here the social marketing message is related to the company's business only in that the firm's designs fall within the category of what is currently known as "urban apparel."

Black Pearls is the name given to an effort in which a number of Brooklyn beauty salons targeting African-American women distribute information on sexually transmitted diseases, breast cancer, heart disease, and other illnesses and also encourage customers to fill out questionnaires measuring their knowledge of various health topics while they are having their hair done. The program is coordinated by the Arthur Ashe Institute for Urban Health (Villarosa 1998). The "message" of the campaign has nothing to do with hair styling, but in this instance the target audiences for the social marketing message and the service provided are the same.

Fidelity Investments, a private-sector corporation, in conjunction with the American Savings Education Council, has sponsored a series of radio commercials featuring the slogan, "Choose to Save." The idea is that if we want to prepare for a comfortable retirement, we should begin saving at as early an age as possible. In this example it is clear that the message is directly associated with the firm's principal business. To the extent the social marketing campaign is effective, the firm as well may benefit.

Giant Foods and **Wegman's** supermarkets advertise "Strive for Five." This is a campaign encouraging people to eat at least five different fruits and vegetables each day. Certainly there is a public benefit to be gained: eating more fruits and vegetables, and by implication less fat and starches, will be healthier for most of us. Supermarket chains stand to benefit not only from a heightened public image but from the increased sales of produce, which carries a higher margin than most grocery products.

The **Newspaper Association of America** has run advertisements encouraging people to improve the reading skills of their children by reading a newspaper to them each day. A more literate, better educated public would indeed be a result of such a change in behavior. Of course, the newspapers would see a direct benefit too in increased circulation.

The **Food Marketing Institute** and the **Grocery Manufacturers of America**, along with a number of individual food processors and supermarket chains, have considered launching a campaign to gain widespread public acceptance of food irradiation as a method of eliminating bacteria such as *E. coli* and salmonella and making our food products safer to eat (Freeman 1998). To date there has been public resistance to using food irradiation because of the mistaken belief or assumption that the process makes food radioactive, and because the word "irradiation" conjures up images of nuclear meltdowns. The hope is to change the public's behavior (i.e., to accept irradiated foods) to reduce death and illness caused by food poisoning.

Denny's, a nationwide chain of restaurants, is running television advertising promoting the benefits of diversity including, specifically, racial diversity. In the mid-1990s Denny's was stung by several well-publicized incidents at several of its restaurants in Maryland, Virginia, and California where African-Americans were subjected to alleged discrimination. A group of black U.S. Secret Service agents waited for more than an hour for their food while their white counterparts and supervisor were served much more quickly. At two other Denny's restaurants an all-black children's choir was refused service because, according to the managers, the restaurants did not have adequate staffing to accommodate the group, although the choir director disputed this claim (Baron 1996, 97–99). These incidents led to lawsuits, threatened boycotts, and a public relations disaster from which the company is striving mightily to recover. The current social marketing message urges all of us to be more accepting of diversity; Denny's hopes to regain some of the legitimacy[1] and good will it has lost.

Pepco and **Pacific Gas & Electric**, along with most other utilities, periodically promote on billboards, television, and bill enclosures various energy saving techniques. These examples of for-profit firms' social marketing efforts are quite different from our previous examples. The hoped-for public benefit is clear enough: reduced energy consumption means the burning of less fossil fuels, cleaner air, less danger of global warming, and so forth. For the utility companies, however, such an outcome would be a *reduction* in their revenues and, therefore, in theory at least, a short-term reduction in their earnings. Presumably, the companies feel that their public reputation will be enhanced, threats to the industry's legitimacy will be reduced, and potential unfavorable government regulation will be forestalled. The assessment is that these longer-term benefits will more than offset any short-run costs.

Anheuser-Busch, along with a number of other brewers and the Beer Institute, have for years urged beer drinkers to know when to say "when," and have preached that "friends don't let friends drive drunk." "Responsible drinking" is the theme, and the public service benefit is the reduction in alcohol-related traffic deaths and accidents as well as the other social costs of alcohol abuse. The distilled spirits industry has run similar campaigns. In theory, these social marketing efforts also could lead to short-term disadvantages: lower revenues and earnings. But the major companies in both the brewing and the distilled spirits industries feel strongly that they must be perceived as pursuing a strong course of self-regulation. Otherwise, the pressure will build to an even greater pitch than there is today to impose some form of additional governmental regulation on top of what we now know.

Our final example concerns the tobacco industry and individual cigarette companies. In December 1998 **Philip Morris,** for example, announced a $100 million campaign to reduce smoking among teens, using the slogan "Think, Don't Smoke." This is only the latest in a series of such campaigns which date to the 1960s after the U.S. Surgeon General's Report first drew widespread attention to the health dangers of smoking. The social marketing goal is clear enough: to reduce the likelihood of teens starting to smoke and becoming addicted to nicotine by portraying that smoking is not "cool." In this example, the potential short-run costs to the firm are even greater. If the campaign is really successful, Philip Morris would lose the very significant revenues and profits generated from cigarette sales to teens. In addition, the company would, in theory, not realize the longer-term sales and profits from those teens who do not become habitual smokers as a result of the social marketing message.

Such potential costs are warranted, presumably, because the industry is under extreme pressure and scrutiny and wants to forestall in any way the very real possibility that draconian marketing regulations will be imposed by federal or state governments. Although a comprehensive tobacco marketing regulation bill failed in the Congress in late 1998, the industry did sign a $200 billion, twenty-five year agreement with the fifty states to settle claims arising from state-paid health costs due to smoking. While the referenced Philip Morris campaign is technically a voluntary effort, it was initiated largely because the industry has lost so much of its legitimacy, and because the adverse pressure from a host of anti-tobacco advocacy groups and the general public has built to such a degree. Various advocacy groups argue that Philip Morris will in fact *not* be harmed by such a campaign, but these arguments will be explored briefly in a later section.

Various Taxonomies

In our description of the eleven examples listed above, there is already evidence of one easy way to group the social marketing programs of these firms. Some of the marketing programs are *entrepreneurial* in the sense that there is some effort, either overt or covert, to increase revenues and earnings. The campaigns of Fidelity Investment, the American Newspaper Association, and Giant Foods fall into this category. The programs of the last four on the other hand, Denny's, the utilities, the breweries, and the cigarette manufacturers, are *defensive*. Their principal purpose is to atone for past sins, regain corporate or industry legitimacy, and/or hold off potentially harmful regulation (see Figure 4-1).

It is also important to note that Pepco, Anheuser-Busch, and Philip Morris are conducting forms of *demarketing* (Kotler and Levy 1971), the purposeful control or limitation of demand (as opposed to the stimulation of demand which most marketing is designed to do). If the social marketing efforts of these three firms are carried out successfully, the results would be an actual *decrease* in revenues and presumably profits. The Denny's program, while defensive by our definition, would not result in the reduction of demand for its products, and so the terms *defensive* and *demarketing* are not synonymous.

We might also consider how direct is the relationship between the social marketing program and the principal revenue source of the firm. The social marketing efforts of Fidelity Investments, Giant Foods, the American Newspaper Association, the Food Marketing Institute, Anheuser-Busch, and Philip Morris all have quite direct relationships with the principal business of the firms. In the case of Pepco there may be at least an indirect relationship between conservation of natural resources and the production and distribution of energy. But with Benetton, Zero Casualties, the beauty salons, and Denny's there is no significant relationship at all (see also Figure 4-1). World peace and racial harmony have no direct relationship with Benetton's apparel business, and improved health and HIV awareness have no connection with hair styling and nail care. The reduction of urban violence relates to the trade name Zero Casualties has chosen, but beyond that there is no connection between the sportswear apparel business and the social cause. And while it may be important to Denny's sales and profits for the firm to repair its public image by *practicing* diversity in its employment and service policies, embarking on a social marketing campaign to promote diversity throughout our society has only an indirect relationship with the fast food business.

In this process it is impossible not to speculate on the motives of the firm. We take it as an axiom that stated or unstated, covert or overt, whether the actions are taken voluntarily or under societal pressure, any

	Entrepreneurial	*Defensive*
Core	Fidelity Investments Giant Foods American Newspaper Association	Pepco Anheuser-Busch Philip Morris
	Food Marketing Institute	
Non-Core	Black Pearls Zero Causalities Benetton	Denny's Restaurants

Figure 4-1. An Organization of Social Marketing Programs

social marketing programs undertaken by for-profit firms will, at some level, be aimed at improving the shareholders' value, if only over the very long term. Even the most altruistic of acts—as a hypothetical example: a firm's anonymous donation to the United Way—would improve the social environment of the community, make it a safer and more pleasant place in which to live, and lead to a stronger economy over the long term, thereby attracting a better pool of potential employees and customers, and so on. It is not possible to conceive of undertaking a social marketing program that would not have some link, however tenuous, to the benefit of the firm.

More specific business goals are also apparent, goals that can accrue from a social marketing program and be realized along a parallel track with the social marketing goals. We can imagine at least five such business goals: a direct, near term increase in revenues and/or earnings; an improvement in employee morale; a heightened public perception that the firm is a good corporate citizen; stabilization or improvement of the legitimacy of the firm; and a reduction or forestalling of onerous government-levied regulations or legislation.

In most circumstances a firm's social marketing program will not be an essential component of its overall marketing strategy even in those examples in Figure 4-1 where the program is directly related to the firm's core business. It is an attractive adjunct which helps the firm carry out its social obligations while at the same time contributing at least in some measure to its profitability. This is quite different from nonprofit organizations where their social marketing efforts are indeed essential elements of their operations.

The important point here is the recognition that for-profit firms have parallel goals or motives when they participate in social marketing programs: economic gain for the firm and social gain for the broader society.

Benetton may be an exception. The company's stated rationale for its controversial social marketing campaign is unusual to say the least:

> Benetton's communication strategy was born of the company's wish to produce images of global concern for its global customers. We realized some time ago that we had a unique tool for communicating worldwide, and that *it would be cynical to waste it on self-serving product promotion.* We trusted in the intelligence of our customers worldwide and decided to give space to issues over *redundant product claims.*
>
> Benetton believes that it is important for companies to take a stance in the real world instead of using their advertising budget *to perpetuate the myth that they can make consumers happy through the mere purchase of their product.*
>
> Our images . . . do not show you a fictitious reality in which you will be irresistible if you make use of our products. They do not tell anyone to buy our clothes, they do not even imply it. All they attempt to do is promote a discussion about issues . . . we feel should be more widely discussed.
>
> We are aware of the controversy some of our images have caused, but we believe that all worthwhile stances will have supporters and detractors. Our hope is that people will move from the sterile discussion of whether or not a company is entitled to illustrate its point of view in its advertising campaigns, to a discussion of the issues themselves. (Benetton 1999, emphasis added)

If we take the company at its word, the Benetton example is the most difficult case in which to make the connection between business and social marketing goals. It is certainly possible that employees of Benetton itself (as opposed to its franchisees) may take pride in the firm's campaign, and it is also possible that some portions of the public would express their approval by buying Benetton apparel. That the firm would continue its controversial advertisements, however, in the face of the boycotts, the lawsuits, and the criticism mentioned above, leads to two conclusions. First,

Benetton really is focusing on changing social behavior: by visibly and viscerally showing the horrors of war and by promoting better understanding and acceptance among diverse peoples, and second, the firm does not have a parallel business-related goal as part of this campaign. Embracing such a controversial social marketing program with no apparent related business goal would be inconceivable were it not for the fact that Benetton is still a family-owned firm.

Entrepreneurial Strategies and Motivations

At Zero Casualties, Nancy Rogers, the company's chief-of-staff, told us explicitly that the firm is pursuing the two parallel goals described above: making a profit and bringing about social change, a reduction in the violence common to our inner cities. She reported that the firm's major retail customers—Macy's, Sears, and Bloomingdale's—have expressed interest in the social marketing goal, and that the goal probably helped influence those stores to place test orders. She declined to speculate whether the retailers would continue with the line in order to promote the reduction of violence even if Zero Casualties did not perform as well as competitors' lines in the stores (Rogers 1999).

The Brooklyn beauty salons cooperating with the Black Pearls program report that their customers appreciate the opportunity to learn more about women's health issues in the comfortable environment of a salon. According to Karla Holloway, director of African and African-American studies at Duke University, "It's a natural, if somewhat unhappy, evolution for black women to get information that might save their lives in beauty salons. Many black women relate the beauty shop to their mothers' kitchens, the kitchen being the first place where we were cared for and got our hair 'done'" (Petty 1998). Over and above the goals of improving their customers' health and creating goodwill in the process, there is also a monetary incentive for the salons: they receive $100 per month from the Arthur Ashe Institute and an additional fifty cents for each health questionnaire that is filled out and returned.

For Fidelity Investments the parallel social marketing and business goals reinforce one another. The firm is performing a public service by sponsoring the "Choose to Save" campaign, urging its radio audience to prepare wisely for their retirement years. But a spokesperson for the American Savings Education Council, which enlisted the help of Fidelity and hopes to take this alliance program nationwide with other regional partners, made no bones about recognizing the profit opportunities for Fidelity and other potential partners. Higher rates of savings mean more customers and more profitable business for commercial banks.

The complementary relationship between social marketing goals and business goals for Giant Foods and the American Newspaper Association has already been covered.

For the Food Marketing Institute, the Grocery Manufacturers of America, and their supermarket partners, the relationship between these goals is slightly less direct. There is no evidence to show that wider acceptance and greater consumption of irradiated foods would result in revenue increases, i.e., more food being sold. A family would presumably buy an irradiated chicken *instead of,* not *in addition to,* a normally processed chicken. The business goal of the firms and the associations would be to reduce certain expenses, for example spoilage, and they could benefit also from a heightened public belief in the safety of supermarket foods.

Defensive Strategies

Denny's social marketing campaign to promote diversity has a different business goal from the previous examples. The media reports and lawsuits resulting from the discrimination incidents left Denny's scrambling to repair its battered public image and regain its lost legitimacy. This we consider a defensive strategy. Any hope of improving revenues and profits by running the diversity campaign is decidedly secondary to this primary goal.

The business goal for Pepco and other utilities running programs urging energy conservation is more difficult to define. It is true that many people who are concerned about environmental issues often view utility companies in a bad light. Pepco, therefore, may be simply trying to enhance its public image among this group and retain its legitimacy. Because such utilities are closely regulated by public utility commissions, it may well be that Pepco and the others want to polish their reputations before their next petition to the commissions to raise their rates. Pepco's use of social marketing, like Denny's, is more of a defensive strategy than an entrepreneurial one.

There are mixed views regarding Anheuser-Busch and other alcoholic beverage producers running "responsible drinking" programs. One representative of the beer distributors believed that the programs were designed, pure and simple, to carve out additional market share. Budweiser advertises "Know when to say 'when,'" the firm is perceived by some as being a responsible corporate citizen, and some of those people will buy Budweiser rather than a competitor's product. We believe a defensive strategy explanation for the campaign is, on balance, more plausible. To the extent this effort at self-regulation is perceived by the public as sufficient to effect a reduction in alcohol-related driving accidents, then more stringent state or federal government regulation will be unnecessary.

We view Philip Morris's "Think, Don't Smoke" campaign as the most defensive of all our examples. Here is an industry that is under severe attack from federal, state, and local regulatory agencies and legislative bodies, and now from international governments, as well; from countless anti-tobacco advocacy and health groups; and from a majority of the population with varying intensities. Here is a company that is the primary target for those attacks because of its dominant position in the industry, because of its flagship Marlboro brand which enjoys the largest market share including a 60 percent share of the underage market, and because of what the anti-tobacco community perceives as sheer arrogance over the past few decades in the way it has spurned all social and legal pressures. If ever a company or an industry has lost legitimacy, this is the quintessential example.[2] Therefore, the primary business goal of Philip Morris in undertaking this \$100 million campaign is certainly to forestall the strict marketing constraints that its attackers would like to see imposed by the federal government.

The Ethical Dimension

It is ironic that we should be raising ethical questions about social marketing at all. Is not social marketing, by definition, meant to improve the welfare of society? Who could object to such a noble goal, and for what possible reasons? Of course, this entire book must deal with that irony; in this chapter we continue to focus on the social marketing efforts of corporations or other for-profit organizations.

Because of our focus on the for-profit sector we need to address the question whether it is appropriate for corporations and other for-profit enterprises to carry on *any* social marketing programs. Milton Friedman, whose landmark article "The Social Responsibility of Business Is To Make a Profit" (1970) still defines the most conservative end of the spectrum of thinking on this subject, would surely question whether corporations should be pursuing any program that does not have some positive effect on the firm's bottom line. That would rule out Benetton's efforts and perhaps those of Pepco and the Food Marketing Institute as well.

This narrow, unidimensional focus on profits and the maximization of shareholder wealth as the only proper goal of the corporation has few adherents today, even within the business community. At least in theory, if less often in practice, business leaders now subscribe to the idea that the corporation must achieve social as well as economic goals. In some academic circles the emphasis of late has been on the stakeholder theory of the firm (e.g., Clarkson 1995; Donaldson and Preston 1995; Windsor 1999). Here it is recognized that the firm does in fact have multiple stakeholders—employees, customers, suppliers, governments, communities, advocacy groups, and often many others—in addition to its shareholders. The challenge for managers is to balance the firm's responsibilities to, and ultimately try to satisfy, all of these stakeholders. How to achieve this balance and whether shareholders still occupy some preeminent position are questions that are yet to be resolved.

In any case, this movement toward a recognition of multiple stakeholders and multiple responsibilities would seem to open the door to a firm's involvement in social marketing. Whether the social marketing program is closely related to the firm's core business as with Giant Foods and the Strive for Five program, where the parallel goals of profits for the firm and benefits to society are quite explicit, or whether the social marketing program is unrelated to the firm's core business as with Benetton, social marketing programs carried on by for-profit firms enjoy greater acceptability today.

We turn, then, to an ethical analysis of social marketing as conducted by for-profit firms. All problems of marketing ethics at the micro level have as their base the fundamental tension that exists between buyer and seller. The ideology of marketing is to satisfy the customer. Theodore

Levitt wrote, "There can be no effective corporate strategy . . . that does not in the end follow this unyielding prescript: The purpose of business is to create and keep a customer" (1986, 19). Long before Levitt, Marshall Field expressed the same idea more succinctly: "Give the lady what she wants." This customer orientation and focus is opposed, however, by the ever-present and equally unyielding necessity of the firm to make a profit. At least in the short run these two forces often conflict, and therein lies the tension. Figure 4-2 sets out the conflicts and tensions related to marketing in general and to social marketing in particular.

At the macro level there is tension and conflict as well. Here also the organization's quest for profit represents one side of the opposing forces. No one would deny that business profits are an absolutely essential element for a capitalistic economy to function successfully. But to what extent must society allow business to pursue its profitability? How single-mindedly? And at what cost to the "greater good?" Concern about the harm done to society by the rapacious nature of business stretches from the Robber Baron days of the nineteenth century, through the birth and growth of environmentalism and consumerism, to Gordon Gekko's celebration of greed in the 1987 movie *Wall Street*. However "the good of society" may be described and/or measured, there is widespread and long-standing belief that the harm done by the business community must be reduced and the net contribution of business to the public good can and must be increased.

Other authors have used a macro-micro framework to help organize ethical issues related to marketing in general (e.g., Laczniak 1983). The same framework helps organize the potential ethical issues related to social marketing that we explore in this paper.

In reviewing our eleven examples of social marketing as conducted by for-profit firms we have identified five ethical issues that can and do arise: (1) Deceiving or confusing the receiver of the message as to the purpose of the message; (2) Offending the sensibilities of the customer/reader; (3) Harmful consequences; (4) the Intrusion and expansion of corporate power and values; and (5) the growth of Cynicism. The first two are micro level issues in that they affect individual consumers. The last two are macro level issues in that they affect our entire society. And the third operates at both the micro and macro levels.

	Marketing (general)	*Social Marketing (for-profit firms)*
Micro level	Takes advantage of consumers — Defective products — Unfair prices — Deceptive advertising — Prey on vulnerable target markets	Deceptive advertising, hidden agenda Offend customers Harmful consequences
Macro level	Wasteful — Unnecessary expense, leads to higher prices — Promotes excessive consumption Promotes harmful values	Harmful consequences Intrusion of corporate power and values Leads to increased cynicism

Figure 4-2. Sources of Conflict and Tension in Marketing

To help us analyze these ethical concerns we turn to two different frameworks. The first, formulated by Laczniak (1983), poses a series of questions for determining if marketing practices are ethical or unethical.

Does action A violate the law?
Does action A violate any general moral obligations:
Duties of fidelity?
Duties of gratitude?
Duties of justice?
Duties of beneficence?
Duties of self-improvement?
Duties of nonmaleficence?[3]
Does action A violate any special obligations stemming from the type of marketing organization in question (e.g., the special duty of pharmaceutical firms to provide safe products)?
Is the intent of action A evil?

Are any major evils likely to result from or because of action A?
Is a satisfactory alternative B, which produces equal or more good with less evil than A, being knowingly rejected?
Does action A infringe on the inalienable rights of the consumer?
Does action A leave another person or group less well off? Is this person or group already relatively underprivileged?

The second framework, presented by Smith (1993), describes the three dimensions of his Consumer Sovereignty Test: the capability of the consumer, the availability and quality of information, and the presence of choice or the opportunity to switch.

We now take a closer look at each of the five problem areas and use both of the above tools to aid our ethical analysis.

Deception

As a general rule, deceiving people is unethical. Deception implies lying (or at best telling half-truths), destroying trust, and taking unfair advantage of others. True enough, interesting ethical questions can be raised, as in the earlier chapter by William Smith, as to whether deception can ever be justified: for example, if a greater harm can be avoided.

It is possible to conjure up a situation where it would be perceived to be ethical for a nonprofit organization to use some degree of deception in a social marketing campaign to achieve an end that promised great benefit for society. But it is considerably more difficult for a for-profit organization to justify the use of deception for a simple reason: that such organizations are usually pursuing two parallel goals as already described, economic and social. Fidelity Investments encourages saving for the future so people will have a safe and comfortable retirement, but the firm also hopes to fatten its bottom line. Such a for-profit firm would sound ingenuous, at the very least, if it were to argue that some degree of deception in the carrying out of its social marketing efforts ought to be accepted.

Is there some element of deception in the social marketing programs under review? When the Newspaper Association of America urges parents to read more to their children, especially newspapers, as a way to achieve higher rates of literacy, there is of course an additional or hidden agenda: to promote the sale of newspapers. We have described this earlier in the chapter as the confluence between business goals and social marketing goals. And we have categorized this as an entrepreneurial effort, because it is designed to increase the firms' revenues, and also as a situation where the social marketing goal is directly related to the firms' core business. Giant Foods and Fidelity fall into the same category. It is fair to say that in all three of these examples the organizations have not told the *whole* truth because they have not told their audiences how the firms might benefit from the social marketing programs. The intent is to highlight the social marketing goal and sublimate the business goal. Do viewers/readers of the ads have a right to be told the whole truth?

Laczniak and Smith would agree, based on their respective schema, that deception of customers (or readers of social marketing messages) is indeed unethical. It violates the marketer's duties of fidelity and nonmaleficence as well as the rights of consumers. Smith would argue that deception or telling less than the whole truth—the hidden agenda of Fidelity Investments, for example—reduces the quality of the information available to the reader and thereby reduces the "choices" available.

One might argue in response that any ethical problem posed here is certainly a small one compared to the goals of the program. After all, the social marketing messages of promoting personal savings (Fidelity Investments), literacy (Newspaper Association), or better health (Giant Foods) are all socially beneficial efforts. Is it necessary that the patrons of a beauty salon cooperating with the Black Pearls program be told that there is some financial reimbursement to the salon for its participation in the program? When Denny's promotes wider acceptance of racial diversity, is it necessary for the firm to tell the public that its endorsement of diversity and its willingness to spend considerable sums of money on the campaign come as part of a consent decree resulting from a class-action lawsuit?

Deciding how much truth needs to be told has always posed a dilemma for marketing ethicists. Social marketing programs add a new dimension to that dilemma.

Offend Customers

Marketers are often faced with questions as to whether their ads or other forms of communication are in "bad taste." Usually, these questions are not so important that they rise to a concern over ethical behavior and obligations. In the case of Benetton's ads, however, some customers are offended to see pictures of gaily colored condoms (promoted to reduce HIV infection) boldly presented in a mainstream publication. Other customers' religious sensibilities will be deeply offended by Benetton's picture of a priest and a nun embracing one another. Similarly, apparel shoppers may be offended by Zero Casualties' graphic reminders of urban violence while shopping at their favorite department stores. These are examples of advertisers going well beyond matters of good or bad taste. Do viewers/readers have a right not to be confronted with such offensive material, and do advertisers have an obligation, therefore, not to present it?

Laczniak might argue that in running its controversial ads, Benetton has ignored its duty of justice or of nonmaleficence. The company has ignored the rights of at least some of its readers, and those who are troubled by being confronted with graphic messages regarding safe sex, interracial relationships, and impious clerical behavior may be less well off.

Smith might object to the "quality" of the information presented to the customer/viewer, and he might also argue that customers have no advance warning and no "choice" about being confronted with such objectionable and disturbing images in magazines or on street posters.

Harmful Consequences

When Philip Morris cautions, "Think, Don't Smoke," and when Anheuser-Busch warns, "Know when to say 'when'," there is the very real possibility that such efforts at self-regulation will result in reduced regulation by state and federal agencies. Indeed, there is little question that this is one of the principal reasons why firms decide to commit their resources to such social marketing messages. Ghingold suggests that such efforts may also have a "subtle subtext" aimed at "liability shifting so that when a drunk driver harms people, Anheuser-Busch can point to its ads on responsible drinking and say, 'We did our part'" (1998).

Depending on one's point of view this "liability shifting" or this diverting of the public policy process away from helpful and necessary regulation, especially of "socially unacceptable" products (Davidson 1996), can lead to harmful consequences, both to individual consumers and to the greater society. Certainly anti-tobacco and anti-alcohol advocates would argue that the consequences of such social marketing campaigns are definitely harmful. It is fair to ask then: Do such programs result in more harm than good?

If the advocates are correct, then Laczniak would surely argue that Anheuser-Busch and Philip Morris have ignored their duty to beneficence. And perhaps, when considering the severity of the problems posed—drunk driving, underage drinking, and the dire health consequences of smoking—that a "major evil" may result from such social marketing efforts. Smith would say that such efforts fall short on the information dimension, that the messages sent in these programs is misleading, implying that the beer and tobacco companies' warnings are sufficient. One can hardly object to the explicit messages of the tobacco and alcohol social marketing programs, but once again there is a hidden agenda. If the alcoholic beverage and tobacco firms really want to stifle the possibility of more stringent government restrictions—as they surely do—then the "information" of the ads is misleading and insufficient to allow readers to make informed judgments on the public policy issues at stake.

Intrusion of Business Power and Values

The conflict between business values and society's values has long been a topic for debate in business ethics circles, as has the concern over the excessive or inappropriate use of business power. To the extent that for-profit firms commit their enormous financial resources to a variety of social marketing programs, can they dominate the marketplace for such ideas? Does society have the right to be protected against business values (profits, power) crowding out social values (justice, social welfare)?

More often than not we would applaud the business community putting its financial muscle behind efforts such as the promotion of literacy, energy conservation, or racial diversity. But the Food Marketing Institute social marketing effort is an example of a more controversial issue: the use of irradiation to protect our food. Here there is real potential for the power of the business community to overwhelm the efforts of those who fear the use of irradiation and to force business values based on maximizing profits ahead of public health concerns.

Laczniak might note that such use of power would disregard marketers' duties of justice and nonmaleficence. It simply would be unfair, in a debate over such a critical matter as the potential harm to public health from irradiated foods, if the food processing industry were to dominate the dialogue by using its considerable financial power. Furthermore, those advocating against the use of irradiated foods would claim that there is the potential for serious harm to the public health from the use of such technology.

On this issue Smith would rely on his dimensions of choice and also of information. Were messages from the business community to drown out arguments from the public health community and were business to succeed in securing its own profit at the expense of the public's health, then the consumer's choice in this marketplace of ideas, i.e., the debate over the irradiation of foods, has been improperly limited.

Cynicism

A common reaction to for-profit firms' use of social marketing is distrust or cynicism. "Benetton doesn't really care about world peace or racial harmony; it just wants to sell more sweaters." Or, "Pepco doesn't really want to reduce pollution; it just wants to look like the good guy instead of like a nasty utility company!" Society expects and accepts that business will promote its goods and services toward the end of making a profit. It is confused and skeptical, however, when business ventures into the area of social marketing to promote the improvement of social good by changing behavior. This leads to an increase in the already worrisome level of cynicism about, and distrust of, business. This type of cynicism is important and dangerous because it means that messages originating with for-profit firms, however well-meant, will be tuned out by the public. And there is at least the beginning of empirical evidence to support this belief. Blazing and Bloom (1998) have presented data showing that the public is less likely to believe a public service message presented by a for-profit firm than the exact same message presented by a not-for-profit organization. Does this admittedly abstract and perhaps immeasurable consequence, cynicism, or lack of trust, outweigh any good accomplished by for-profit firms' social marketing efforts? Is cynicism the mirror image of legitimacy?

There is an ample, and still growing, stream of literature which argues this lack of trust increases transaction costs (Noordewier, John, and Nevin 1990; Ring and Van de Ven 1992), and so the economic consequences of cynicism are easily imaginable. But what of the ethical consequences? Any decision or action which adds to this level of cynicism or distrust would seem to violate Laczniak's duty of nonmaleficence, and to the extent that our market system, i.e., our entire economy, is damaged, then there is the potential here for a "major evil." Under such conditions—heightened cynicism and the absence of trust—consumers' "information" is limited and skewed. This would jeopardize Smith's quest for consumer sovereignty.

By searching out, exploring, and analyzing these ethical questions there is no intent on the authors' part to proscribe the use of social marketing by for-profit organizations. Nor do we try to measure any harm done against the benefits. Especially with the last of our five ethical concerns, cynicism or distrust, which appear only at the macro level, we are at a loss to offer solutions. It is important to recognize, however, that there is the potential for ethical breaches in such social marketing efforts. To the extent such problems can be avoided in the creation and implementation of the social marketing strategies, any harm will be diminished and the net good from the results will be increased.

Conclusions

First, we emphasize that for-profit firms can indeed carry on social marketing programs, and that such programs should not be dismissed merely because the firms have mixed motives including their own economic benefit. These programs warrant further attention on the part of social marketers because they are being created and implemented by organizations highly skilled in the use of marketing tools. It would be short-sighted to ignore this category simply because of a definitional bias that excludes the study of for-profit programs.

Second, there is certainly the potential for ethical problems to arise when for-profit firms use social marketing programs as a part of their overall business strategies. These problems may concern deception, offending viewers/readers of ads, creating harmful consequences, contributing to the dominance of corporate power and values, and increasing the level of cynicism to the point that trust in the business system is harmed. This is a different set of ethical questions than those raised when social marketing programs are conducted by nonprofit and government organizations. The difference is largely due to the parallel activities, business marketing and social marketing, pursued by the firm. Where there is little or no conflict between these activities, as with our Benetton or Fidelity Investments examples, the ethical problems are likely to be less serious. Where there is a direct conflict, however, as with the alcoholic beverage and tobacco industries, the ethical problems are likely to be considerably greater.

Finally, it is important that mainstream marketing scholars and managers explore this category because it will extend our understanding of the increasingly important fields of philanthropy, cause-related marketing, and sponsorship, and the relationship of those fields to the broader area of corporate social responsibility. We need a focused look at the intersection between a firm's marketing or overall business strategy and the use of social marketing. We know very little at this stage about the effectiveness of social marketing programs as part of a firm's overall business strategy. Nor do we know for what industries or what types of firms social marketing is most appropriate.

Marketers must always be aware of unintended consequences resulting from their actions. The use of social marketing is no exception. Initially, a conscientious marketer might conclude that contributing to the solution of social problems by promoting behavioral change would be a fine way to fulfill the firm's social responsibility. It would be ironic indeed if the firm were met with increasing ethical criticism for its pains.

Notes

1. We use the term "legitimacy" to mean acceptance of the organization by the society in which it is embedded. Others have stressed that legitimacy indicates congruence or alignment with social values (Hurst 1970) and that legitimacy is essential for the long-run viability of organizations (Boulding 1978). For a look at legitimacy as it applies to the tobacco industry, see Davidson (1992).

2. In its November 29, 1999, cover story *Business Week* calls Philip Morris "arguably the most reviled corporation in America. . . . Rarely has . . . a company been so deeply vilified and so thoroughly discredited as . . . Philip Morris."

3. Not doing harm, or the quality of doing good.

References

Andreasen, Alan R. 1995. *Marketing Social Change*. San Francisco: Jossey-Bass Publishers.

Baron, David P. 1996. *Business and Its Environment*, second edition. Upper Saddle River, New Jersey: Prentice Hall.

Benetton, 1999. "Communication Policy. http://www.benetton.com/wws/aboutus/ourcomms/file1946.html.

Blazing, Jennifer, and Paul Bloom. 1998. "How Perceptions about the Purity of Sponsor Motives Affect the Persuasiveness of Socially-Oriented Communications." Paper presented at the meetings of the American Marketing Association, August 15, Boston, Massachusetts.

Boulding, Kenneth. 1978. "The Legitimacy of the Business Institution," in *Rationality, Legitimacy, Responsibility*. Edwin M. Epstein and Dow Votaw, eds. Santa Monica, California: Goodyear Publishing Company, Inc.

Clarkson, M.B.E. 1995. "A Stakeholder Framework for Analyzing and Evaluating Corporate Social Performance." *Academy of Management Review*, 20:39–48.

Conference Board. 1999. "Corporate Contributions: the View from 50 Years." Research Report 1249-99-RR. http://www.prnewswire.com.

Davidson, D. Kirk. 1992. "Legitimacy: How Important Is It for the Tobacco Strategies?" in *Contemporary Issues in the Business Environment*. Dean Ludwig and Karen Paul, eds. Lewiston, New York: Edwin Mellen Press.

———. 1996. *Selling Sin: The Marketing of Socially Unacceptable Products*. Westport, Connecticut: Quorum Press.

Donaldson, Thomas, and Lee Preston. 1995. "The Stakeholder Theory of the Corporation." *Academy of Management Review*, 20:65–91.

Fine, Seymour H. 1981. *The Marketing of Ideas and Social Issues*. New York: Praeger.

———. 1990. *Social Marketing: Promoting the Causes of Public and Nonprofit Agencies*. Boston: Allyn and Bacon.

Freeman, Laurie. 1998. "'Irradiation' Designation May Finally Become a Sales Pitch." *Marketing News*, September 14, p. 1.

Friedman, Milton. 1970. "The Social Responsibility of Business Is to Increase Its Profits." *The New York Times Magazine*, September 13, p. 32f.

Fry, Marie-Louise. 1998. From personal correspondence with the authors. Email: mgmlf@cc.newcastle.edu.au.

Ghingold, Morry. 1998. From personal correspondence with the authors. Email: mghingol@husky.bloomu.edu.

Ho, Rodney. 1998. "Start-Up Urban-Apparel Maker Declares Peace Mission." *The Wall Street Journal*, December 15, p. B2.

Hurst, James Willard. 1970. *The Legitimacy of the Business Corporation in the Law of the United States, 1780–1970*. Charlottesville, Virginia: The University Press of Virginia.

Klages, Gregory. 1994. "Begging the Question: Is Benetton Using Innovative Advertising or Commercial Exploitation?" Web site: http://www.peak.uoguelph.ca/peaksters/gklages/Toscani.html.

Kotler, Philip, and Sidney J. Levy. 1971. "Demarketing, Yes, Demarketing." *Harvard Business Review*, November–December.

Kotler, Philip, and Gerald Zaltman. 1971. "Social Marketing: An Approach to Planned Social Change." *Journal of Marketing*, 35 (July): 3–12.

Laczniak, Gene R. 1983. "Framework for Analyzing Marketing Ethics." *Journal of Macromarketing*, (Spring): 7–18.

Lazer, William, 1973. "Marketing's Changing Social Relationships." In *Social Marketing: Perspectives and Viewpoints*. William Lazer and Eugene J. Kelley, eds. Homewood, Illinois: Irwin.

Levitt, Theodore, 1986. *The Marketing Imagination*. New York: Free Press.

Noordewier, T. G., G. John, and J. R. Nevin. 1990. "Performance Outcomes of Purchasing Arrangements in Industrial Buyer-Vendor Relationships." *Journal of Marketing*, 54(4): 80–93.

Petty, Jill. 1998. "Coloring, Styling, Perming–and Lifesaving Info." *Ms*. magazine. August 24.

Ring, P. S., and A. H. Van de Ven. 1992. "Structuring Cooperative Relationships Between Organizations." *Strategic Management Journal*, 13:483–498.

Rogers, Nancy. 1999. From a telephone conversation with the author on January 13.

Rothschild, Michael L. 1999. "Carrots, Sticks and Promises: A Conceptual Framework for the Management of Public Health and Social Issue Behaviors." *Journal of Marketing*, in press.

Smith, N. Craig. 1990. *Morality and the Market: Consumer Pressure for Corporate Accountability*. London: Routledge.

———. 1993. "The Role of Ethics in Marketing Management." In *Ethics in Marketing*. N. Craig Smith and John A Quelch, eds. Homewood, Illinois: Irwin.

Varadarajan, P. Rajan, and Anil Menon. 1988. "Cause-Related Marketing: A Coalignment of Marketing Strategy and Corporate Philanthropy." *Journal of Marketing*, 52 (July), 3: 58.

Villarosa, Linda. 1998. "Tailoring a Healthy Message to Blacks." *The New York Times*, August 18, p. C 7, (New England edition).

Windsor, Duane. 1999. "Can Stakeholder Interests Be Balanced?" Paper presented at the International Association for Business and Society annual meeting, Paris, France, June 24–27. *Proceedings*, Donna J. Wood and Duane Windsor, eds.

CHAPTER FIVE

Alliances and Ethics in Social Marketing

Alan R. Andreasen and Minette E. Drumwright

It has long been accepted that social marketing is significantly different from commercial marketing despite the fact that its hallmark is the borrowing of the latter's concepts and tools (Andreasen 1995; Bloom and Novelli 1981). One of these differences is that social marketing is charged with dramatic goals—getting all Americans to eat five fruits and vegetables a day, getting all gay men to practice safe sex, or getting 90 percent of all children in developing countries fully immunized by age two. Consider the following mission statements:

> Share Our Strength works to alleviate and prevent hunger in the United States and around the world.
>
> The Alzheimer's Association . . . creating a world without Alzheimer's disease while optimizing quality of life for individuals and their families.
>
> Goodwill Industries will actively strive to achieve the full participation in society of people with disabilities and special needs by expanding their opportunities and occupational capabilities. . .
>
> The Environmental Defense Fund is dedicated to protecting the environmental rights of all people, including future generations.
>
> Project Inform is . . . working to end the AIDS epidemic.
>
> Boys & Girls Clubs [aims] . . . to inspire and enable all young people, especially those from disadvantaged circumstances, to realize their full potential as productive, responsible, and caring individuals.

By contrast, commercial marketers' missions are more often concerned with achieving modest gains in market penetration or brand market share. A second difference is that social marketers typically have only limited resources for achieving such impressive objectives, whether these resources emanate from taxes, charitable donations, or the organization's own commercial activities. Commercial marketers often have millions of dollars to spend on annual campaigns or product launches such as the $300 million launch of Gillette's Mach 3 razor.

A significant and inevitable consequence of these differences is that, in order to have significant impact, social marketers must seek the help of other organizations and individuals to achieve their objectives (Austin 2000). They need others to build and staff health centers, design and place advertisements, carry out field research, and so on. In many cases, this help emanates from government or quasi-government agencies, especially in developing countries. However, in developed economies, it is much more common for help to come from the commercial sector.

There are two primary reasons for this. First, the commercial sector very often has the skills and personnel that social marketing organizations lack. Commercial marketers know how to develop and test promotional programs. They know how to carry out cost-effective and timely marketing research. They know how to translate customer research into effective strategies. Thus, they have significant *potential* to help. And, because of a recent change in the way marketers view social enterprise, they now have the *motivation* to help.

As Craig Smith pointed out in 1994, a significant change has taken place in the relationship of the private sector to social issues and social organizations. Commercial organizations have realized that resources of personnel and dollars that they formerly gave away to nonprofit charities as handouts from surplus profits could, with careful thought, be put to strategic use (Smith 1994). That is, instead of giving $100,000 to Harry's Homeless Shelter for Harry to do with pretty much as he wished, a major corporation might use the same funds to organize a fundraising event such as a 10K run or a mini-fair at which there would be significant benefits to Harry but also there would be great publicity, TV and newspaper coverage, and product giveaways, all of which could increase brand sales. Such events would also improve staff morale and therefore hiring potential, and position the corporation as a caring community enterprise.

Further, corporations have seen that the operating budgets that were formerly used for conventional advertising and promotion could, in part, be diverted to campaigns with social—as well as commercial—impacts and obtain greater effectiveness and efficiency than they would otherwise achieve. Finally, many of the more farsighted commercial organizations have seen that improvements in community infrastructure and welfare can have major payoffs for corporations and their commercial goals. Thus, a healthier, less worried workforce will perform better. A developing country with improved telecommunications infrastructure will be a better location for selling cell phones and business software. And so on.

This confluence of for-profit and nonprofit needs has led to a dramatic growth in the number and scope of alliances between these organizations to achieve individual and mutual goals. As Weeden has noted, the relationship for social marketers has shifted from *begging* to *partnering* (1998, 14). However, this shift is not without its perils for both sides. Businesses find that venturing into social enterprise can pose important risks to the firm's reputation when it is found to step over ethical bounds (Sarner and Nathanson 1996). At the same time, nonprofits have found themselves in new partnerships and networks where the norms of behavior are unclear and the nonprofits are at risk of being exploited intentionally or unintentionally by more powerful and more sophisticated commercial partners.

In the present article, we outline—with examples—the motivations and character of what Drumwright, Cunningham, and Berger (2000) have called "social alliances," partnerships between for-profit and nonprofit organizations[1] and distinguish them from strategic alliances among purely for-profit organizations. We then discuss ways in which social alliances can present ethical challenges for one or both partners.[2] Finally, we discuss the alternatives available to social marketers to both detect and resolve ethical dilemmas in social alliances.

Marketing Alliances

At the outset, it is critical that we define what we mean by "marketing alliances." A marketing alliance is a formal or informal arrangement between organizations where each seeks through marketing activities gains that would not be available to either without such an alliance. In our view, the term alliances encompasses two of the three types of marketing exchange characterized by Gundlach and Murphy (1993). These authors distinguish among transactional, contractual, and relational exchanges. A typical *transactional exchange* is a one-time event where, for example, A sells to B. A *contractual exchange* is where A and B agree to a joint undertaking for some fixed period of time, for example, where A and B agree to carry out a six-month promotion of complementary product lines. A *relational exchange* is one that theoretically has no limits, as when A and B conduct a joint venture to market Product Y in Country Z. The last two may be considered "alliances," differing mainly in their time frame and, by extension, the attitudes, intentions and behaviors of the parties. In the commercial sector, such alliances may involve equity investments by one or—more typically—all parties (cf. Varadarajan and Cunningham 1995; Bucklin and Sengupta 1993; Lei and Slocum 1992; Lorange, Roos, and Bronn 1992; Milne, Iyer, and Gooding-Williams 1996).

The forms that marketing alliances in the private sector take are diverse:

1. Vertical distribution alliances: e.g., Giorgio Armani and Neiman Marcus contract for the latter to carry the products of the former on an exclusive basis and perhaps feature these items in certain ways.
2. Franchise arrangements: e.g., Domino's allies with an investor in Bangkok to develop and open Domino's outlets throughout central Thailand.
3. Joint ventures: e.g., America Online and Sun Microsystems work together to develop new e-commerce tools and internet services using Sun's Java technology.
4. Co-branding alliances: e.g., Keebler, Hershey, and Kraft Foods jointly create and sponsor advertising for S'Mores (a confection combining Kraft marshmallows, Keebler graham crackers and Hershey chocolate);
5. Horizontal alliances among competitors: e.g., Lufthansa, United, and several other airlines agree to combine routes, reservation codes, and frequent flyer programs in the "Star Alliance."

Many scholars divide the objectives of alliances into two categories, *operational* and *strategic* (Spekman et al. 1996). Operational alliances involve partnerships designed to make marketing transactions more efficient. Thus, Procter & Gamble and Wal-Mart may form distribution partnerships that involve sharing data electronically in order to speed deliveries, minimize stock-outs and so on. However, both P&G and Wal-Mart have such arrangements with other firms that do not offer unique strategic advantages. Strategic alliances on the other hand, such as that between AOL and Sun, offer partners potential competitive advantages unavailable to rivals. And, of course, some alliances may have both operational and strategic objectives.

Other explanations offered in the literature as to why firms first engage in such alliances (Osborn and Hagedoorn 1997; Smith, Carroll, and Ashford, 1995; Hymer 1960) include:

1. Increasing a firm's access to assets, both financial and personnel, often to allow expansion of the enterprise into new countries or new markets.
2. Reducing monitoring costs of carrying out business, e.g., spending less time and money on administering a distribution alliance between partners with shared interests and a level of trust than in arm's length transactions between non-partners (Buckley and Casson 1989; Dunning 1993).
3. Providing access to new markets. The legal and social structure of many countries and some markets within countries (e.g., some U.S. government contracts) requires partnering with firms with specific characteristics (e.g., that they be local nationals or members of minority groups) (Mowery 1988).
4. Acquiring new knowledge (Ordover and Willig 1985; Tirole 1988; Lei and Slocum 1990) as when GM creates an alliance with Toyota in part to learn more about Japanese manufacturing techniques.

Lorange and Roos (1993) divide such motivations for alliances into those that are offensive (e.g., gaining access to markets) and those that are defensive (e.g., sharing risks of a new, expensive technology). Haspeslagh and Jemison (1991) note that alliances (especially relational exchanges) can also be the first, lower-risk steps toward formal mergers.

Social Alliances

For present purposes, we define social alliances as any formal or informal agreement between a nonprofit organization and one or more for-profit organizations to carry out a marketing program or activity over a significant period of time where:

1. both parties expect the outcome to advance their organization's mission;
2. the corporation is not fully compensated for its participation; and
3. there is a general social benefit expected.

These alliances may be either contractual or relational, i.e., having or not having a fixed termination point. If one considers the first cause-related marketing venture by American Express in 1981 as the starting point of the recent intense interest in social marketing partnerships, it seems fair to conclude that most reported social alliances to date have been contractual alliances. The early American Express project to contribute to the restoration of the Statue of Liberty was a contractual arrangement with a fixed closing date. The dominance of the contractual form may be changing as commercial organizations see the strategic potential of social alliances and so develop longer-term, more open-ended relationships. One example of a longer term alliance is the agreement recently signed between Coca-Cola and the Boys & Girls Clubs of America (BGC) through which Coca-Cola will invest $60 million and significant staff time over ten years to help BGC increase the number of young people participating in its programs. Such a relationship meets our criteria in that:

1. Coca-Cola will significantly increase its exposure to a prime market target—young people—improve staff morale in local community activities, and improve its corporate image;
2. BGC will receive significant investment capital and volunteer assistance, and new promotional opportunities;
3. BGC does not pay Coca-Cola for the services it renders to BGC; and
4. The result should be a significant increase in the number of at-risk young people involved in positive after-school activities.

It should be noted that our definition of social alliances *excludes* contractual agreements between nonprofit and commercial organizations where the former merely hires the latter (sometimes at below-market rates) to perform specific services. Such arrangements are increasingly common for such service areas as advertising, public relations, research, and distribution.

Contractual and strategic alliances are becoming more and more common and have proved to be very successful. For example, consider the ongoing Avon Breast Cancer Awareness Crusade, which was initiated in 1993 and is based on a partnership between Avon Products and the National Alliance of Breast Cancer Organizations (NABCO).[3] Through the crusade, Avon sales representatives have raised $37 million for breast cancer education and increased access to early detection by selling special merchandise (e.g., pins with the insignia of the pink breast cancer ribbon). NABCO distributes the funds to community programs throughout the U.S. that promote education and access to screening services for underserved women. In addition, Avon's 480,000 U.S. salespeople have been trained to talk about breast cancer and the importance of early detection. They have distributed more than 80 million flyers on breast cancer detection. Some of them volunteer through local breast cancer-related organizations or through special events such as one of the Avon Breast Cancer Walks. The Crusade has generated more than one billion media impressions.

Since the Crusade began, NABCO has been transformed. Prior to its involvement with Avon, NABCO was an information and education resource with an annual budget of less than $2 million. In addition to augmenting NABCO's education and information efforts, the Crusade has enabled NABCO to expand its mission, its clientele, and its annual budget. According to Amy Langer, NABCO executive director:

> Before the Crusade, we were busy empowering those patients who are information seekers, which meant that we were serving educated, white women—"the haves." I had begun to feel an ethical imperative about who we weren't serving—the "have nots"—the medically underserved women. Through Avon, NABCO was allowed to direct money and focus on an unsexy area—underserved women.

Share Our Strength (SOS), the anti-hunger nonprofit, more than doubled its grant-making capacity through its collaboration with American Express for the Charge Against Hunger campaign during the fourth quarters of 1993–1995. City Year, the national corps of young adults involved in community service, has expanded from a single city operation to a 10-city operation in nine states since its partnership with Timberland began. With Timberland's help, it has initiated two revenue-generating ventures—a line of clothing, "City Gear," and a team building and training service for managers (Austin 2000).

Similarities and Differences between Social and Purely Commercial Alliances

Social alliances have important similarities—and some differences—with commercial alliances. First of all, social alliances are different in that they are almost always strategic rather than operational and almost always non-equity rather than equity. On the other hand, they are similar in that both parties see advantages that they would not achieve without the partnership. For corporations, four advantages for engaging in social alliances are typically cited (Alperson 1994):

1. Enhanced corporate image;
2. Increased employee involvement;
3. Improved customer ties; and
4. Increased efficiency in giving programs.

From the social marketer's perspective, a wide range of benefits is possible:

1. Increased input resources addressing the organization's mission, including investment capital and volunteer help;
2. Increased promotional exposure primarily through advertising, public relations, and special events;
3. Increased knowledge and growing sophistication in management.

Social and commercial alliances are also similar in that, as with any "marriage," differences between the organizations require adjustment and tolerance for the partnership to work effectively.

However, there are some important differences that affect both outcomes and the potential for ethical problems to arise. Consider again the social alliance between Avon and NABCO at its beginning in 1993. Though both organizations were headquartered in New York City, Avon's offices sprawled through a contemporary high-rise building near Central Park close to the Park Plaza Hotel, while NABCO's office was nestled in a modest building on East 34th Street. The differences in the office locations and styles only hint at differences that must have existed in organizational cultures and circumstances. Avon had worldwide revenues of more than $5.2 billion and employed more than 2.8 million representatives worldwide, while NABCO had an annual budget of less than $2 million and employed only a handful of people. Avon's expertise was in the direct selling of cosmetics and gifts, while NABCO's expertise was in providing information regarding breast cancer detection, treatment, and research. One of Avon's prime performance measures would be sales, while one of NABCO's would be the number of individuals provided with information.

In social marketing alliances, the parties will often have significant differences in:

1. Size
2. Expertise
3. Objectives and performance measures
4. Cultures.

Differences in size and expertise can lead to important differences in power in the relationship, and thereby the potential for the abuse of that power. Differences in objectives and culture can lead to differences in propensity for opportunism on the one hand and wariness on the other. Among the differences in culture between social and commercial marketers that have been noted are those cited in Table 5-1.

There is some dispute in the management literature as to whether cultural differences across organizations affect the success of alliances. In a study of 98 commercial partnerships, Saxton recently concluded that "alliances are economic actions embedded in a social structure" which can affect outcomes (cf. Granovetter 1985; Hill 1990; and Nooteboom 1992). However, his quantitative analysis found that "similarities between partners with respect to specific organizational characteristics, including cul-

Table 5-1. Differences between Social and Commercial Marketers

Social Marketers	*Commercial Marketers*
Want to do good	Want to make money
Funded by taxes, donations	Funded by investments
Publicly accountable	Privately accountable
Performance hard to measure	Performance measured in profits, market share
Behavioral goals long term	Behavioral goals short term
Often target controversial behaviors	Typically provide noncontroversial products/services
Often choose high-risk targets	Choose accessible targets
Risk-averse managers	Risk-taking managers
Participative decision making	Hierarchical decision making
Relationships based on trust	Relationships often competitive

ture and human resources, were negatively related to alliance outcomes" (Saxton 1997, 456). Saxton did find that alliance performance was positively related to:

- reputation of the partner
- shared decision making
- similarities between partners in strategy and organizational processes.

As with other researchers, Saxton indicates that trust is a very important factor affecting alliance outcomes. However, Osborn and Hagedoorn suggest that "there is growing recognition that sponsors may have incompatible expectations for a given alliance" (1997, 268). This can have important effects on trust, and thus sabotage a potentially satisfactory arrangement.

A final difference between social and commercial alliances is that, in the former, much more often there is an imbalance in the emotional and organizational stake in the alliance. For the corporation, the alliance is often just one of a great many corporate marketing activities whereas the nonprofit partner may have much more invested in the venture. Among other things, such an imbalance can lead to differences in the perceived magnitude of ethical lapses or conflicts and, for the nonprofit, possibly raise the "heat" of the reaction.

Ethical Challenges

When do marketing alliances and social alliances become problematic? A first question is: problematic for whom? In this volume, William Smith proposes that, in social marketing, we need to be concerned about the impacts of social marketers' actions on two parties, those directly affected by the social marketing program (e.g., the target audience or audiences) and those who are indirectly affected by the program. We propose here that the latter category be partitioned to include:

1. The social marketer (what Smith refers to as "the Actor");
2. Any ally, corporate, nonprofit or government that is in some sense also "an Actor";
3. The stakeholders of the latter, including stockholders, employees, other suppliers, their customers, etc.;
4. Other members of society; and
5. The social marketing "profession."

Again, following Smith's framework, we are here concerned with an "act" or "acts" that comprise the formation and operation of the social alliance, per se. We do not consider tactical decisions to be problematic—such as advertising that is deceptive for audiences—since these are ethically questionable no matter who undertakes them. On the other hand, Smith would argue that the existence of the alliance is germane because whether an action is unethical may depend on the character of the actor and the context of the action. Others in this volume take up the latter issue.

We now consider ethical issues at the macro and micro levels.

Macro Ethical Issues

We begin from the perspective of the society in general and ask whether social alliances are unethical in and of themselves. Writers who have considered how we take care of social problems have distinguished among three sectors: government, the private sector, and the nonprofit sector. Clearly, social alliances blur this distinction. Moreover, the creation and sustenance of the nonprofit third sector is seen by many as a reaction to a combination of market failure and inattention by government (Hansmann 1980). Milton Friedman (1970) and Herbert Stein (1983) have been consistent advocates of the position that the social responsibility of corporations is simply and only to generate profits for its stockholders and jobs for its workers. Any attempt to use corporate resources for social ends, in their view, would represent both a misappropriation of stockholder assets and a meddling of corporations in areas where they have no skills or standing.

The opposite side of this argument is the position advocated by Donaldson and Dunfee (1995) and Quinn and Jones (1995) that corporations are responsible to multiple stakeholders, a prominent one of which is society. Further, the fact that society allows corporations to exist implies a social contract imposing *obligations* on the corporation to consider society's interests in its actions. Others take a different, more empirical tack. Weeden (1998) among others has asserted that social alliances are just good business—i.e., systematic social investing can have direct, positive payoffs for the corporation's bottom line. Drumwright, Cunningham, and Berger found that social alliances can result in increases in financial, human, and social capital (2000). However, one can question whether the activities of nonprofits merit societal support such as freedom from taxes if their activities in part benefit profit-making corporations.

A second issue of importance to society is whether the involvement of corporations in social marketing has the effect of distorting the allocation of the nonprofit sector's attention to the range of problems it has undertaken to address. Popular, attractive causes often are selected by corporations, while the less popular, less attractive, or less acceptable causes are neglected—a practice often described as "cherry-picking." For example, more than seventy companies have become affiliated with some aspect of breast cancer. Breast cancer as a cause is attractive for a variety of reasons. Many affluent women are concerned about it, and it is currently on the nation's agenda, which creates fertile ground for favorable publicity. Its incidence is fairly high, and it is not associated with any "sins" or with disreputable socioeconomic classes. Many people with no family history contract it, and it is difficult to predict who will be affected. And it need not be fatal; with early diagnosis and treatment, the survival rate is high. Cherry picking can even occur within a single cause. With breast cancer, many companies prefer to be involved with the more glamorous aspects of the cause, such as funding high profile research efforts. Fewer are willing to fund less glamorous endeavors such as transportation to and from mammography clinics.

Unfortunately, the importance of a cause is not necessarily correlated with popularity or attractiveness. Early on, this was true for AIDS, which was a potential major epidemic but was associated with populations looked upon unfavorably by many segments of the general population: male homosexuals and intravenous drug users. Similarly, issues such as domestic violence and date rape are important, but not particularly attractive. Some men, both consumers and employees, have reacted negatively to cause-related marketing efforts related to causes such as these.

In a sense, a "market mentality" is imposed on the universe of social alliances. That is, the most appealing and least objectionable causes receive support rather than the neediest causes. Does this market mentality substantiate Friedman's argument that companies have no business using their resources for social ends because this will only result in social distortions? Are they indeed meddling in areas in which they have no expertise nor the appropriate motives, and in the process, creating macro level problems for society? Is society then better off if companies see their social responsibility merely as creating jobs and generating profits for shareholders? In response to these concerns, Bloom, Hussein, and Szykman (1995, 11) propose that corporate social marketing programs be put to the following two-question test: (1) "Is society better off because of this program?" and (2) "Has corporate involvement allowed this program to perform better than it would if it were managed by only a nonprofit or government agency?" Drumwright and Murphy (2000) argue that social alliances and other forms of corporate societal marketing can result in compelling benefits not only for companies but also for nonprofits, consumers, and society—a "win/win/win/win." James Austin (2000) provides several vivid examples of social alliances where the participants believe that the result is greater than could be accomplished without the alliance, but the participants, of course, cannot be the sole judges from a societal perspective.

Another macro level concern involves the aggregate effect of social alliances on the total amount of charitable giving. For example, if individuals perceive that they have contributed to charity through buying a product promoted by cause-related marketing, will they reduce their personal charitable giving? Likewise, if companies are contributing to nonprofits through their marketing initiatives, will they give less through philanthropy? Could the net effect of social alliances be a lower level of charitable giving? No data shed light on these tradeoffs at present. Further, one might argue that individuals and corporations have no ethical obligation to contribute at a particular level. On the other hand, should it be discovered that some corporations were, in effect, hiding behind well-publicized alliances to reduce their charitable giving, this would raise ethical concerns.

A final macro issue is the use of social alliances by corporations to cover over or excuse anti-competitive or anti-social activities in the corporations' core businesses. Many have argued that the flurry of alliances between the tobacco industry and arts organizations and government projects is really a smokescreen intended to divert attention from the danger of their products.

Micro Ethical Issues for Alliance Participants

Within a specific social alliance, ethical issues arise out of three kinds of dissatisfaction: (a) dissatisfaction with outcomes or results, (b) dissatisfaction with procedures or processes, and (c) dissatisfaction with a partner's behavior (including its actions regarding matters that may be unrelated to the alliance). Of course, many alliances in both the for-profit and nonprofit worlds are unsuccessful. Partners are disappointed and sometimes angry because outcomes are not as expected in kind or amount. Procedures can be neglected or botched. Partners have partings of the way. These are expected and, while disappointing and sometimes the focus of much name-calling, they do not necessarily raise ethical concerns. Dissatisfaction suggestive of an ethical problem occurs when an element of *hurt* is felt by one or both of the parties.

Parties may feel hurt if they believe the other party failed to meet one or more of the following ethical standards (cf. Gundlach and Murphy 1993):

a. Honesty
b. Equity
c. Fairness

d. Trust
e. Commitment
f. Responsibility

Failures of an alliance to meet these standards in some cases can be redressed legally. Indeed, as Gundlach and Murphy point out, much of contract law that guides such alliances is based on moral principles (1993). However, our concern here is with cases where the standard is ethical, not legal.

Outcomes and Issues of Fairness and Equity

Social alliances, in the main, seek one or both of two kinds of outcomes. Many, particularly those under the label of cause-related marketing (Varadarajan and Menon 1988; Andreasen 1996), are designed to provide new sources of funding for the social marketer—while achieving marketing, public relations, and/or human relations objectives for the partnering corporation. Others are designed to increase the impact of some particular program, as when soap makers in South America promote handwashing (BASICS 1997).

Frustrations about the success of fundraising can come from many sources. For example, ethical concerns can arise over how a company specifies exactly how it will determine what its donation will be. If the company commits to passing on to the social marketer a percentage of profits, companies can abuse their discretion in the allocation of costs to minimize or even eliminate the pass-along. On the other hand, should a corporation be ethically bound to turn over an agreed upon share of profits if the corporation's basic financial circumstances change. Should a company keep its commitment if its own employees are suffering income loss and layoffs?

A company's donation to a nonprofit often is based on a cause-related marketing initiative in which the company commits to make a donation based on sales. For example, Avon contributes profits from the sales of pink-ribbon merchandise to promote breast cancer access and screening. Each time its private label candy bar is purchased, Wild Oats Markets makes a donation to charity. Sears donates all proceeds from sales of a specific CD of Christmas music to Gilda's Club. The commitment to donate can be structured and stated in a variety of ways, some of which can be problematic.

One source of problems is if either the nonprofit partner—or consumers more generally—are misled to think that the donation will be much larger than it is in actuality. Intentional deception would be the most egregious form such miscommunication could take, but absence of rigorous efforts to assure that there is no deception could also be viewed as an ethical breach as well. In this context, neither caveat emptor nor "caveat nonprofit" is wise or ethical. For example, managers at a company with a chain of retail stores had been advertising that 100 percent of profits on a given day each month was being donated to charity. The company was acquired by another company that had been donating 5 percent of its revenues on a given day each month. An internal audit revealed that the acquired company's 100 percent of profits was substantially less than the other company's 5 percent of revenues because of the manner in which costs, particularly indirect costs, were allocated.

In contrast, Avon specifically chose to have its cause-related contributions tied to specialty products (e.g., ink pens or jewelry pins with the pink breast cancer ribbon) and to make the accounting highly transparent. Salespeople receive no commission on the products, and the company covers only its direct costs. All proceeds over and above the direct costs go to fund the grants made by its nonprofit partner, NABCO. While one could argue that contributing a percentage of the sales or profits from one of its existing products, say a lipstick, during a specified period might provide more money, Avon executives have said that doing so would not preserve the integrity of the program.

Problems differ depending on whether the company makes its donation commitment as fixed or variable. Examples of fixed commitments were Timberland's pledge to donate $5 million to City Year over a five-year period, and Avon's pledge of $5 million to the Statue of Liberty Renovation Fund, which was to be raised through a cause-related marketing effort. After making these commitments, each company experienced disappointing financial performance. Timberland reported its first loss since becoming a public company and underwent painful restructuring and the accompanying plant closings and layoffs (Austin and Elias 1996). Likewise, Avon's cause-related marketing program commemorating both the 100th birthday of the Statue of Liberty and the 100th birthday of Avon failed to capture the imaginations of Avon's sales representatives or consumers outside of New York City, and the results were disappointing. Simultaneously, the company was experiencing financial difficulty. Both companies faced difficult ethical dilemmas regarding their pledges. One can easily imagine that a laid-off employee (or a stockholder suffering a loss) would see it as unethical for the company to keep the commitment to the nonprofit. Likewise, a nonprofit that has entered into a partnership in good faith with the promise of specified funds would see it as unethical for the company not to keep its commitment. After all, the nonprofit delivered on its part of the partnership. Both organizations honored their commitments.

As a result of this experience, Avon decided to avoid fixed commitments that might be awkward to fulfill and structured the Breast Cancer Awareness Crusade so that donations vary with sales. Joanne Mazurki, director of the Crusade, said that this aspect, the absence of a fixed commitment by Avon to turn over a set amount, was a big "turn-off" and "deal breaker" to many of the nonprofits that Avon approached as potential partners. However, Avon felt that the variable approach was more responsible because it communicated the uncertainty from year to year. Many nonprofits that demurred undoubtedly were uncomfortable operating without the kind of certainty afforded by the foundation grants that are a more common form of nonprofit transfers.

Companies may be criticized for taking an unfair portion of the money raised as well as for their means of raising it. Consider the case of Pallotta Teamworks, a for-profit corporation that organizes walks and rides to benefit charity. Pallotta Teamworks has organized both a series of bicycle rides benefiting AIDS organizations and the Avon Breast Cancer Crusade Walks. The company has been harshly criticized for the relatively small percentages of the proceeds actually provided for charity. On average, 62 to 50 percent of the amount raised goes to charity, and at times the percentage has been as low as 6.5 percent (Christian 1999; Franklin 1999). Pallotta Teamwork's expenses, which include its fees, have been criticized as excessive and greedy (Wise 1997). The defense offered by Dan Pallotta, the president and founder of the company, is that these events are expensive to run, and without the events, the vast amounts of money that they produce would not be raised. As an example, the Avon Breast Cancer Walk in California in October 1998 netted $5 million for the Crusade. The rationale is that any percentage is better than nothing.

Procedures and Issues of Fairness and Equity

A concern for many social marketers is whether the extent and character of the efforts of both parties are appropriate and equitable. Because marketing communications in general and advertising in particular are central to most social alliances, procedural ethical issues are often embedded in decisions about them. One issue involves the ratio of the money spent promoting the alliance to the money contributed to the cause. American Express has been subject to criticism for both "Charge Against Hunger" and the "Statue of Liberty" campaigns because far more was spent advertising the campaigns than was contributed to the causes (Ratnesar 1997; Smith and Stodghill 1994). For example, American Express's annual contribution to Share Our Strength was capped at $5 million, while the amount spent on advertising was surely at least two to three times greater. One could argue that a 2:1 or 3:1 advertising-to-donation ratio represents an irresponsible lack of equity. On the other hand, one could argue that the $10–$15 million was going to be spent by American Express on advertising during the fourth quarter anyway, irrespective of whether "Charge" and "Share Our Strength" were part of the campaign. The question then becomes, in one sense, not whether the split in resources between advertising and the cause was equitable, but whether the cause will be a part of the "normal" advertising budget at all. On the other hand, if it is agreed that the cause will be part of the ad budget, is it less equitable if the ratio of ad budget to donations is 10 to 1 than if it is 2 to 1?

Part of the source of friction here is the difference in organizational cultures and experience. Nonprofits often have little experience with promotional budgets—especially large ones—often relying on donated time and promotional services. Further, they have little experience with brand building which—the company feels—may require inordinate amounts of near-term spending. Thus, there may be legitimate corporate reasons for a high ratio. On the other hand, many alliances involve corporate promotional expenditures that seem less inequitable. For example, Avon's Breast Cancer Awareness Campaign has raised $37 million to date on an annual budget of less than $500,000. It is primarily a direct selling effort with minimal advertising expense.

Another ethical issue related to marketing communications involves cobranding or the licensing of a nonprofit's name or logo to a company for use in marketing its products. In 1998, companies paid nonprofits more than a half billion dollars for the use of their names (Abelson 1999). Such arrangements can be very problematic.

Perhaps the most publicized example of co-branding gone wrong is the 1997 agreement between the American Medical Association (AMA) and Sunbeam, which permitted Sunbeam to put AMA's name on products ranging from blood pressure monitors to heating pads (Collins 1997; Johnson 1999). This was an exclusive agreement whereby the American Medical Association name could not be used with rival products. AMA members raised a storm of protest over this agreement, fearing that the AMA name on these products would imply an endorsement and/or signify that the products were superior to competitive products. The AMA paid Sunbeam $10 million to settle a breach-of-contract lawsuit.

On the other hand, despite the Sunbeam example, licensing agreements between companies and social marketers have abounded. For example, Bristol-Myers Squibb has run full page advertisements for Pravachol, a cholesterol-lowering drug, that featured the name and logo of the American Heart Association. Electrolux negotiated an exclusive arrangement with the Asthma and Allergy Foundation to use its name and logo on the cartons in which its vacuum cleaners are packaged and in product literature. SmithKline Beecham runs television ads for NicoDerm, its nicotine patch, in which the company and the American Cancer Society were described as "partners in helping you quit."

Such co-branding may not be problematic in and of itself, but it becomes a potential ethical problem if consumers are misled regarding the nonprofit's endorsement of the product and its degree of involvement with the product. Unlike companies, nonprofits typically assert that they endorse no commercial products, *even when their names and logos are used.* Thus, a number of state attorneys general have become concerned that advertisements using nonprofit names and logos are misleading (Ableson 1999). As one example, SmithKline Beecham settled with a dozen attorneys general who were concerned that the NicoDerm ads were misleading by agreeing to pay $2.5 million and to spell out in its ads that it "makes an annual grant to the American Cancer Society for cancer research and education and for the use of its seal." Further, state attorneys general have proposed a possible code of conduct for such co-branding alliances. This code is discussed further below.

As noted above, one of the differences between nonprofits and for-profits is a difference in size and sophistication. This can lead to another area of procedural unfairness where the corporate partner imposes unfair restrictions on the actions of the social marketer. Is it ethical for companies to require the kinds of exclusivity agreements noted above, ensuring that the nonprofit will not enter into collaborative initiatives with competitors? Is it right for a company to require an exclusive agreement from a nonprofit, while it continues to accord itself the right to work freely with multiple nonprofits? Drumwright, Cunningham, and Berger (2000) have observed that exclusivity agreements often are not mutual. That is, the company assumes that it is free to work with multiple nonprofits related to the same cause while making it clear that the nonprofit is not to work with companies in similar industries. This appears to be a reflection of the relative power of the players. Could it also be exploitative? On the other hand, if the company helps the social marketer make contact with non-competing companies, does this mitigate the "unfair" restrictions of an exclusivity agreement? For example, during the Charge Against Hunger campaign, American Express, although requiring exclusivity among credit card companies, provided Share Our Strength entree to retailers and encouraged the latter to match the American Express contribution for the charges made in their store.

Should a company—after an agreement is signed—be able to object to a social marketer's actions, e.g., lobbying for some controversial social change or partnering with some other nonprofit that the corporation finds objectionable? Companies may want to place requirements on grant making. For example, companies may require nonprofits to make grants within certain geographical areas, such as the regions in which the company operates. Or the company might request that the nonprofit not make grants to organizations that the company finds troublesome on some dimension, such as the political persuasion or sexual orientation of their clienteles. The ethical issue arises when the corporation appears to be exerting unconscionable power.

Imbalances in power or asymmetries have been shown to be a major source of difficulty for alliances (Bucklin and Sengupta 1993; Varadarajan and Cunningham 1995). Drumwright, Cunningham, and Berger (2000) observed that companies tend to perceive that they "own" the collaborative initiative; after all it is funded through their marketing budgets, and they may expect to call the shots. This perspective is often reflected in the program names. For example, Avon's Breast Cancer Awareness Campaign makes no mention of its nonprofit partner. Charge Against Hunger ads prominently displayed the American Express logo, but the Share Our Strength logo was not included. Are the nonprofit interests receiving short shrift? Does the corporation have an ethical obligation to give their partner equal billing and visibility?

A related problem is the tendency of companies to micromanage the nonprofit's part of the collaboration. This can come about because of the company's feelings of ownership of the collaboration, or perhaps because they question the nonprofit's competence. Nonprofit managers can perceive this micromanagement as intrusive, highly inappropriate, and arrogant; they often complain that the company is moving beyond its own expertise and is not respecting the nonprofit's special skills. Again, the ethical issue concerns the corporate partner's possible use of power to force the social marketing partner to take actions that the latter believes are not in its own interests.

Another source of potential problems identified by Drumwright, Cunningham, and Berger (2000) is how or when a social alliance will end. This difficulty typically stems from neglect in the negotiation and planning stages. It can become problematic when the social marketer is relying heavily on the partner for funds and assistance and the corporation decides to sever the relationship, often for little good reason and/or with little warning. Among equal corporations, such shifts in alliances are presumably common and offer little long-term damage. In a social marketing context with unequal partners and a tendency among nonprofits to avoid contingency planning, the responsibilities on the corporate partner would seem to be much greater.

A final process-oriented problem may develop when there is disagreement regarding what is "right" in some strategic or tactical decision. Such arguments often stem from the differences in culture and values outlined in Table 5-1. They can poison the partnership culture to the extent that nonprofit staffers feel that either their organization and/or the commercial partner is unethical and to the point that the corporate partner becomes completely frustrated. Because the rightness of an action is an ethical issue, this potential for conflict argues forcefully for early agreement on partnership ethical standards.

Behavior and Issues of Trust and Responsibility

An alliance partner's behavior outside the relationship may be problematic if it appears that this partner is behaving unethically. The other "innocent" partner may feel that its own reputation is tainted by the questionable actions. Nike engages in many social marketing ventures and their nonprofit partners have been troubled by charges that Nike products may, in some cases, have been produced by child labor.

Nonprofit leaders sometimes must take stands and speak out on controversial or highly polarized subjects such as welfare, healthcare, or prison reform, not to mention abortion, gay rights, and other topics corporate leaders typically avoid. Companies involved in social alliances could create pressure, even if subtle, on nonprofit leaders to hold their tongues or refrain from governmental coalition building. At what point does such pressure become an ethical issue? On the other hand, could the nonprofit's stand on a controversial issue with which the company has a conflict of interest create an ethical dilemma for the company?

Finally, there is the question of requests that a partner makes that are formally beyond the terms of the partnership. Is it ethical for a corporation to try to coerce a social marketer into using the company's products or services? Suppose the corporation asks its nonprofit partner to intervene with someone else on the corporation's behalf? The latter may be relatively common where at least one objective of the partnership is to associate a firm with reputation problems with a squeaky-clean nonprofit. Is it acceptable for the corporation to ask the social marketer to speak out in praise of the company should the press or activist groups challenge it? What if the corporation wants the nonprofit to use its relationship with government agencies to get favorable treatment for corporate actions? When does help for a partner compromise a partner?

Preventing Ethical Lapses

How, then, can ethical lapses be prevented or, barring this, detected and resolved? These issues are dealt with elsewhere in this volume. In our view, solutions may be divided roughly into four categories: symbolic, contractual, educational, and procedural. We consider each briefly in turn.

Symbolic Solutions

A first, perhaps necessary, step is the formulation of a set of ethical standards governing social marketing as a whole and, specifically, social marketing alliances. The American Marketing Association Code of Ethics could be a useful starting point as it has among its provisions the following standards that would apply to social marketing alliances:

> Marketers shall uphold and advance the integrity, honor, and dignity of the marketing profession by . . . not knowingly participating in conflicts of interest without prior notice to all parties involved;
>
> Participants in the marketing exchange process should be able to expect that . . . all parties intend to discharge their obligations, financial and otherwise, in good faith;
>
> [Rights and duties of the parties] would include, but is not limited to . . . not using coercion in the marketing channel [and] not exerting undue influence over the reseller's choice;
>
> They should not demand, encourage, or apply coercion to obtain unethical behavior in their relation with others;
>
> [Social marketers should] Apply confidentiality and anonymity in professional relationships with regard to privileged information;
>
> [Social marketers should] Meet their obligations and responsibilities in contracts and mutual agreements in a timely manner;
>
> [Social marketers should] Avoid manipulation to take advantage of situations to maximize personal welfare in a way that unfairly deprives or damages their organization or others.

While the American Marketing Association Code is a good starting point, alliance partners must still consider whether the threshold for unethical behavior should be higher where a major objective of the partnership is the promotion of some social good. Is "upholding the integrity, honor, and dignity" of social marketing different from upholding that of the commercial marketing profession? If so, what additional obligations or responsibilities should be included? Does a company have a greater responsibility in dealing with a nonprofit partner than it would have with a commercial partner? Does it have an obligation to protect the nonprofit's best interests? On the other hand, is such an approach condescending and patronizing?

It is the authors' view that (a) corporations that enter into social alliances are implicitly accepting some responsibility for what might be called "social stewardship"; (b) social marketing organizations are agencies that society has chartered to advance society's welfare; (c) therefore, corporations' social stewardship should extend to society's designated agents. This means that corporations should have a special obligation to advance—or at least not harm—the social marketer, just as they have undertaken an implicit obligation to advance the welfare of society.

This special responsibility has been recognized in a recent report issued by sixteen state attorneys general and the Corporation Counsel of the District of Columbia ("What's In a Nonprofit's Name? . . ." 1999). This report focuses on advertisements that result from cause-related marketing partnerships. The report states, in part, "public trust is the true currency supporting nonprofit organizations . . . [and therefore] The Attorneys General believe that careful consideration should be given to the potential impact on nonprofit organizations' independence that marketing alliances offering substantial payments to nonprofit organizations in exchange for the use of their names and logos may have." The attorneys general suggest a number of "guidance principles" to guide future alliances, including:

Adherence to all existing consumer and commercial legal standards;

Not representing in advertisements for commercial products that a nonprofit organization has endorsed the advertised product;

Not representing that such commercial products are superior unless the claim is true and substantiated and the nonprofit has determined the product to be superior;

Revealing any commercial payments for the use of the nonprofit's name and logo;

Not deceiving consumers about the effect of consumer purchases on charitable contributions by the consumer or the commercial sponsor;

Avoiding *exclusive* relationships between the nonprofit and the commercial sponsor.

Contractual Solutions

In the absence of a code by which the alliance partners agree to abide, standards can be set out in their contractual relationship about what each partner will or will not do as part of the relationship. Bucklin and Sengupta's research suggests that the negative effects of managerial imbalance in alliances can be countered by increases in the formality of the relationship, exit barriers and exclusivity among the partners (1993). Contractual agreements will give each organization a basis for precluding unethical pressures as well as providing a basis for legal action in the case of serious organizational injury. Exhibit 1 outlines the terms that the Health Promotion Directorate of HealthCanada (albeit a government agency) includes in any agreement it makes with the private sector. Exhibit 2 outlines "Guidelines and Principles for Strategic Alliances" prepared by the Boys & Girls Clubs of America.

While fair and equitable standards of ethical conduct can protect both sides, there still remains a question of whether the process of writing such terms is *itself* fair and equitable. The authors would again argue that, even though corporations typically have greater experience in negotiating contracts and more power in the social marketing alliance, their social stewardship imposes a special obligation to negotiate a fair and equitable arrangement.

Educational Solutions

Codes of ethics and contractual agreements only set out the standards for ethical conduct, they do not ensure that such conduct will follow. Individuals commit ethical lapses, and they may do so out of ignorance that an ethical challenge exists, misinterpretation of the standards that ought to apply, or, in the worst case, a willingness to ignore the applicable standards. This implies clearly that formal ethical standards must be accompanied by ethical training of those who must apply them. This is a topic dealt with extensively by Michael Basil in chapter 8.

Procedural Solutions

Of course, the presence of codes, contractual terms, and ethically trained managers is seldom sufficient to prevent the emergence of potential ethical conflicts. For social marketing alliances to remain healthy and effective, procedures must be established for discussing and resolving ethical issues. Such discussions may not be free of controversy as alliance partners come from very different cultures and may have different views of what is ethical or unethical. Some possible subjects of debate are:

- What constitutes acceptable puffery in promotions?
- What constitutes acceptable decision-making risk when spending scarce resources?
- Under what circumstances can a desperate market be ignored if it is not cost-effective to target it?
- Under what conditions should market values or efficiency criteria prevail over social goals?

Conclusion

Social alliances appear to be here to stay, and thus it is incumbent upon both companies and nonprofits to give considerable attention to developing ethical standards and procedures for addressing ethical issues when they arise. A combination of four approaches outlined above appear essential to creating ethically sound social alliances in which there is a minimum of opportunistic behavior and little or no hurt feelings. A wide range of research consulted for this paper makes clear that: (a) the longer the relationship, the more that unexpected considerations will become part of the partnership dynamic, and (b) flexibility and survival can be enhanced if there is both trust and commitment in the relationship (Zaltman and Moorman 1988; Morgan and Hunt 1994; Bonoma 1976; Heide and John 1988; Moorman, Zaltman, and Deshpande 1992; John 1984; Heide 1994). Careful attention to ethics and potential ethical conflict will go far to establish these necessary conditions.

Notes

1. Note that this article focuses on alliances between nonprofits and corporations. However, alliances between government and quasi-government organizations are becoming increasingly common. For example, the Health Promotion Programs Branch of HealthCanada lists over 200 partnerships between 1990 and 1996 contributing an estimated $60,000,000 (Canadian) in new resources.

2. For simplicity, we consider only bilateral partnerships. We recognize that many social alliances may involve multiple parties from public and private sectors.

3. Information regarding the Avon Breast Cancer Awareness Crusade was taken from presentations that Amy Langer, executive director of the National Alliance of Breast Cancer Organizations, and Joanne Mazurki, director of the Avon Breast Cancer Awareness Crusade, made at the annual national conference of Business for Social Responsibility in Boston on Nov. 19, 1998, and from public lectures that Mazurki gave at the University of Texas at Austin on Nov. 10–12, 1997.

References

Abelson, Reed (1999), "Sales Pitches Tied to Charities Attract Scrutiny," *New York Times* (May 3): 1.

Alperson, Myra (1994), *Corporate Giving Strategies That Add Business Value.* New York: The Conference Board.

Andreasen, Alan R. (1995), *Marketing Social Change: Changing Behavior to Promote Health, Social Development and the Environment.* San Francisco: Jossey-Bass.

Andreasen, Alan R. (1996), "Profits for Nonprofits: Find a Corporate Partner," *Harvard Business Review* 74 (November-December): 47–59.

Austin, James (2000), *The Collaboration Challenge: How Nonprofits and Businesses Succeed Through Strategic Alliances.* San Francisco: Jossey-Bass.

Austin, James E., and Jaan Elias (1996), "Timberland and Community Involvement," *Harvard Business School Case* No. 9-796-156. Boston: Harvard Business School.

BASICS (1997), "The Promise of Partnerships," *Social Marketing Matters* December: 15–16.

Bloom, Paul N., Pattie Yu Hussein, and Lisa R. Szykman (1995), "Benefiting Society and the Bottom Line: Businesses Emerge from the Shadows to Promote Social Causes," *Marketing Management* 4 (Winter): 8–18.

Bloom, Paul N. and William D. Novelli (1981), "Problems and Challenges in Social Marketing," *Journal of Marketing* 45 (Spring): 79–88.

Bonoma, Thomas V. (1976), "Conflict, Cooperation and Trust in Three Power Systems" *Behavioral Science* 21: 499–514.

Buckley, P. J., and M. Casson (1988), "A Theory of Cooperation in International Business," in F. J. Contractor and P. Lorange, eds., *Cooperative Strategies in International Business.* Lexington, MA: Lexington Books.

Bucklin, Louis P., and Sanjit Sengupta (1993), "Organizing Successful Co-Marketing Alliances." *Journal of Marketing* 57 (April): 32–46.

Christian, Carol (1999), "Bicycle Event for AIDS Will Scale Down," *Houston Chronicle* (February 23): 15.

Collins, Glenn (1997), "A.M.A. to Endorse Line of Products," *New York Times*, (August 13): section A, 1.

Donaldson, Thomas, and Thomas W. Dunfee (1995), "Integrative Social Contracts Theory: A Communitarian Conception of Economic Ethics," *Economics and Philosophy* 11 (April): 252–84.

Drumwright, Minette E., Peggy H. Cunningham, and Ida E. Berger (2000), "Social Alliances: Company/Nonprofit Collaboration," Report No. 00-101, Cambridge, MA: Marketing Science Institute.

Drumwright, Minette, and Patrick E. Murphy (2000), "Corporate Societal Marketing" in Paul N. Bloom and Gregory Gundlach, eds., *The Handbook of Marketing and Society.* Newbury Park, CA: Sage.

Dunning, J. H. (1993), *Multinational Enterprises in the Global Economy.* Wokingham Berks, U.K.: Addison Wesley.

Franklin, Robert (1999), "AIDS Charities Got 28 Cents Per Dollar in '98 Bike Rides," *Minneapolis Star Tribune* (March 9): 1B.

Friedman, Milton (1970), "The Social Responsibility of Business Is to Increase Its Profits," *New York Times Magazine* (September 13).

Granovetter, Mark (1985), "Economic Action and Social Structure: The Problem of Embeddedness," *American Journal of Sociology* 91 (November): 481–510.

Gundlach, Gregory D. and Patrick E. Murphy (1993), "Ethical and Legal Foundations of Relational Marketing Exchanges, " *Journal of Marketing* 57 (October): 35–46.

Hansmann, Henry (1980), "The Role of Nonprofit Enterprises," *Yale Law Journal* (April): 835–901.

Haspeslagh, P., and David Jemison (1991), *Managing Acquisitions: Creating Value through Corporate Renewal.* New York: Free Press.

Heide, Jan B. (1994), "Interorganizational Governance in Marketing Channels," *Journal of Marketing* 58 (January): 71–85.

Heide, Jan B., and George John (1988), "The Role of Dependence Balancing in Safeguarding Transaction-Specific Assets in Conventional Channels, " *Journal of Marketing* 52 (January): 20–35.

Hill, C. W. L. (1990), "Cooperation, Opportunism, and the Invisible Hand: Implications for Transaction Cost Theory." *Academy of Management Review* 15: 500–513.

Hymer, S. (1960), *The International Operations of National Firms: A Study of Foreign Direct Investment.* Cambridge, MA: MIT Press.

John, George (1984), "An Empirical Investigation of some Antecedents of Opportunism in a Marketing Channel." *Journal of Marketing Research* (August): 278–289.

Johnson, Greg (1999), "Officials Urge Limits On Use of Nonprofit Logos," *Los Angeles Times* (April 7), Part C, p. 1.

Lei, David, and John W. Slocum (1990), "Global Strategy and Reward Systems: The Key Roles of Management Development and Corporate Culture," *Organizational Dynamics* 19 (Autumn): 27–41.

——— (1992), "Global Strategy, Competence Building and Strategic Alliances." *California Management Review* (Fall): 81–97.

Lorange, P., and J. Roos (1991), "Why Some Alliances Succeed and Others Fail," *Journal of Business Strategy* (January/February): 25–30.

Lorange, P., and J. Roos (1993), *Strategic Alliances: Formation, Implementation and Evolution*. Cambridge, MA: Blackwell.

Lorange, Peter, J. Roos, and Peggy Simcic Bronn (1992), "Building Successful Strategic Alliances," *Long Range Planning* 25(6): 10–17.

Milne, George R., Easwar S. Iyer, and Sara Gooding-Williams, (1996) "Environmental Organization Alliance Relationships Within and Across Nonprofit, Business, and Government Sectors." *Journal of Public Policy and Marketing* 15; 203–215.

Moorman, Christine, Gerald Zaltman, and Rohit Deshpande (1992), "Relationships Between Providers and Users of Market Research: The Dynamics of Trust Within and Between Organizations," *Journal of Marketing Research* 24 (August): 314–328.

Morgan, Robert M., and Shelby D. Hunt (1994), "The Commitment-Trust Theory of Relationship Marketing," *Journal of Marketing* 58 (July): 20–38.

Mowery, D. C. (1988) "Collaboration Ventures Between U.S. and Foreign Manufacturing Firms: An Overview," in D. C. Mowery, ed., *International Collaborative Ventures in U.S. Manufacturing*. Cambridge, MA: Ballinger, 37–70.

Nooteboom, Bart (1992), "Marketing, Reciprocity and Ethics," *Journal of Business Ethics* 7 (December): 907–915.

Ordover, J. A., and R. D. Willig (1985), "Anti-trust for High Technology Industries: Assessing Research Joint Ventures and Mergers," *Journal of Law and Economics* 28: 311–333.

Osborn, Richard N., and John Hagedoorn (1997), "The Institutionalization and Evolutionary Dynamics of Interorganizational Alliances and Networks," *Academy of Management Journal* 40(2): 261–278.

Quinn, Dennis P., and Thomas M. Jones (1995), "An Agent Morality View of Business Policy," *Academy of Management Review* 20(1): 22–42.

Ratnesar, Romesh (1997), "Doing Well By Doing Good," *The New Republic* (Jan. 6): 18.

Sarner, Mark, and Janice Nathanson (1996), *Social Marketing for Business*. Toronto: Manifest Communications.

Saxton, Todd (1997), "The Effects of Partner and Relationship Characteristics on Alliance Outcomes," *Academy of Management Journal* 40(2): 443–461.

Smith, Craig (1994), "The New Corporate Philanthropy," *Harvard Business Review* 72(May-June): 105–116.

Smith, Geoffrey, and Ron Stodghill II (1994), "Are Good Causes Good Marketing?" *Business Week* 3364 (March 21): 64.

Smith, K. G., S. J. Carroll, and S. J. Ashford (1995), "Intra- and Interorganizational Cooperation: Toward a Research Agenda," *Academy of Management Journal* 1: 7–23.

Spekman, Robert E., Lynn A. Isabella, Thomas C. MacAvoy, and Theodore Forbes, III (1996), "Creating Strategic Alliances Which Endure," *Long Range Planning* 29 (June): 346–357.

Stein, Herbert (1983), *Agenda for the Study of Microeconomic Policy.* Washington, D.C.: American Enterprise Institute.

Tirole, J. (1988), *The Theory of Industrial Organization*. Cambridge, MA: MIT Press.

Varadarajan, P. Rajan, and Margaret H. Cunningham (1995), "Strategic Alliances: A Synthesis of Conceptual Foundations," *Journal of the Academy of Marketing Science* 23 (Fall): 282–296.

Varadarajan, P. Rajan, and Anil Menon (1988), "Cause-Related Marketing: A Coalignment of Marketing Strategy and Corporate Philanthropy," *Journal of Marketing* 52 (July): 58–74.

Weeden, Curt (1998), *Corporate Social Investing: New Strategies for Giving and Getting Corporate Contributions*. San Francisco: Berett-Koehler.

What's In a Nonprofit's Name? Public Trust, Profit and the Potential for Public Deception, (1999), A Preliminary Multistate Report of Commercial/Nonprofit Product Marketing, (April).

Wise, Jeff (1997), "Altruism for Fun and Profit," *New York Times* (Sept. 7): 64.

Zaltman, Gerald, and Christine Moorman (1988), "The Importance of Personal Trust in the Use of Research," *Journal of Advertising Research* 28 (October-November): 16–24.

CHAPTER SIX

Social Marketing and Social Contracts: Applying Integrative Social Contracts Theory to Ethical Issues in Social Marketing

N. Craig Smith

The practice of social marketing is generally founded on good intentions. Nonetheless, in seeking to do good, social marketers can face many ethical issues. Indeed, as later discussed, in some respects there may be greater scope for unethical practice in social marketing than in for-profit marketing by business. This chapter illustrates the range of ethical issues arising in social marketing and examines the potential of normative marketing ethics to inform decisions about these issues. More specifically, it explores the possible application of social contract theory to social marketing.

Social marketers can confront many of the same ethical issues as commercial marketers. Accordingly, the broader topic of ethics in marketing is introduced in the next section, followed by a more focused discussion of ethics in social marketing. Having considered the potential of the major approaches to ethical issues from the marketing ethics literature, more specific attention is given to social contract theory in the next section. Social contract theory is gaining increased recognition within business ethics, particularly in a specific formulation known as Integrative Social Contracts Theory (Donaldson and Dunfee 1994; 1995). ISCT's focus on communities and their norms makes this approach particularly appropriate to social marketing because it often involves competing claims of different communities. Following an overview of ISCT, the chapter discusses how the theory might be applied to a family planning social marketing campaign. The chapter concludes with a discussion of ISCT's strengths and limitations in application to social marketing.

Ethics in Marketing

Managers make decisions that have ethical content, be they decisions about human resources (e.g., redundancies), finance (e.g., recommending a takeover bid that is not in the interests of shareholders), or marketing (e.g., product safety). Marketing managers appear more likely to face ethical issues than managers in other business functions because of their boundary-spanning role (especially their involvement with multiple stakeholders) and their capacity for exercising economic power (through their involvement in sales transactions and their control of large promotional budgets).

Making decisions about these ethical issues is important, but often quite difficult. It is important because of possible negative consequences of unethical conduct, such as adverse publicity and harm to the organization's reputation, lower employee morale, and possibly legal or regulatory sanctions. Conversely, there may be positive consequences of ethical conduct, such as improved employee morale or more favorable consumer sentiment. These arguments have prompted advocacy of the maxim "good ethics is good business." More important perhaps, at least from a non-consequentialist perspective, is the moral imperative to which all human beings are subject; we attempt to be ethical in our conduct because, quite simply, it is "the right thing to do." Nonetheless, decision making about many ethical issues in marketing can be complex. Often, it is difficult to determine the morally right course of action. It is clear, however, that ethical considerations should be an integral part of marketing decision making.

Normative marketing ethics, as a subset of business ethics (itself a subset of the field of ethics), identifies moral principles and methods of moral reasoning that justify rules and judgments of what is morally right and wrong. It is prescriptive and primarily concerned with what marketing managers ought to do when making decisions with ethical content. Hence, it may provide marketers with guidance in managing ethical issues.

Ethical issues can arise in any part of the marketing program (Laczniak and Murphy 1993; Smith and Quelch 1993). In marketing research, there are issues of research integrity in data collection, analysis, and interpretation, for example. In market selection, there are decisions made about who will *not* be targeted by marketing campaigns, such that some segments may be denied products and services (sometimes referred to as "redlining"). Product policy can include decisions about how safe a product will be. Pricing decisions can involve issues of fairness (e.g., the price of a life-saving drug). Channel decisions may involve the abuse of power by one channel intermediary in relation to another. Personal selling may present unscrupulous customers with opportunities for bribery requests. And advertising may be deceptive. Chonko and Hunt surveyed marketing practitioners, asking them to describe the job situation that poses the most difficult ethical problem (1985). A ranking of the issues they identified is reported in Table 6-1. How are marketers to deal with such issues?

At the most basic level, making marketing decisions with ethical content requires, first, that there be recognition of an ethical issue. This is believed to be prompted by "ethical sensitivity" (Hunt and Vitell 1993; Sparks and Hunt 1998). Next, from a deontological perspective, there needs to be an understanding of any moral duties associated with the ethical issue (e.g., promise-keeping) and, from a consequentialist perspective, an assessment of who (which "stakeholders") could be affected (Hunt and Vitell 1993). Analysis is then required of the associated moral duties, including any conflicts of duties; of how the stakeholders are affected; and of the values relevant to the decision. Nash (1989) has suggested that questions to consider at this stage might include the following: How would you feel in their place (i.e., as the stakeholders)? How might others judge your action? What is your intention? To whom and to what do you give your loyalty as a person and as a member of the corporation? Will your position be as valid in the future? Under what conditions would you allow exceptions to your stand? In practice, sources of guidance for this analysis might include the individual's own values and ethical maxims, such as "do unto others as you would have them do unto you" (the Golden Rule) and "when in doubt, don't" (Laczniak and Murphy 1993). The experience of others; ethical "vignettes" (often acquired during ethics training); and organizational, industry, or professional codes (e.g., the code of ethics of the American Marketing Association) may also provide guidance. For many issues, these sources may be sufficient, though it is quite possible that an individual's values, for example, could be at odds with justified normative principles. Often, for more complex issues, marketing decision-makers may need to use marketing-specific heuristics or frameworks and possibly even apply general ethical theories.

Smith (1995) has proposed the consumer sovereignty test (CST) as a marketing-specific approach that managers can use to evaluate marketing

Table 6-1. Ethical Issues in Marketing Management: Survey Findings of Chonko and Hunt (n = 281)

Rank	*Issue (with illustrations)*	*Frequency*
1	*Bribery* (gifts from outside vendors, "money under the table," payment of questionable commissions)	(15%)[1]
2	*Fairness* (manipulation of others, unfairly placing corporate interests over family obligations, inducing customers to use services not needed, taking credit for work of others)	(14%)
3	*Honesty* (misrepresenting services and capabilities, lying to customers to obtain orders)	(12%)
3	*Price* (differential pricing, meeting competitive prices, charging higher prices than firms with similar products while claiming superiority)	(12%)
5	*Product* (products that do not benefit consumers, product and brand infringements, product safety, exaggerated performance claims)	(11%)
6	*Personnel* (hiring, firing, employee evaluation)	(10%)
7	*Confidentiality* (temptation to use or obtain classified, secret or competitive information)	(5%)
8	*Advertising* (misleading customers, crossing the line between puffery and misleading)	(4%)
9	*Manipulation of Data* (distortion; falsifying figures or misusing statistics or information, internally and externally)	(4%)
10	*Purchasing* (reciprocity in the selection of suppliers)	(3%)

[1]. *To be read:* 15 percent of the 281 respondents referred to bribery in response to the open-ended question: "Would you please briefly describe the job situation that poses the most difficult ethical or moral problem for you?"

Source: Lawrence B. Chonko and Shelby D. Hunt, "Ethics and Marketing Management: An Empirical Investigation," *Journal of Business Research,* 13 (1985): 339–59.

decisions. Its purpose is to establish that consumers can exercise informed choice as a necessary but not sufficient basis for evaluating the ethics of marketing practices. Its domain is limited to corporate impacts on customers; therefore, the framework does not directly address marketing impacts on other stakeholders. The CST identifies an obligation of the mar-

Dimension	*Establishing Adequacy*
• **Consumer capability**	Vulnerability factors — age, education, income, etc.
• **Information**	
• Availability and quality	Sufficient to judge expectations at time of purchase will be fulfilled.
• **Choice**	
• Opportunity to switch	Level of competition Switching costs

Source: Smith, N. Craig (1995), "Marketing Strategies for the Ethics Era," *Sloan Management Review,* 36 (Summer): 92.

Figure 6-1. Consumer Sovereignty Test

keter to take account of consumer capability, information and choice, even where there is an absence of market pressure to do so.

Figure 6-1 summarizes the test, including criteria for determining the adequacy of performance along each of the three dimensions of capability, information, and choice. So, for example, tobacco marketing is ethically problematic under two, if not all three dimensions of the CST. Most people start smoking in their early teens and thus there is diminished consumer capability. Further, the addictive nature of tobacco diminishes consumer choice. Finally, although there is generally abundant information about the adverse health effects of smoking in developed countries, this is less true in Less Developed Counries (LDCs) where many tobacco companies are now focusing their marketing efforts. The CST is relatively robust, generally easily understood, and justified to marketing managers, but it has limitations. It is specific to company-customer conflicts and thus is not applicable to some marketing ethics issues (e.g., abuse of channel power, environmental impacts of products), and there may be uncertainty about the adequacy of performance on the CST dimensions. Also, it has potentially paternalistic consequences, particularly with marketing managers making judgments of consumer capability (see Smith 1995 for a more detailed discussion of the limitations of the CST).

Laczniak and Murphy (1993, 49–51) incorporate a broad range of ethical theory by recommending the following questions for evaluations of the ethics of marketing practices:

> Does the contemplated action violate the law? (legal test).
>
> Is this action contrary to widely accepted moral obligations? (duties test).
>
> Does the proposed action violate any other special obligations that stem from the type of marketing organization at focus? (special obligations test).
>
> Is the intent of the contemplated action harmful? (motives test).
>
> Is it likely that any major damages to people or organizations will result from the contemplated action? (consequences test).
>
> Is there a satisfactory alternative action that produces equal or greater benefits to the parties affected than the proposed action? (utilitarian test).
>
> Does the contemplated action infringe upon property rights, privacy rights, or the inalienable rights of the consumer? (rights test).
>
> Does the proposed action leave another person or group less well off? Is this person or group already a member of a relatively underprivileged class? (justice test).

Answering any of the questions affirmatively suggests that the marketer's decision could be unethical and therefore needs to be revised. However, as Laczniak and Murphy (1993) acknowledge, for many marketing practices there may well be conflicting responses to their questions; for instance, perceived good consequences often conflict with widely accepted moral duties (e.g., a firm might defend its use of bribery to obtain an order on the basis that it is required for the firm to stay in business, though its action could be in conflict with a moral duty not to engage in bribery).

In many respects, this difficulty in applying multiple theories of moral philosophy is not surprising. Indeed, applying only one theory may often produce conflicting outcomes. For example, utilitarian analysis may require comparisons of different types of utilities that may well be incommensurate (e.g., jobs retained for workers that result in higher prices for consumers). Duties may be difficult to identify under deontological analysis and, if identified, may point to conflicting obligations. These and other widely acknowledged problems of the general ethical theories have often frustrated attempts by business ethicists to make definitive ethical evaluations of business practices. Robin and Reidenbach have gone so far as to suggest that the "grand narratives" of moral philosophy are unsuitable for adaptation to marketing and that the field needs to develop its own workable ethical philosophy (1993).

One response to the problems in applying the general ethical theories to business ethics is the work on Integrative Social Contracts Theory (ISCT) by Donaldson and Dunfee (1994; 1995), and by Dunfee, Smith, and Ross (1999). Before turning to ISCT, more specific attention to ethics in the practice of social marketing is required. Hence, the next section classifies the range of ethical issues found in social marketing, in relation to commercial marketing, and considers whether the approaches to marketing ethics discussed above may assist in managing the ethical issues faced by social marketers. It also includes discussion of why attention to ethical issues may be particularly important in social marketing.

Ethics and Social Marketing

Andreasen, noting problems with prior definitions, defines social marketing as "the adaptation of commercial marketing technologies to programs designed to influence the voluntary behavior of target audiences to improve their personal welfare and that of the society of which they are a part" (1994, 110). He suggests that the differentiating characteristic of social marketing as opposed to, say, health education, is that it applies commercial marketing technology. This includes understanding and segmenting the target audience, and utilizing the full complement of marketing mix elements, in contrast to many practitioners who only do social advertising but consider it to be social marketing.

Ethical conduct is a fundamental requisite of a profession. Social marketers consider themselves to be professionals and thus are expected to be ethical in the practice of their profession. Yet it may be argued that their ethical obligations may be greater than those of their professional counterparts in commercial marketing, for the following reasons:

1. As Andreasen (1994) and many others claim, there is much potential for social marketing to do good. Its aim is not to serve the practitioner's self-interest, but to improve individual and/or societal welfare. Unethical conduct would reduce the likelihood of this outcome and discredit the field.

2. Because social good is generally the goal, many social marketers act in the public trust and unethical conduct is in violation of that trust.
3. Ethical concern of social marketers may have a humanizing effect that enhances their dealings with clients.
4. While there is the potential for social marketing to do great good, there is also the potential for it to do great harm. This may result through misuse of marketing technology (e.g., promotion of a behavior change that is actually harmful to the target audience) or through undesirable program aims (it is typically the social marketer who determines whether a program promotes the individual and societal welfare).

If social marketers do adapt commercial marketing technologies for their purposes and utilize all marketing mix elements, then potentially they may face many of the same ethical issues as commercial marketers. This would include issues of deception in advertising for social marketing campaigns, and other issues identified earlier, such as product safety and bribery. However, some ethical issues in marketing may be more likely in the commercial context and some may be more likely in the social marketing context, if not be unique to these contexts. This is illustrated in Figure 6-2.

Laczniak and Murphy (1993, 243–49) identify ethical issues common, though not unique to the social marketing context (issues that largely fall within box 4 of Figure 6-2). They suggest that there are generic ethical problems for marketers stemming from charges that marketing may be unfair, manipulative, wasteful, play favorites, and be intrusive. Questions about unfairness in the social marketing context include: How much disclosure is sufficient (e.g., advertising of a contraceptive that has side effects)? What is a reasonable level of fear (e.g., safe-driving campaigns that may create anxieties about road safety)? Are sales tactics appropriate (e.g., high-pressure selling)? Questions about inappropriate manipulation in the social marketing context include: Is the idea or cause worthy (e.g., "drink milk")? Will there be unintended consequences or side effects (e.g., weight gain as a result of a smoking cessation program)? Questions about wastefulness include: Should scarce resources be used to promote offerings that are intrinsically valuable (e.g., nutrition campaigns)? How much should be spent on reluctant consumers (e.g., seat belt campaigns)? The concern about marketing playing favorites includes the exclusion effects of mar-

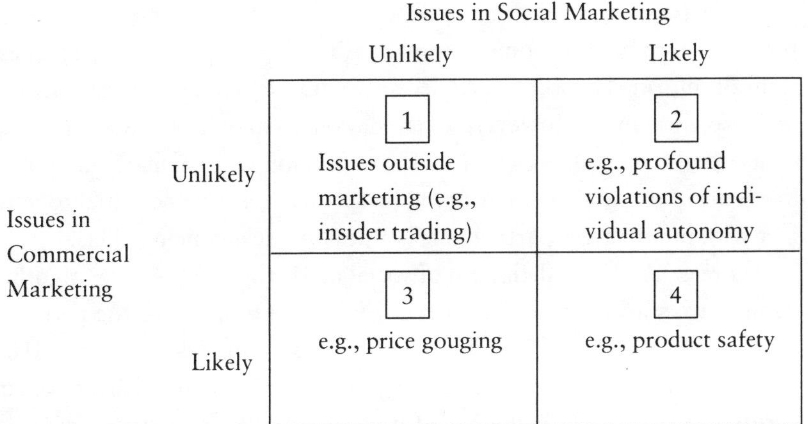

Figure 6-2. Ethical Issues in Commercial versus Social Marketing

ket segmentation. Social marketers make decisions about which segments to target and, hence, who will *not* benefit from social marketing programs (e.g., an anti-smoking campaign targeting better-educated people who are more likely to quit). Finally, the charge that marketing is intrusive raises questions of taste or offensiveness in social marketing campaigns (e.g., family planning campaigns that do not respect religious/cultural traditions) and questions about how much information may be obtained in research on target populations (e.g., research on sexual practices for AIDS prevention campaigns).

In addition, there are issues in social marketing that are much less likely to occur within commercial marketing (issues that fall within box 2 of Figure 6-2). There may be values conflicts among program partners or stakeholders (e.g., when a program involves social marketers from developed countries operating with agencies in developing countries). However, this type of problem is increasingly evident among strategic alliance partners in commercial marketing, particularly with globalization and the growth of relationship marketing. There may also be values conflicts among social marketers who agree on a program mission, but disagree on its implementation (e.g., should an Outward Bound organization, founded to provide developmental experiences for disadvantaged youth, also provide revenue-generating executive training?). Do the ends justify the means? Also in box 2 of Figure 6-2, and potentially unique to social marketing, are those issues that result from concerns about the informed consent of program participants. Some commercial marketing practices raise questions of informed consent (e.g., deceptive practices in marketing research or personal selling). However, social marketing may raise more profound concerns about challenges to individual autonomy, particularly in light of the goals of many social marketing programs and their potential to conflict with many target participants' values and deeply held beliefs.

Andreasen's (1994) definition of social marketing, consistent with other definitions, states that it is an activity intended to improve the personal welfare of program participants and the welfare of society. Commercial marketing, in contrast, has as its purpose the creation and delivery of superior customer value as the basis for an organization to achieve its profit and other goals (Webster 1994). While there may be many exceptions, in commercial marketing the interests of the customer and the producer are typically closely aligned: provision of superior customer value by the firm (relative to competitors) leads to increased customer satisfaction which, in turn, leads to increased sales and greater potential profits for the firm. Moreover, in competitive markets, customers have considerable choice.

As Rangan, Karim, and Sandberg observe, "conventional marketing methods are generally designed for situations in which benefits to the consumer from choosing the advertised product or service clearly outweigh the cost" (1996, 42). However, some social marketing situations entail significant costs to targeted participants and they may not be the primary beneficiaries: "With social marketing . . . the benefits are not always so concrete. They often accrue to society, sometimes over the long term. In fact, in some cases, the individuals, communities, or organizations targeted by the change effort may feel that the costs of change exceed the benefits" (Rangan, Karim, and Sandberg 1996, 42). Figure 6-3 shows how Rangan, Karim, and Sandberg classify social marketing initiatives according to the costs and benefits of behavior change (44).

Hence, a close alignment of interests is not always the case in social marketing. Conceivably, social marketers might attempt to influence the behavior of target individuals because it is in the best interests of society (at least in their opinion), though not necessarily in the best interests of the individuals targeted. In other words, the personal welfare of program participants and society's best interests may conflict, as may potentially be the case with social marketing initiatives in cell D of Figure 6-3. This is

		Benefits of the Program	
		Tangible, personal	Intangible, societal
Costs (to the target of behavior change)	Low	Cell A (e.g., persuading men to be examined for colon cancer)	Cell B (e.g., recycling programs)
	High	Cell C (e.g., smoking cessation program)	Cell D (e.g., reducing chlorofluorocarbon production)

Source: V. Kasturi Rangan, Sohel Karim, and Sheryl K. Sandberg (1996), "Doing Better at Doing Good," *Harvard Business Review* 74 (May-June): 44.

Figure 6-3. Types of Social Marketing Initiatives

evident, for example, in some family planning programs, as later discussed. It is also conceivable, though perhaps much less likely, that social marketers may attempt behavior change that is beneficial to the program target but not the broader society, at least as currently organized. (This is one criticism, however ill-founded from a Western perspective, of social marketing programs to promote education of women in traditional societies, such as Bangladesh.)

Furthermore, consumer choice may be less apparent in the social marketing context. While marketing has often been subject to charges of manipulating consumers (e.g., Farmer 1967), these charges may be more warranted when applied to social marketing, where competition is limited and, in some respects, the social marketer is the only game in town. The good intent of social marketers may also lead to the use of more coercive tactics (e.g., fear appeals in advertising), relative to commercial marketing, with the practice rationalized by claiming that the ends justify the means. Social marketers may also be too ready to exploit suspect scientific findings to advance their case for behavior change. For example, recent campaigns against smoking in public places were often justified by relatively weak evidence of adverse health effects from passive smoking. This, in turn, may well have contributed to the intensified stigmatization of smokers and increasingly coercive methods used against smokers, such as smoking bans.

In light of these distinctions between commercial and social marketing, it seems possible that there may be ethical issues unique to the social marketing context. More specifically, issues can arise in social marketing (but not in commercial marketing) where the individual autonomy and best interests of the program target may be compromised by a program goal of serving the broader society.[1]

In sum, most social marketing campaigns seek to influence behavior to benefit the target audience and the broader society. However, at its core, social marketing may challenge the autonomy of the individual who is the subject of a social marketing campaign. Further, some social marketing campaigns may be of benefit to the wider society, but benefits to the target individual may be less evident (and possibly vice-versa). Even where target individuals would give informed consent to social marketing campaigns and see benefits to themselves, there may be ethical issues arising in the development and execution of marketing programs. Hence, social marketers can be faced with many of the ethical issues found in commercial marketing as well as a set of issues that may be more common if not unique to the social marketing context.

Just like commercial marketers, social marketers may find that they can respond to many of the ethical issues they encounter by recourse to their own values, ethical maxims or codes of conduct (though, again, it should be noted that there is the possibility that the social marketer's values are erroneous). For example, a social marketer's own belief in the importance of truth-telling may lead easily to a decision to reject a proposal from an advertising agency that might mislead the target audience by overstating possible positive consequences of a behavior change. Similarly, recalling the Golden Rule might persuade a social marketer to adopt a less coercive strategy or reference to the AMA Code of Conduct might remind the social marketer of the obligation to disclose all substantial risks associated with product or service usage.

Social marketers might also turn to the Consumer Sovereignty Test. Given its underlying rationale, its scope is more appropriately limited to customer-company conflicts in a for-profit marketplace context. But the CST is a useful, if indirect reminder of the importance of the informed consent of the target participants of social marketing programs. It asks: Can they exercise informed choice?

However, again like commercial marketers, social marketers may find that these sources provide insufficient guidance, especially for more complex issues. General ethical theories have more potential perhaps, but they too have problems, as already noted. It is against this backdrop that the social contract approach is introduced. This approach is gaining increased interest within business ethics (including a special issue of *Business Ethics Quarterly* devoted to the topic) and, in the formulation known as Integrative Social Contracts Theory, could be particularly appropriate to some of the more difficult ethical issues in social marketing.

Social Contracts

Origins of Social Contract Theory

Social contract theory originated with the major social changes in seventeenth and eighteenth century Europe and the search for a political philosophy legitimizing state authority. One of the earliest contributors was Thomas Hobbes (1588–1679). Hobbes's *Leviathan* (1651) describes a "state of nature," a world without a state, wherein people act to satisfy their desires, principally self-preservation, and life would be "solitary, poor, nasty, brutish, and short" (Hampton 1992, 544). Under these conditions, Hobbes argues, people would agree to the only alternative of a state ruled by an absolute sovereign.

Hobbes was a major influence on John Locke (1632–1704). Locke's *Two Treatises of Government* (1690) was published in justification of the Whig rebellion and revolution of 1688. He wished to defend the new regime by showing that the rebellion by Williamites (who put William of Orange on the English throne) had been legitimate and that the rebellion by Jacobites against King William was not (MacIntyre 1966). More fundamentally, Locke sought to identify a basis for the legitimacy of state authority. He proposed a philosophy providing a justification for the existence of the state and identified the reciprocal obligations of citizen and state. As MacIntyre (1966) observes, Locke's doctrine of consent is the doctrine of every modern state that claims to be democratic but which also wishes to possess some measure of coercive power over its citizens.

More common in the twentieth century are questions about the legitimacy of business than questions about the legitimacy of the state (Berger 1981). However, the marketing ethicist's search for a basis for establishing that a new product is "good" or an advertising campaign is "right," is in some ways similar to Locke's search for a basis for obedience to the state. More specifically, from the social marketing perspective, we might be interested in identifying a basis for establishing, for example, when and to what extent the use of coercive tactics by social marketers is justified.

Common to most social contract theories, is an agreement (typically hypothetical) among moral agents that warrants individual consent (e.g., to state authority) and a device or method whereby such an agreement may be logically justified. Accordingly, the French philosopher Jean-Jacques Rousseau (1712–1778) identifies a pre-social condition from which society develops. *The Social Contract* (1762) examines the problem of finding a form of social organization that provides the benefits of social life, but avoids its disorders. Rousseau's solution is for all individuals to agree to place themselves in common under the direction of the "general will" (Reath 1992, 1114).

Key to the revival of social contract theory is *A Theory of Justice* (1971) by John Rawls. He proposes the device of "a veil of ignorance." Accordingly, Rawls asks what principles of justice autonomous agents would collectively agree on, were they *not to be aware* of their specific individual circumstances, such as sex, race, education, religion, and social class (Becker 1992, 1176). Thus, Rawls identifies an "original position" so as "to set up a fair procedure so that any principles agreed to will be just . . . [and] nullify the effects of specific contingencies which put men at odds and tempt them to exploit social and natural circumstances to their own advantage" (1971, 136).

Social Contract Theory Applied to Business

Donaldson, the leading proponent of social contract theory applied to business ethics, has constructed a social contract for business (1982), illustrated its application to international business (1989), and (with Tom Dunfee) refined its content and developed a methodology for its application to many business contexts (Donaldson and Dunfee 1994; 1995). His social contract for business (SCB) is founded on consent, i.e., that corporations exist only through the cooperation and commitment of society. This suggests an implied agreement between the corporation and society. The simplest form of the contract is to specify what business needs from society and what, in turn, are its obligations to society.[2] More specifically, Donaldson argues that the contract should be viewed as existing between productive organizations ("where people cooperate to produce at least one specific product or service") and individual members of society (1982, 42). He suggests society's obligations to productive organizations are: (1) to provide recognition to the firm as a single agent, especially in the eyes of law; and, (2) to grant the authority to use or own land and natural resources, and to hire employees.

Donaldson's device for agreement (akin to Hobbes's "state of nature," Rousseau's "pre-social" condition, and Rawls's "original position") is to imagine a society without the productive organizations being analyzed. This he calls the "state of individual production" (1982, 44). In keeping with the social contract tradition, his analysis requires: (1) a characterization of the conditions existing in the state of individual production; (2) recognition of the problems solved by the introduction of productive organizations; and (3) specification of the terms of the agreement or social contract that individuals and productive organizations would agree to as a result of seeing how the introduction of productive organizations benefits or harms society.

Donaldson suggests two principal classes of people would stand to benefit or be harmed by the introduction of productive organizations: consumers and employees. The hypothetical consumers of Donaldson's state of individual production would benefit from enhanced satisfaction of economic interests; by: (1) improved efficiency through maximizing advantages of specialization, improving decision-making resources, and increasing the capacity to use or acquire expensive technology and resources; (2) stabilized levels of output and channels of distribution; and (3) increased liability resources (1982, 45–47). Benefits for employees would include increased income potential and capacity for social contribution, diffused personal liability, and needs-oriented personal income allocation (1982, 47–49). These are the reasons why ordinary people, economically interested and rational, would agree to productive organizations. In keeping with Locke, Donaldson argues that the SCB would aim to minimize the prima facie drawbacks of the introduction of productive organizations, as well as maximize the prima facie benefits, for both consumers (e.g., minimize environmental impacts) and employees (e.g., minimize possible worker alienation and loss of pride).

In sum, Donaldson writes, "corporations considered as productive organizations exist to enhance the welfare of society through the satisfaction of consumer and worker interests, in a way which relies on exploiting corporations' special advantages and minimizing disadvantages. This is the *moral foundation* of the corporation" (1982, 54, emphasis in original). The performance of the corporation can thereby be assessed by a measure of how well it fulfills this social contract. However, the inevitable tradeoffs that must be made, especially between the interests of consumers and workers (lower prices or higher wages?) require that the contract must not violate certain minimum standards of justice; while welfare tradeoffs are permissible, organizational acts of injustice are not. Hence, at the minimum, productive organizations must "avoid deception or fraud . . . show respect for their workers as human beings, and . . . avoid any practice that systematically worsens the situation of a given group in society" (Donaldson 1982, 53).

Criticisms of Social Contract Theory

Some moral philosophers are critical of social contract theory. They note that no such contracts actually exist and, as hypothetical contracts, do not provide for meaningful consent and agreement. Hume (1711–76), for example, uses the analogy of the press-ganged seaman, asked when at sea to "consent" to service. As Becker (1992, 1172) puts it, in reference to Hume's analogy, "when we come to moral consciousness, the only viable option we have is to stay on board—at least for quite some time." A hypothetical contract is not a contract at all—"not worth the paper it is not written on"—to these critics.

Anticipating this criticism, Donaldson writes: "There may never have been a pen and ink contract, but remarkably enough, thousands of people have acted *as if* there were" (1982, 40, emphasis in original). This did not satisfy Kultgen, who suggests that it is necessary to claim that the contract is a mere heuristic device or that it exists or that it could be made to exist (1986). Kultgen does not entirely dismiss the SCB; he sees the potential for an actual ("genuine") social contract for business, though this "would not be an unmixed blessing" (Kultgen 1987). Donaldson's subsequent work on ISCT is partly in line with this suggestion, by incorporating the "microsocial contracts" of actual communities, as later discussed.

Social Contract Theory and Social Marketing

Under Donaldson's social contract for business, the legitimacy of the corporation rests on societal consent and is subject to the firm providing needed goods and services while conforming to certain minimum standards. A social contract approach might extend this formulation to include social marketing organizations. Social marketers might also be viewed as subject to a social contract, though perhaps with somewhat different terms to those applying to commercial organizations. For example, in return for providing unpaid services intended to improve the welfare of individuals and society as a whole, we might envisage greater scope for social marketers to use coercive tactics (e.g., fear appeals in advertising). However, rather than develop this hypothetical general social contract for social marketers, in the next section a more elaborate formulation of social contract theory is introduced.

There has been a growing recognition of the potential of social contract theory in business ethics. Frederick, for example, has referred to its "compelling theoretical significance" (1995, 270). Particularly noteworthy is the contractarian approach of Integrative Social Contracts Theory proposed by Donaldson and Dunfee (1994; 1995). ISCT utilizes a social contract approach that typically operates at the level of specific situations or issues. In contrast to the abstraction of the basic social contract approach, it can more readily contribute to ethical evaluations of complex, real-life social marketing situations. Moreover, it focuses on communities and their norms and thus may be especially relevant to the ethical issues in social marketing that often involve competing claims of different communities.

Integrative Social Contracts Theory[3]

ISCT integrates two types of contracts. A hypothetical macrosocial contract provides the overall framework and is a heuristic device comparable to the classic social contracts of Locke, Hobbes, Rousseau, and Rawls. In keeping with these philosophers, Donaldson and Dunfee (1994;

1995) view global humanity as seeking to design a binding, though unwritten agreement that establishes the parameters for ethics in economic relationships. Within this framework are actual, community-based microsocial contracts. These contextual, more narrowly prescribed social contracts reflect the norms used by specific communities in evaluating business ethics. Hence, ISCT (under certain conditions) gives normative status to the norms or "rules of behavior" that govern everyday life in most communities. In order to justify consent on the part of the contractors, Donaldson and Dunfee (1994; 1995) limit themselves to two parsimonious assumptions and a minimalist global social contract, as follows.

Bounded Moral Rationality

First, it is assumed that the contractors are aware of, and concerned about, bounded moral rationality. In a similar way to bounded economic rationality, it is assumed that individual moral agents lack the information, time and emotional strength to make perfect judgments consistent with their moral preferences. Further, moral agents may not have developed clear preferences due to lack of time or understanding. The bounded moral rationality assumption also relates to the question of whether the global contractors would be able to agree to a comprehensive moral theory or set of principles specifying the parameters of ethics in economics. ISCT assumes that the individual contractors would wish to retain the right to select their own values to the maximum extent possible and that they would "desire to participate in economic communities that reflect their personal and cultural values" (Donaldson and Dunfee 1995, 93). In so doing, the contractors would be recognizing bounded moral rationality as a limit on the ability of moral theorists to design a moral calculus applicable to all decision contexts for all of diverse humanity.

The Need for Community-Based Moral Fabric

The second assumption is that the global contractors would, in response to bounded moral rationality, recognize the need for a community-based moral fabric as a necessary condition for both the generation of wealth and for the maintenance of an environment conducive to a good and productive life. Without this moral fabric, which is the purpose of the global convention, there is the threat of social degeneration into Hobbes's "warre" of man against man.[4]

In response to these core assumptions, Donaldson and Dunfee hypothesize that the global contractors would wish to set up an arrangement—the global social contract—that recognizes the key role of human relationships and groups (or "communities") and that allows them the ability to confront the specific context in which moral judgments must be made before they are required to develop in detail the ethical rules for proper behavior. This arrangement would be a binding macrosocial contract, applicable to all on the basis of their assumed consent to these arrangements. Donaldson and Dunfee's claim is that the global macrosocial contract derived is the only rational solution to the need for a moral fabric in the face of bounded moral rationality (1994). Its four key terms are spelled out below.

1. Local economic communities may specify ethical norms for their members through microsocial contracts (the "moral free space" term). Communities are the core focus of the macrosocial contract. A community is defined in ISCT as "a self-defined, self-circumscribed group of people who interact in the context of shared tasks, values, or goals and who are capable of establishing norms of ethical behavior for themselves" (Donaldson and Dunfee 1994, 262). Corporations, subsidiaries, even departments or informal units within an organization, along with partnerships, professional groups, trade associations, and nation states may all be ISCT communities in the context of a given ethical decision. In focusing on communities, ISCT recognizes that norm-governed group activity is a critical component of economic life.

The idea of moral free space is consistent with the desire of the contractors to keep their options open. It also recognizes that communities are entitled to have differing norms. Acting within their own moral free space, each of these communities is allowed to generate indigenous "authentic" ethical norms. A norm is defined as authentic when it is supported by the attitudes and behavior of a substantial majority of the members of a community.

2. Norm-generating microsocial contracts must be grounded in informed consent buttressed by rights of exit and voice (the "protected informed consent" term). A major impact of ISCT is to establish that norms are obligatory for dissenting members of communities when an authentic norm has been identified and it satisfies the other requirements of ISCT given below. In keeping with classical social contract theory, the obligation stems from the consent given when one acts as a member of a community (perhaps by accepting the benefits of the community environment). However, ISCT imposes some additional requirements on the operation of the community. The community must respect the right of members to withdraw or exit from group membership. Thus, a dissenting member of a community who is quite distressed about a particular authentic norm may elect to leave the community.

Similarly, ISCT (at least as formulated by Dunfee, Smith, and Ross 1999) emphasizes that an individual should have the opportunity to exercise voice within the community. Individuals desire the right to influence the development and evolution of norms, and, perhaps most importantly, to be able to influence changes in norms they find objectionable. In sum, so long as the requirements of community recognition of voice and exit are met, and a given norm is supported by the attitudes and behavior of a substantial majority of the membership of a community, it qualifies as an authentic norm.

Thus far in the exposition of ISCT, the only mechanism that would protect a dissenting individual from having an ethical obligation to comply with a distasteful norm is the right to leave the community or to try to change the norm. Beyond that it appears as though the "is" has become the "ought" and that values and moral judgments are largely relative. To avoid excessive relativism, it is assumed in ISCT that the original contractors would wish to recognize a thin set of universal principles that would constrain the normative relativism of community moral free space. This is the role of the third term of the macrosocial contract.

3. In order to be obligatory, a microsocial contract norm must be compatible with hypernorms (the "hypernorms" term). Under ISCT, a hypernorm is a norm by which authentic norms are tested. The term "legitimate" is used to describe an authentic norm that has passed the hypernorm test. Hypernorms are defined as "principles so fundamental to human existence that . . . we would expect them to be reflected in a convergence of religious, philosophical, and cultural beliefs" (Donaldson and Dunfee 1994, 265). This is a high standard for a set of universal principles and, presumably, their number and scope would be, as Walzer (1992) suggests, rather thin. This is appropriate when one considers the dominant role of hypernorms and their effect of constraining choice within local communities by overriding any and all inconsistent norms or standards. However, how does one ascertain the existence of particular hypernorms?

In support of the claim for the existence of hypernorms, one can point to studies finding similar methods of moral reasoning across cultures (Kohlberg 1968), and agreement concerning certain core principles across large samples of managers (Kanter 1991). Can examples be provided? Frederick studied six intergovernmental compacts (including the OECD Guidelines for Multinational Enterprises, the Helsinki Final Act, and the ILO Tripartite Declaration of Principles Concerning Multinational Enterprises) to identify principles common to the set (1991). Similarly, one could look to the statements of global organizations as potential sources of hypernorms. The Principles for Business developed by the Caux Round Table (which meets annually in Caux, Switzerland) is a prime example, as is the document "Toward a Global Ethic," produced by the Council for a Parliament of the World's Religions. One might also look to the United Nations Universal Declaration of Human Rights, and Donaldson proposes a minimal set of ten fundamental international rights (1989, 81). Dunfee, Smith, and Ross propose an anti-bribery hypernorm, at least for public sector bribery (1999). Donaldson and Dunfee, in their most recent work on ISCT, advance further hypernorms (1999).

Hypernorms do not provide a complete bounding of the moral free space of communities. The issue may still arise of conflict between two or more norms that are legitimate. This problem is addressed by the final term of the macrosocial contract.

4. In the case of conflicts among norms satisfying terms 1–3, priority must be established through the application of rules consistent with the spirit and letter of the macrosocial contract (the "priority rules" term). It will often be the case that multiple legitimate norms applicable to the same ethical judgment will come in conflict. This may happen when a transaction crosses two distinctly different communities, as is often the case in marketing and in social marketing in particular. To resolve problems of this type, ISCT specifies a loose set of six priority rules which are influenced by the concepts underlying principles of international conflicts of law and dispute resolution (Donaldson and Dunfee 1995, pp. 105–06). They are derived from the basic assumptions and terms of the macrosocial contract and are as follows:

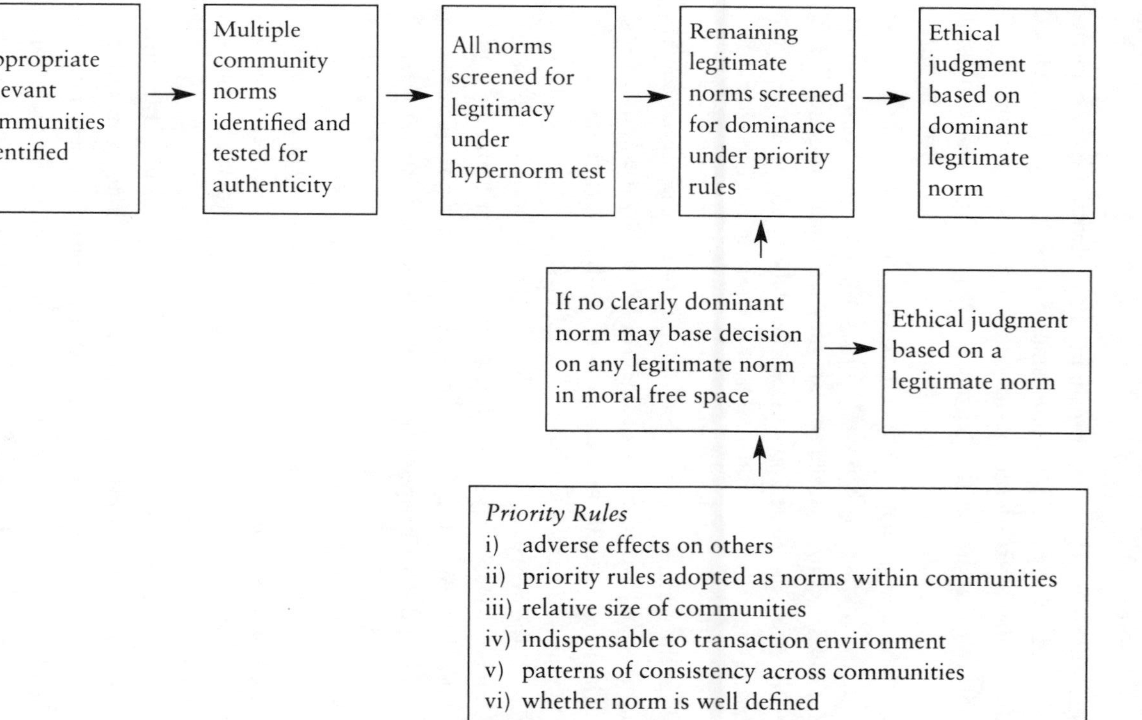

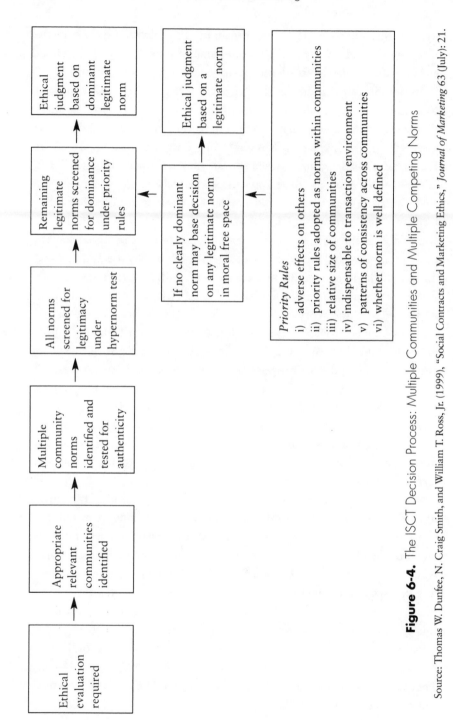

Figure 6-4. The ISCT Decision Process: Multiple Communities and Multiple Competing Norms

Source: Thomas W. Dunfee, N. Craig Smith, and William T. Ross, Jr. (1999), "Social Contracts and Marketing Ethics," *Journal of Marketing* 63 (July): 21.

1. Transactions solely within a single community, which do not have significant adverse effects on other humans or communities, should be governed by the host community's norms.
2. Community norms for resolving priority should be applied, so long as they do not have significant adverse effects on other humans or communities.
3. The more extensive the community that is the source of the norm, the greater the priority which should be given to the norm.
4. Norms essential to the maintenance of the economic environment in which the transaction occurs should have priority over norms potentially damaging to that environment.
5. Where multiple conflicting norms are involved, patterns of consistency among the alternative norms provide a basis for prioritization.
6. Well-defined norms should ordinarily have priority over more general, less precise norms.

The more complex issues of marketing ethics may well involve conflicts of legitimate norms. Under ISCT, the priority rules are to be applied as a set, not in isolation, though the rules aren't given priority themselves. For a given dilemma, several might be involved, loosely weighed without a strict calculus of relative value. In sum, Figure 6-4 shows how ISCT might be applied to an ethical issue involving multiple communities and multiple competing norms.

Applying ISCT to the PSI Case

The classic (and best-selling) Harvard Business School social marketing case study, "Population Services International: The Social Marketing Project in Bangladesh" (Rangan 1985) can be used to illustrate the application of ISCT. This case raises a number of ethical issues for social marketers, including questions about the appropriateness of an intensive mass media campaign for family planning that conflicted with important religious and cultural values in Bangladesh. However, the analysis that follows will focus on the issue of whether individual autonomy and the best interests of the program target were compromised by a program goal of serving the broader society. The case does not contain all the data necessary for a fully developed analysis using ISCT. However, it can serve well as an illustration of how ISCT might be applied to this and other troubling ethical issues in social marketing, including issues that may be more common if not unique to the social marketing context relative to commercial marketing (i.e., box 2 of Figure 6-2).

Population Services International

PSI is a not-for-profit agency that was founded in 1970 with the fundamental objective of "disseminating family planning information and marketing birth control products to people who needed to avert births but did not know where to seek the information or products" (Rangan 1985, 2). Its programs were directed primarily at LDCs and described as a response to the "population explosion" in these countries. In 1976, PSI reached an agreement with the government of Bangladesh to conduct a family planning program in collaboration with the United States Agency for International Development (USAID) and the United Nations Fund for Population Activities (UNFPA). Its program involved the aggressive marketing of Raja brand condoms and Maya brand oral contraceptives direct to consumers at nominal prices via local retail outlets. This strategy was consistent with the beliefs of one of the two founders of PSI who said that "if contraceptive products such as pills and condoms are made the leading vehicles of family planning . . . the entire society would be better off" (Rangan 1985, 2). By 1983 (the case study decision point), PSI had become the second largest advertiser in Bangladesh. Promotional themes of "happy marriage" and "the confident choice of the prudent family" were repeatedly communicated through radio, press, billboards, and posters. Results for Maya were considered disappointing. Raja became the leading brand of condom available in Bangladesh, with a 59 percent volume market share. However, with unit sales of 50 million pieces, this was only equivalent to 500,000 CYPs (couple years protection); only one half million couples were protected in a country with a fertile population of 20 million couples.

Rangan, Karim, and Sandberg (1996) suggest that behavior change in social marketing programs is more difficult when the costs of change for the target participant are high (monetarily or in other ways, such as the difficulty of quitting smoking) and where personal benefit is unclear or nonexistent (cell D in Figure 6-3). Both of these obstacles are evident in the PSI case and they point to possible conflicts of interest and a major ethical issue in the case. In 1983, Bangladesh was one of the poorest countries of the world, its health care and education were very limited, and literacy levels were low. The large rural population (91 percent of a total population of 100 million) was more disadvantaged than the urban population. Bangladeshi people, particularly in rural areas, had good reasons not to practice family planning:

- Most parents counted on their children to support them in their old age; there was no pension or social security system.
- Many Bangladeshi children die before reaching adulthood, as a result of natural calamities and disease.
- Daughters require dowries at marriage, suggesting a need for at least as many sons as daughters.
- Large families provide sufficient labor for family farming.
- Eighty-five percent were conservative Muslims, for whom family planning is inconsistent with religious beliefs (though research found only 6 percent cited religion as a reason for not adopting family planning).

As Rangan, Karim, and Sandberg note (1996), most of the citizens of Bangladesh at this time did not understand the long-term benefits to the country of curbing population growth. Given the limited economic resources of Bangladesh, reducing the rapid growth in population would be prudent from the perspective of the society as a whole. The government had set the goal of zero population growth by 1995. In this situation, PSI's program was clearly consistent with its founder's belief that promoting contraceptive products could make the entire society better off, but to what extent would it better the individual program participant? Would Bangladeshi society gain at the individual's expense? Moreover, were changes in behavior a result of the free choice of target participants, or coercion? Did the program compromise the autonomy of participants? Finally, society would only gain if the program succeeded; as Rangan, Karim, and Sandberg observe: "A critical obstacle to implementation is that *early adopters stand to lose,* . . . if only a few couples in Bangladesh chose to have smaller families, those couples would be at a disadvantage among their peers, and there would be no ensuing benefit to society. Schools would become less crowded, food more plentiful, and medical facilities widely available only if the society as a whole reduced its birthrate" (1996, 43, emphasis in original).

Notwithstanding the obstacles (and ethical issues), the Bangladesh family planning program is reported to be a success, with estimates of couples practicing family planning in the 1990s ranging from 45–60 percent, a dramatic improvement over the 4 percent rate of the 1980s. Rangan, Karim, and Sandberg, in reference to Figure 6-3, suggest that "the first thing marketers should do when they have a Cell D challenge on their hands is determine whether the initiative can be repositioned in Cell C. . . . try to figure out whether there is some way to show the target community a more direct benefit" (1996, 51). In the PSI case, research showed that although Bangladeshi men were unable to see the long-term economic and quality-of-life benefits of family planning, women could (see Table 6-2). Women were receptive to family planning as a way of improving their health and that of their existing children, and saw opportunities for better education and greater overall prosperity. However, men usually did the household shopping, they did not generally discuss personal issues such as family size with their wives, and women would be embarrassed to buy contraceptives in a public place.

In the mid-1980s, a revised strategy was introduced whereby oral contraceptives would be promoted and made available to women through the country's one hundred thousand Rural Medical Practitioners. As important, a communications program was targeted at men (Rangan, Karim, and Sandberg, 1996, 51). This aimed "to break down cultural barriers" and "to encourage men to discuss family planning issues with their wives." It included film ads shown at travelling cinema shows that "co-opted the men by portraying one of their peers discussing the subject with his wife and drawing the conclusion that he should be supportive of the idea" (Rangan, Karim, and Sandberg, 1996, 51).

How ISCT Might Inform Ethical Evaluations of PSI

ISCT can be applied to two decision points in the PSI case. First, the initial decision to develop a family planning social marketing program, as described in the case. Second, the later decision to adopt the revised strategy, as reported in Rangan, Karim, and Sandberg (1996). To better illustrate ISCT, analysis of the former is focused on the ethics of family plan-

Table 6-2. Specific Family Planning Meanings Mentioned by Participants in a PSI Survey

	Female		Male	
Specific meanings mentioned	*Rural*	*Urban*	*Rural*	*Urban*
Limit family size	48.9[1]	53.1	73.7	48.9
Have small/happy family	16.4	30.3	12.2	36.0
Stop having children	48.4	31.4	16.9	13.7
Two children are enough	2.7	5.7	8.5	15.8
Space childbirth	5.5	6.3	—	3.6
Preserve health of mother	20.1	21.7	3.3	2.2
Assure healthy children	2.7	1.1	4.2	5.0
Assure good health for mother and children	8.2	6.9	—	3.6
Assure good health for all	3.7	3.4	8.9	12.9
Assure food and clothing	58.0	57.1	32.9	38.8
Less poverty	21.5	19.4	33.3	43.2
Live within means	8.7	9.7	12.7	9.4
Saving for future	8.7	15.4	9.4	4.3
Avoid subdividing property among children	8.7	1.7	6.1	3.6
Peace and happiness in the family	48.4	48.6	35.7	40.3
Happier family life	4.1	6.9	0.5	—
Assure education for children	42.0	62.9	17.4	53.2
Rearing children properly	12.8	10.3	2.3	4.3
Number interviewed	219	175	213	139

[1]. *To be read:* 48.9 percent of the 219 interviewed, mentioned that "limit family size" was one of the meanings they got out of family planning communication.

Source: V. Kasturi Rangan (1985), "Population Services International: The Social Marketing Project in Bangladesh," *Harvard Business School* case study no. 9-586-013. Boston, MA: Harvard Business School, 16.

ning without regard to program implementation. Program elements are given more attention in the analysis of the second decision.

In keeping with Figure 6-4, the conduct in question is morally permissible under ISCT if all four of the following conditions hold: (1) The conduct is consistent with an authentic norm of the communities involved. (2) The norms of all relevant communities have been considered. (3) The conduct in question does not violate a hypernorm. (4) Any conflict among communities' norms is resolved via the priority rules.

In evaluating the PSI case, we might initially conclude that family planning was not an authentic norm of the Bangladeshi community. Evidence for this claim may come from the information in the case about cultural and religious values and family economics (i.e., the reasons not to practice family planning, listed above). However, ISCT requires that all relevant communities be considered. As well as the people of Bangladesh, we may also wish to consider the norms of the government of Bangladesh. While the case does not provide information on the norms of government officials, it might be reasonable to assume that their norms are supportive of family planning, in light of the government's stated goal of zero population growth and its backing of PSI's program. USAID and UNFPA might also be treated as relevant communities with norms that endorse family planning.

Thus, we have multiple communities with conflicting norms. Under ISCT, authentic norms must be checked for legitimacy using the hypernorm test. If we specify the authentic community norms as referring to a belief in the appropriateness of family planning (ignoring, at this point, how the social marketing program might be executed) it seems reasonable to claim that there may not be a constraining hypernorm on a belief in either direction. Religious beliefs notwithstanding, it is difficult to imagine a hypernorm that would condemn uncoerced family planning in Bangladesh, particularly in light of welfare considerations. Hence, our analysis requires recourse to the priority rules.

Priority rules (3) and (4) would appear to be most relevant to our ethical evaluation. In accordance with the third priority rule, we might conclude that the norm of the more extensive community of Bangladeshi people takes precedence. However, the fourth priority rule (that gives preference to norms indispensable to the transaction environment relative to norms potentially damaging to that environment) might be interpreted to give precedence to the norm favoring family planning of the Bangladeshi government, USAID and UNFPA. We might conclude that family planning is essential to the maintenance of the economic environment of Bangladesh, and giving priority to a norm that precludes family planning would be potentially damaging to that environment.

The outcome of this analysis suggests there is no clearly dominant norm. Our ethical judgment would be that either norm is legitimate and can be used to justify the decision to be made. In some respects, this is not an entirely satisfactory outcome. However, our analysis does point to the potential for further guidance on developing a social marketing program. More specifically, in making decisions about program implementation, which includes market segmentation and targeting, we may wish to subdivide the Bangladeshi people and identify different relevant communities within this larger group. In addition, the hypernorm test referred specifically to uncoerced family planning, suggesting that decisions about program execution need to consider the extent to which its different elements might be coercive. These concerns become more evident in an ISCT analysis of the decision to adopt the revised strategy.

Inevitably, perhaps, analysis of the decision to adopt the revised strategy is much more speculative. In particular, less data are available on relevant community norms. However, some insight may be gleaned from the research results shown in Table 6-2, if they may be treated as representative and a possible basis for inferring community norms. These data suggest that when identifying all relevant communities, Bangladeshi men and women need to be treated separately, and urban and rural Bangladeshis also need to be considered as separate communities.[5]

The findings in Table 6-2 suggest that women may be more supportive of family planning as, indeed, PSI concluded.[6] At least 50 percent of urban females associated family planning with assuring education for children, and assuring food and clothing. At least 50 percent of rural females associated family planning with assuring food and clothing. Rural males, by contrast, overwhelmingly associated family planning with limiting family size (74 percent of respondents), and only a third or less identified any benefits of doing this (33 percent mentioned assuring food and clothing). Just over 50 percent of urban males associated family planning with assuring education for children, though close to 50 percent also associated it with limiting family size.

Again, inferring authentic community norms from these data is extremely speculative. Nonetheless, there may be sufficient basis for concluding that treating the Bangladeshi people as one community with an authentic norm opposed to family planning is inappropriate. It may be more appropriate to treat it as multiple communities with different norms on the appropriateness of family planning. Alternatively, depending on the ratio of males to females and urban to rural males and females, the Bangladeshi people may be considered a single community that does not hold an authentic norm on the appropriateness of family planning (there is not a substantial majority that approves or disapproves).

This conclusion influences analysis of family planning program implementation and may also influence our analysis of the initial decision about developing a family planning social marketing program. More important, perhaps, when we consider the revised strategy, is the extent to which norms supportive of particular types of programs are in conflict with hypernorms. At one extreme, the coercive approach to family planning adopted by the Chinese government, requiring couples to have only one child, could well conflict with a likely hypernorm. This might be a putative hypernorm protecting individual liberty or a more narrowly crafted hypernorm. For example, Article 16 of the United Nations Universal Declaration of Human Rights gives men and women the right to marry and found a family. At the other extreme, making family planning products available to well-educated citizens who would freely choose to use them without being influenced by a heavy-handed communications campaign, would not appear likely to violate a hypernorm.

In the PSI case, the approach adopted appears to fall somewhere between these two extremes, although again there are limitations to the data. Troubling elements include the use of saturation advertising and attempts to "co-opt" males in the face of good arguments not to adopt family planning (Rangan, Karim, and Sandberg 1996, 51). In the absence of necessary facts, no definitive ethical evaluation is offered. However, this analysis suggests possible causes for concern and, more broadly, points to the potential of ISCT as an approach to evaluating ethical issues in social marketing, particularly where communities have competing claims.

Discussion and Conclusions

The Merits of ISCT Applied to Social Marketing

The ethics of the PSI social marketing program could well have been analyzed using the more familiar deontological and teleological (or consequentialist) theories. The obligations of social marketers to their target audiences could have been identified, noting possible constraints on coercive tactics. Likewise, both good and bad potential consequences of the social marketing program could have been identified. It is unlikely that such an analysis of this complex case would produce a definitive ethical evaluation. Nonetheless, it would still have merit and provide insight on the ethical issues. Although ISCT may be viewed as an alternative approach, it is perhaps better considered as complementary. While for many of the more complex issues of marketing ethics definitive ethical evaluations can be elusive, we may come closer to this goal by benefiting from the insight of multiple theories. Moral judgment may be better informed overall; though, if possible, it is preferable to identify a method that provides a more compelling justification than the alternatives.

Dunfee, Smith, and Ross applied ISCT to commercial bribery, illustrating the theory's potential to better inform ethical judgments of this practice, when contrasted against the well-established standard ethical treatments of the issue (1999). This approach was not possible in this chapter—there are few ethical evaluations of social marketing practices. However, the above illustration of ISCT applied to the PSI case, notwithstanding its more speculative elements, does point to some of ISCT's strengths and limitations. Its strengths lie principally in its normative legitimization of the relevance of community (and professional) norms, the requirement to identify all relevant communities (or stakeholders), its reliance on a thin set of hypernorms (or universal standards), and its procedure for resolving conflicts in norms across communities. The latter strength makes it particularly appropriate to ethical issues where complexity results from multiple stakeholders (or communities). This is often found in cross-cultural and many other social marketing situations. Of course, ISCT has limitations.

Authentic and legitimate norms of communities are given normative status under ISCT as a result of how the macrosocial social contract is formulated and its underlying assumptions. It must be accepted that these assumptions and the contract terms derived are logically compelling. In applying ISCT, care must be exercised in identifying and defining all relevant communities. Moreover, there is not a definitive set of hypernorms. However, as in the PSI analysis, a case can be advanced for particular hypernorms that might challenge the legitimacy of community norms. Again as illustrated in the PSI analysis, priority rules may conflict and they do not have priority in themselves, suggesting the potential for an uncertain resolution. Finally, there may be uncertainty about the norms of communities, suggesting a need for empirical research. However, this, in turn, may raise questions about the permanence of norms. For example, did the intervention of the Rural Medical Practitioners, particularly in their educational role, change the norms of female Bangladeshis with regard to the appropriateness of family planning?

Conclusions

In conclusion, this paper has argued, first, that attention to ethical issues may be particularly important in social marketing, especially given its potential for both great good and great harm. Second, social marketers face many of the same ethical issues found in the commercial marketing context, but there may be some issues that are more common, if not unique to social marketing, particularly issues arising where the individual autonomy and best interests of the target are potentially compromised. Third, although heuristics such as the Consumer Sovereignty Test may be helpful in evaluating some ethical issues in social marketing, more comprehensive theories will often be required. However, there are widely acknowledged drawbacks to the standard ethical theories.

Fourth, social contract theory, particularly in the formulation of ISCT, may provide a complementary if not alternative approach that addresses some of the drawbacks of the traditional theories. It gives recognition to community norms; provides a process for determining their appropriateness ("authenticity" and "legitimacy"); proposes a method for resolving differences in norms across communities; and while providing "moral free space," reduces the risk of moral relativism by bounding decisions by a core set of moral principles ("hypernorms"). Fifth, and finally, while it has limitations, ISCT may be particularly appropriate to some of the more troubling issues in social marketing, especially issues that are cross-cultural and, more generally, issues that result from differences in norms across communities.

Notes

This chapter substantially draws upon "Social Contracts and Marketing Ethics." The author acknowledges with gratitude Tom Dunfee and Bill Ross for their many insights on social contract theory and business ethics. The helpful comments of Alan R. Andreasen and George G. Brenkert on an earlier version of this chapter are also gratefully acknowledged.

1. To some extent, Andreasen addresses the concern that social marketing programs may not be in the target individual's best interests. He suggests that target participants should "embrace the values that permit the behavior to be considered for adoption" (1994, 112). However, his purpose, apparently, is not to claim autonomy on the part of the program participant; rather, it is to argue that social marketers should not attempt campaigns that require major shifts in target participants' values and that would likely be unsuccessful for this reason.

2. This exchange characteristic of the social contract approach makes it particularly appealing as a way of thinking about ethics in marketing, a field that often treats exchange as a paradigm for marketing thought and practice.

3. This section draws substantially upon Dunfee, Smith, and Ross (1999). Readers seeking a more detailed exposition of the theory should turn to this source, and to Donaldson and Dunfee (1994, 1995, 1999).

4. In addition to these express assumptions, there appears to be an implicit assumption in the creation of the hypothetical contract of ISCT (Dunfee, Smith, and Ross 1999). The global contractors must also recognize the importance of organizations and relationships in business. Individuals must work as part of organizations and they must interact with others in order to carry on the functions of economic life. In turn, those organizations and relationships are based upon implicit understandings concerning the proper bounds of behavior.

5. An important consideration in applying ISCT is how relevant communities are defined and who defines them. Potentially, social marketers might attempt to define relevant communities in ways that favor their preferred outcome of the analysis (i.e., they engage in a form of gerrymandering). Under ISCT theory, communities are self-defined, though this might present problems in implementation of the theory and we may well worry about the notion of communities being manipulated by marketers and others.

6. Note, however, that these study results did not show that a substantial proportion of women, at least at the time surveyed, associated family planning with improving their own health or that of their children, apparently an important rationale for the revised strategy (Rangan, Karim, and Sandberg 1996).

References

Andreasen, Alan R. (1994), "Social Marketing: Its Definition and Domain," *Journal of Public Policy and Marketing* 13 (Spring): 108–114.

Becker, Lawrence C. (1992), "Social Contract," in *Encyclopedia of Ethics*, Lawrence C. Becker and Charlotte B. Becker (eds.). New York: Garland, 1170–76.

Berger, Peter L. (1981), "New Attack on the Legitimacy of Business," *Harvard Business Review* (September-October): 82–89.

Chonko, Lawrence B., and Shelby D. Hunt (1985), "Ethics and Marketing Management: An Empirical Investigation," *Journal of Business Research* 13: 339–59.

Donaldson, Thomas (1982), *Corporations and Morality*. Englewood Cliffs, NJ: Prentice Hall.

Donaldson, Thomas (1989), *The Ethics of International Business*. New York: Oxford University Press.

Donaldson, Thomas, and Thomas W. Dunfee (1994), "Towards a Unified Conception of Business Ethics: Integrative Social Contracts Theory," *Academy of Management Review* 19 (April): 252–84.

——— (1995), "Integrative Social Contracts Theory: A Communitarian Conception of Economic Ethics," *Economics and Philosophy* 11 (April): 85–112.

——— (1999), *Ties That Bind: A Social Contracts Approach to Business Ethics*. Boston, MA: Harvard Business School Press.

Dunfee, Thomas W., N. Craig Smith, and William T. Ross, Jr. (1999), "Social Contracts and Marketing Ethics," *Journal of Marketing* 63 (July): 14–32.

Farmer, Richard N. (1967), "Would You Want Your Daughter to Marry a Marketing Man?" *Journal of Marketing* 31 (January): 1–3.

Frederick, William C. (1991), "The Moral Authority of Transnational Corporate Codes," *Journal of Business Ethics* 10 (March): 165–77.

——— (1995), *Values, Nature, and Culture in the American Corporation*. New York: Oxford University Press.

Hampton, Jean (1992), "Thomas Hobbes," in *Encyclopedia of Ethics*, Lawrence C. Becker and Charlotte B. Becker (eds.). New York: Garland.

Hunt, Shelby D., and Scott J. Vitell (1993), "The General Theory of Marketing Ethics: A Retrospective and Revision," in N. Craig Smith and John A. Quelch, *Ethics in Marketing*. Homewood, IL: Irwin, 775–784.

Kanter, Rosabeth Moss (1991), "Transcending Business Boundaries: 12,000 World Managers View Change," *Harvard Business Review* 69 (May-June): 151–66.

Kohlberg, Lawrence (1968), "The Child as a Moral Philosopher," *Psychology Today* 2(September): 25–30.

Kultgen, John (1986), "Comments on Donaldson's Corporations and Morality," *Business and Professional Ethics Journal* 5 (1): 28–39.

Laczniak, Gene R. and Patrick E. Murphy (1993), *Ethical Marketing Decisions: The Higher Road*. Needham Heights, MA: Allyn and Bacon.

MacIntyre, Alasdair (1966), *A Short History of Ethics*. New York: Collier Books.

Nash, Laura (1989), "Ethics Without the Sermon," in *Ethics in Practice: Managing the Moral Corporation,* Kenneth R. Andrews (ed.). Boston: Harvard Business School Press.

Rangan, V. Kasturi (1985), "Population Services International: The Social Marketing Project in Bangladesh." Harvard Business School case study no. 9-586-013. Boston, MA: Harvard Business School Press.

Rangan, V. Kasturi, Sohel Karim, and Sheryl K. Sandberg (1996), "Doing Better at Doing Good," *Harvard Business Review* 74 (May-June): 42–54.

Rawls, John (1971), *A Theory of Justice*. Cambridge, MA: Harvard University Press.

Reath, Andrews (1992), "Jean-Jacques Rousseau," in *Encyclopedia of Ethics*, Lawrence C. Becker and Charlotte B. Becker (eds.). New York: Garland.

Robin, Donald P., and R. Eric Reidenbach (1993), "Searching for a Place to Stand: Toward a Workable Ethical Philosophy for Marketing," *Journal of Public Policy and Marketing* 12 (Spring): 97–105.

Smith, N. Craig (1995), "Marketing Strategies for the Ethics Era," *Sloan Management Review*, 36 (Summer): 85–97.

Smith, N. Craig, and John A. Quelch (1993), *Ethics in Marketing*. Homewood, IL: Irwin.

Sparks, John R., and Shelby D. Hunt (1998), "Marketing Researcher Ethical Sensitivity: Conceptualization, Measurement, and Exploratory Investigation," *Journal of Marketing* 62(April): 92–109.

Walzer, Michael (1992), "Moral Minimalism," in *The Twilight of Probability: Ethics and Politics*, W. R. Shea and G. A. Spadafora (eds.). Canton, MA: Science History.

Webster, Frederick E., Jr. (1994), *Market-Driven Management: Using the New Marketing Concept to Create a Customer-Oriented Company*. New York: John Wiley and Sons.

CHAPTER SEVEN

Marketing Ethics to Social Marketers: A Segmented Approach

Susan D. Kirby and Alan R. Andreasen

Ethical behavior is by its nature individual behavior. We choose to act ethically or to ignore ethical considerations when faced with conflicting behavioral alternatives. The consequences of such behaviors are similarly personal in that we are the ones who will feel the guilt of acting unethically, the pangs of conscience of skirting the "ethical fine line" or the pleasure at "doing what is right."

But ethical behavior also has implications for others—not only for the person or persons who are the target of the behavior. One's personal ethical behavior has implications for organizations or groups with which one is associated, especially if the behavior in question is taken in one's role as a member of the organization or association. Because unethical—or even ethically questionable—behavior can reflect negatively on such institutions, their stewards have a vested interest in ensuring that (a) ethically relevant decisions and behaviors are recognized by institutional members and (b) high standards of ethical behavior are maintained. Elsewhere in this volume, Michael Basil addresses the challenges facing social marketing organizations in promoting ethical behavior. In the present chapter we shall consider how the social marketing *profession* might raise its ethical standards.

Because we are seeking to influence the future behavior of our social marketing colleagues, it is appropriate that we apply our own discipline to this task. In this chapter, we begin with the important premise that, as in most social marketing situations, it makes no sense to treat all members of the profession as a single target audience, but to segment them in meaningful ways that have implications for future interventions. Further, relying on the work of Andreasen (1995), and others, we recognize that the desired behaviors will only come about if the target audience becomes aware of the need and desirability of such behavior, believes others who are important to them are supportive of the behavior and believes that he or she can actually carry such behavior out. To assist the latter, we offer a formal framework whereby conflicted social marketers can wrestle with difficult ethical dilemmas. We recognize that considered ethical choices may still be unpopular with many in the institutional environment. Thus, an important outcome of a subset of ethical decisions—i.e., controversial ones—is that relevant stakeholders should be apprised of likely backlash and given the opportunity to inoculate themselves from possible reputational damage.

Who Should Market Ethical Behavior to Social Marketers?

Ours is a practical profession which is resistant to abstract explorations that have no practical consequences. Thus, merely urging higher ethical standards on the profession—when no one is given responsibility for achieving this—would prove ineffective. Thus, we argue that the profession needs to create or designate an institution to meet this challenge. Two obvious candidates emerge. First, promoting ethically responsible behavior is clearly part of the mission of the recently formed Social Marketing Institute, which has a mission of "advancing the science and practice of social marketing." A second candidate would be ethics programs in schools of business. A number of universities including Georgetown, Virginia, Harvard, and others have faculty and, in some cases, centers devoted to ethical issues in business practice. It would be a reasonable challenge for such individuals or centers to stretch their purview to include social marketing, which is, of course, an application of commercial marketing concepts.

Why Should the Profession Care About This?

Does the social marketing profession have a stronger obligation to ethical practice than commercial marketing? Our conclusion is that, yes, social marketers do have a stronger obligation to assure that social marketing programs are ethical. As has been argued in other chapters in this volume, social marketing is a profession that seeks to improve societies. This is true even if those societies value multiple voices, and different groups have different ideas of what is "good" for their society. It is not generally up to social marketers to define what is "good" for society—this is done through both the political system (for government programs) and deliberations of trustees (for programs supported by private foundations).[1] Because, as Kotler and Andreasen have noted (1996), these sponsors are subject to the glare of publicity, the ethical demeanor of practicing social marketers must be above reproach. If program managers behave unethically and are caught and criticized, funding for—and credibility of—future programs may be in jeopardy. Certainly, this has practical implications for social marketing organizations—unethical practice means less "business."

But, there is a second, moral reason for social marketers to behave ethically: their programs are typically focused on inducing socially "good" behavior in target audiences. Social marketers urge individuals to exercise, stop using drugs, immunize their children, and wear seat belts. It would be hypocritical for social marketers to urge "good" behavior while at the same time behaving "badly" themselves. Of course, there are cases in which the social marketing manager could be working to do good, but might unintentionally harm society, thus undermining the goal and definition of social marketing. This, however, does not absolve the profession from seeking to do good in good ways!

Segmenting the Social Marketing Profession

Crooks, legalists, rationalizers, seekers, and moralists. These are the labels that Eugene Laczniak attached to the five segments into which he divided all commercial marketing managers in terms of their approach to ethical behavior (1993). *Crooks* know what is right but often act unethically to achieve personal or organizational gain. *Moralists* are the managers who act on principle, who always try to do the right thing. Because Crooks are unlikely to change their values and Moralists are trying to do what is right, Laczniak argued that it is a waste of resources to target these segments for behavior change. Rather, he saw the best improvements in ethical practice in the commercial marketing profession likely to come from targeting the *Legalists*, *Rationalizers*, and *Seekers*. All three groups comprise individuals who recognize ethical dilemmas when they encounter them—but treat them differently. *Legalists* address ethical dilemmas by doing no more than what is legal. *Rationalizers* take actions that often are in their self-interest and then minimize the ethical implications of what others might categorize as unethical. The last segment, *Seekers*, want to be ethical but are uncertain about what they can and should do.

Laczniak concludes that those seeking to influence the ethical practices of the marketing profession should plan programs that address the intrapersonal and interpersonal factors that influence ethical practice in each of these segments. For the Legalists, he suggests that an introduction to *ethical theory* would be beneficial. The Rationalizers would benefit most from *ethics education* to heighten their sensitivity to the unethical implications of many of their actions. Finally, for the Seekers Laczniak sees the development of *ethical reasoning skills* as a step toward more ethical practice.

Ethical Behavior of Social Marketers

Segmenting Social Marketers and Identifying "At-Risk" Social Marketing Managers

Do the Legalists, Rationalizers, and Seekers describe the audience segments in the social marketing profession? How can social marketing academics or the Social Marketing Institute help these segments improve the ethics of our profession? Is this a marketing problem? As Rothschild might ask, should we market ethical behavior (1999)? Would education be sufficient? Or, at the other extreme, do we need the force of law? We could argue that education is the best strategy, that social marketing professionals are wise, educated individuals who need simply to be informed about potential ethical dilemmas and how to deal with them. In this case, teaching ethics theory and ethical reasoning may be sufficient. On the other hand, maybe the force of law should be the only course—perhaps social marketers will only "do right" if there are likely consequences to their pocketbook or freedom.

Of course, if we think about Laczniak's segments for commercial marketing managers (1993), we recognize that the appropriate course of action will vary by segment and the segment's characteristics. If we apply

Table 7-1. Ethics Strategy Segmentation Categories

Laczniak Categories	*Kirby/Andreasen Categories*
Crooks	Crooks
Legalists	Legalists
Moralists	Moralists
Rationalizers	Rationalizers
Seekers	Seekers
	Do-Gooders
	Tryers

Laczniak's segmentation distinctions to social marketing managers, we might have somewhat different labels and two additional categories (see Table 7-1). We propose that the social marketing segments be called *Do-Gooders, Rationalizers, Seekers, Tryers, Moralists, Legalists,* and *Crooks.*

Crooks and *Legalists* have the same definition in both sectors. While there is at present no data that permit estimation of the size of the various segments, we believe that Crooks—who will do anything to achieve their ends and thus ignore ethical considerations—are rare in social marketing because of the typical glare of publicity that surrounds social marketing programs. On the other hand, for the same reason, we suspect that Legalists may be more common in social marketing where a legal defense of actions may deflect public criticism. Because these two groups are relatively indifferent—even hostile—to strictly ethical cautions, they will receive limited attention here, as will Moralists. *Moralists* are those social marketers who are consistently conducting ethical assessments of their programs, are convinced that the advantages outweigh the disadvantages, and intend to conduct ethical assessments on future programs. One of the new segments, the Do-Gooders will also receive limited treatment. *Do-Gooders* are convinced that what they are doing is for the good of society, so it must be ethical, and therefore an ethical assessment is unnecessary. They, too, are presumably relatively impervious to future ethical marketing efforts.

On the other hand, we will focus on the remaining three segments, *Rationalizers*, *Seekers*, and *Tryers*. *Rationalizers* are pretty sure what they are doing is ethical, but fear that dedicating resources to this minor activity will deter them from achieving their overall goals, so they rationalize that doing an ethical assessment and acting on it is a waste of precious resources. *Seekers* are a group of social marketing professionals who are convinced that the advantages of doing an ethical assessment outweigh the disadvantages, but are unsure how to go about doing one, who should be involved, and what to do with a negative finding. The *Tryers* are a group who have done at least one ethical assessment, but are unsure if the advantages of this assessment outweigh the disadvantages. Tryers are unsure if they will dedicate resources to this effort in the future.

Stages of Change

In order to develop strategies for influencing the ethical behavior of these segments, we must turn to our own frameworks. One of the most commonly used frameworks is Prochaska and DiClemente's *Transtheoretical Stages of Change* (Prochaska and DiClemente 1984). This approach provides a valuable framework for understanding the target segments and what interventions may be useful in effecting change in them. Their model proposes that people change behaviors in a progressive, developmental manner and that most influence attempts work best at moving people from one stage to the next instead of directly from stage one to stage five. Prochaska and his colleagues have proposed five stages of development toward behavior change, Precontemplation, Contemplation, Preparation, Action, and Maintenance. In the first stage, Precontemplation, the intended audience, is not thinking about changing his/her behavior and does not usually even consider the desired behavior change to be on his/her radar screen. This can occur either because the person at this stage is unaware of the need/opportunity for desired behavior or believes that the behavior is not appropriate for them—for one reason or another. If enough education, social force, personal persuasion, or self-enlightenment occurs at this stage, the Precontemplator may move into Contemplation. A Contemplator is considering the change in question, actively weighing the advantages and disadvantages of adopting the behavior. In order to move on to Preparation, the Contemplator will have to make some small steps, or trial behaviors, to establish his or her intention to change behavior.

Once a Preparer has made the commitment to act and, in fact, taken some action, he/she begins movement into the Action stage, where he/she will firmly begin the new behavior at the desired level (e.g., undertaking moderate physical activity for at least thirty minutes five days per week). The person in Action is no longer trying out the behavior, but has made a commitment to adopt it at the recommended level for some period of time. The target audience member is not considered to be in Maintenance (the final stage) until a sufficient time period has passed for the person to assume a reasonable sense of his/her ability to maintain the behavior. During the Maintenance stage, he/she will need to address environmental stimuli that could induce recidivism, such as social group influence and easy access to the old behavior. In the present context, the ultimate behavior in question is to practice social marketing ethically and the initial behavior is to conduct an ethical assessment of a program's plan.

With respect to ethical behavior, Stage 1 (Precontemplation) is the starting point at which the "actor" has little or no interest in ethics or in ethical behavior from a personal or organizational perspective. Stage 2 (Contemplation) is characterized by an awareness that ethical situations exist, that these situations might create problems, and that there may be some value in behaving more ethically. Someone in Stage 3 (Preparation) is best described as a person who has weighed the pros and cons and decided to make a small level of commitment to pursue ethical behavior. Stage 3 usually involves some skill-building before people can be fully committed to detecting and addressing ethical dilemmas at Stage 4 (Action). In the Action stage, people are seeking out and reacting to ethical dilemmas, but have not been doing so for a very long period of time (often designated as six months in empirical studies). Stage 5 (Maintenance) is characterized by being fully committed to ethical practice for a sufficient period of time that greatly reduces the risk of relapse to earlier stages. In the present context, we define a "gold standard" for ethical practice as a personal and/or organizational commitment to regularly seek out and address ethical dilemmas, as contrasted with ignoring such issues or simply reacting to them when forced to by others such as competitors or the media.

A comparison of the ethical market segments outlined earlier with the Stages of Change model suggests that the former are really descriptors of groups "stuck" at a particular stage of progression toward committed ethical practice. That is, one can see the Do-Gooders, Crooks, and Legalists as all in the Precontemplation Stage in that they are not at all thinking about changing their behavior. On the other hand, Rationalizers are target audience members who are contemplating ethical practice but have convinced themselves that they do not need to prepare and take any further actions—i.e., they are in Stage 2. Seekers are clearly in Stage 3 in that they are looking for ways to implement an ethical orientation while Tryers have moved beyond preparation to actually undertaking new approaches to ethical action. And, finally, the group we have labeled Moralists are those who have reached Stage 5, Maintenance, and are routinely detecting and acting on ethical issues.

This comparison of stages and segments for both commercial and social marketing segments is outlined in Table 7-2. Table 7-2 also contains suggestions (after Prochaska and DiClemente 1983) about processes that might be useful in moving segments to the next stage in the model's progression.

Marketing Development: Applying the 4 Ps to the Marketing of Ethical Practice

Now that we have identified the target segments, we can begin to plan for behavior change. Using Stages (and Processes) of Change Theory, we can make some assumptions about what may work to move social marketing segments from one stage to the next. While academic ethics centers or the Social Marketing Institute in future should collect market research data on the proposed segments and their likely responsiveness to the processes of change, we may speculate on approaches that might prove effective in changing ethical behavior. Among those in the Precontemplation Stage, it is very unlikely that Crooks would ever be interested in pursuing ethical behavior, although Rothschild's Force of Law (Rothschild 1999) may be the one tool to get their attention. Legalists are probably immune from influence unless they can be shown examples where a lack of attention to ethical considerations *beyond legal mandates* has cost other organizations revenue and growth opportunities. Do-Gooders are also difficult to approach in that they are aware of the importance of ethics but think that the "goodness" of their mission means that what they are doing is *de facto* ethical. Here, the best tactic will be to provide them with examples where blindness to ethical considerations has led to tarnished reputations. Do-Gooders are a group that highly values their reputations and such messages may be powerful.

Table 7-2. Stages of Change and Hypothetical Segmentation of Commercial and Social Marketers

Stages of Change Toward Ethical Assessment	*Laczniak's Ethical Segmentation of Commercial Marketers*	*Hypothetical Social Marketing Manager Segments*	*Processes for Moving to Next Stage*
Precontemplation (no interest in ethical assessment)	*Legalists,* have no use for ethics; if it's legal it's ethical.	*Legalists*, believe that one must only obey the law and no more.	Consciousness raising, confrontations
	Crooks, believe that self-interest makes ethical considerations irrelevant.	*Crooks*, believe that self-interest makes ethical considerations irrelevant.	
		Do-Gooders, believe no assessment of ethical decisions is necessary. Know that what they are doing is ethical because it's for the good of society.	
Contemplation (some interest, weighing pros and cons)	*Rationalizers,* aware of ethical problems, but haven't yet been convinced that they can act ethically and get what they want, so they rationalize unethical acts.	*Rationalizers*, believe that what they are doing is socially "good" and worry that spending time on minor issues like ethics means they might never achieve their big goals, so they rationalize that no ethical assessment is necessary.	Continuing consciousness raising, dramatic relief, role playing, values clarification

Table 7-2 (continued). Stages of Change and Hypothetical Segmentation of Commercial and Social Marketers

Stages of Change Toward Ethical Assessment	*Laczniak's Ethical Segmentation of Commercial Marketers*	*Hypothetical Social Marketing Manager Segments*	*Processes for Moving to Next Stage*
Preparation (some action toward ethical assessment, but need skills to maintain behavior)	*Seekers* recognize situations with moral consequences but cannot properly address them.	*Seekers*, want to conduct ethical assessments but are not sure how to proceed, whom to involve, and how to handle negative outcomes.	Continued dramatic relief, role playing, values clarification Commitments to act, public pledges
Action (doing some ethical assessments but not institutionalized yet)		*Tryers,* have done some ethical assessments, but not sure they will dedicate the resources and time to engage in this for every decision-making opportunity. An intermittent behavioral commitment. Not sure the benefits outweigh the cost.	Continuing commitments, rewards, countering, controlling environment including interpersonal contacts, social support
Maintenance (institutionalized ethical assessments)	*Moralists* generally are making ethical decisions on a routine basis.	*Moralists,* generally are making ethical decisions on a routine basis.	Continuing rewards, countering, environmental controls, and social support

Rationalizers in Stage 2 are a more promising prospect in that they *might* consider conducting an ethical assessment, even a minor one, if they can be convinced that the pros outweigh the cons. The main barrier keeping Rationalizers from moving to Stage 3 is their perception that there are either more disadvantages than advantages, or that the disadvantages are more heavily weighted than the disadvantages. It is the change agent's job then to present the target segment, Rationalizers, with either more or stronger advantages for conducting an ethical assessment. Another method for moving people from the contemplation stage (Rationalizers), according to Prochaska and DiClemente (1983), is to provide *consciousness raising* or *dramatic relief*, generally in the form of a communication. In order to market ethical practice to specific Rationalizers, a marketing manager would need to implement some audience research to determine the most prevalent and heavily weighted advantages and disadvantages to ethical practice and then develop a program designed to maximize the advantages and minimize disadvantages using some consciousness-raising, role-playing, or dramatic relief tactics.

In social marketing, it is important to use all of the 4 Ps, so any market research aimed at a target segment should investigate how ethical practice is packaged (product), how it is delivered (place), why, where, and how social marketers would participate in ethical practice (price and place), and how the change agent can promote routine ethical assessment and consideration (promotion). In a simple program, this design could consist of a series of social marketing newsletter stories. The first in the series could be about a social marketing manager who is thinking about conducting an ethical audit and is currently weighing the pros and cons. The newsletter could develop an "interview from the field" talking with a social marketing manager about his/her attitudes toward an ethical audit and what benefits and costs he/she expects to encounter. The feature story would have to demonstrate that there are more or stronger benefits to conducting than not conducting an audit, in order to address concerns of the Rationalizers segment. The change agent could also introduce ideas in the interview that explore the potential negative effects of not conducting an ethical assessment and make clear the interviewee's intentions to conduct future ethical assessments.

The second story in the series could focus on another factor important to moving social marketing managers from Contemplation to Preparation by presenting an interview with someone to explore the cost of conducting an ethical assessment based on real experience. The interviewee could explain the process he or she used, the costs involved, and the program changes that have been implemented based on the audit. This interview would provide social modeling of the desired behavior, social pressure to perform ethical assessments, and real information about the costs of such an audit that can replace misperceptions about such costs.

Thus far, the intervention directed at Rationalizers is mostly about pros and cons of the specified behavior change, a benefits-cost approach. Andreasen's (1995, 272) and Prochaska and DiClemente's (1983) work suggest that a cost/benefit focus for those in contemplation, especially the early stages, would likely create the most change. Of course, such an intervention appears to be much more of an *education* intervention than marketing, except that the emphasis is on *perceived* benefits and costs, instead of just urging the target audience to do an ethical assessment. Further, as Andreasen (1995) urges, a social marketing approach would place a strong emphasis on addressing the cost side of the equation whereas traditional education and communication approaches would simply communicate benefits. One of the characteristics of Rationalizers is that they cannot be bothered with ethical dilemmas. They rationalize their neglect. Clearly, one explanation for such an attitude would be that they think the costs of paying attention to ethical considerations are too high in terms of time and organizational effort. An effective campaign to market ethical practice must address this concern. This is where an effective process for routinely identifying ethical issues and resolving them could mitigate the concerns and provoke movement to Stage 3 where the Rationalizers would become Seekers.

The *Seekers* segment in Preparation is characterized as planning to conduct an ethical audit, but having few skills to do so and therefore a low sense of self-efficacy (Bandura 1992). Skill development can come from educational opportunities promoted by ethics academics or the Social Marketing Institute at conferences, training courses, short internal seminars, list-serve discussions, web sites, textbooks, and other communication activities. A Social Marketing newsletter, suggested as a channel to reach the Rationalizers, could also be used to reach the Seekers. In the newsletter series, an interview could provide intensive background on how to conduct an ethical audit, impart specific skills and help social marketing managers anticipate challenges with managing the process. The newsletter could refer readers to web sites that offer assistance with ethical audits, or link them to people who have conducted an ethical audit in the past. Ethical assessments or audits could be a packaged product provided by the Social Marketing Institute. Such communications and products would not only teach skills but would also bring to bear some amount of social pressure, which theory suggests is important for individuals in the Preparation stage. The web sites could serve both as a distribution network for ethical management products as well as a direct promoter of desired actions. As Smith argues in this volume, to secure desired behavior, it is important to make it fun, easy, and popular. Much of the marketing at this stage should focus on making attention to ethical issues popular by making clear that the approach is widely followed—particularly by leaders in the field. Once skills are developed and social influence is brought to bear, it is much more likely that the Seekers will become Tryers.

The final segment that ethical social marketers need to address is the *Tryers*. This segment can be characterized as having some commitment to ethical practice, but currently unsure of their intentions to permanently dedicate resources to this in the future. So, the major issue with the Tryers segment is to solidify their commitment. The principal method of ensuring this behavior is to reinforce such efforts. There are many ways to do this. First, Tryers can be the focus of the newsletter stories mentioned above, implicitly legitimizing and praising their efforts. Tryers can also be invited to participate in panels on ethical issues at conferences and universities. Awards and recognition for ethical audits could be sponsored by social marketing conferences.

Another important issue in moving target audiences to the Maintenance Stage is controlling expectations. Individuals who have made progress up to the Preparation and Action stages are sometimes frustrated by the outcomes of their experiences in identifying and acting on ethical dilemmas. Sometimes the problem is that their expectations are unrealistic. For example, a social marketer will carefully consider the ethical implications of some potentially offensive communication, evaluate the alternatives (perhaps using the framework outlined by William Smith in the first chapter in this book) and make his or her ethical judgment. However, their subsequent action raises vocal criticism offending the social marketer who thought that his/her choice would be respected. The expectation that ethical choices would always be honored for their sincerity was not met. There is therefore the risk that the frustrated marketer will recycle back to earlier stages, for instance becoming Rationalizers who simply justify their inaction. It is important, therefore, that those who wish to promote more ethical commitment make clear that ethical decisions are often difficult and not all observers will agree with the outcome. But, it is important that the Tryer persist in the conviction that he/she is satisfied that the right course has been taken. Reinforcement by significant others should help solidify this conviction.

Social marketing professionals can also help by sharing with colleagues the benefits they have experienced from pursuing ethical courses of action. Again, the proposed newsletter can be helpful here. The newsletter series on ethics in social marketing could present an interview with a noted and respected social marketing professional who could describe realistic expectations of an ethical audit and ethical choices and ways to anticipate difficulties they have overcome.

A Program of Action

So what is the social marketing field to do to market ethical behavior to its professionals? The first step, obviously, is to identify a group or institution that will shoulder the responsibility of promoting ethical behavior for the profession. The next step would then be to identify potential allies within existing social marketing organizations. The latter would be responsible for internal marketing of ethical practice within their own organizations as well as serving as promoters and reinforcers of the behavior of others.

Those responsible should then do as all good social marketers do—conduct formative research, in this case on themselves. In particular, such research should assess the validity of the segments hypothesized here. In the course of that research, we need to learn the principal benefits and costs of instituting ethical assessments and decisions. It is to be expected that one of the findings of this research is respondents' complaints about the absence of a simple, usable framework and guide for introducing and managing a social marketing ethical practice that is easy to use, easy to distribute, and accessible around the world. As noted earlier, there are several components to a "gold standard" ethical practice. First, there must be mechanisms put in place for detecting and addressing ethical issues in the field. For example, as Andreasen and Drumwright indicate in their chapter, organizations might rely on an Ethics Monitor to watch over potential ethical lapses or, alternatively, schedule monthly meetings to review programs and tactics for possible ethical problems. Second, there must also be a framework for evaluating ethical dilemmas once detected. We present one such possible framework below.

Mechanisms must also be put in place to routinely share successful ethical assessments with other social marketers to increase social pressure. If individual organizations' personnel resources are too strained to conduct their own audit, it would be important to develop a system of sharing auditing expertise. Providing technical assistance with ethical audits is perhaps one of the best areas in which social marketing practitioners could collaborate with social marketing academics and/or the Social Marketing Institute.

But over the long haul, social marketing practitioners themselves must come to accept that ethical assessments should be an integral part of program planning and resources should be specifically allocated for this activity. Of course, the field is a long way from such institutionalization of ethical assessments. That is the focus of the next section of this chapter.

Ethical Assessment Guide

Duke et al. (1993) have proposed a process for evaluating the ethics of fear appeals in marketing communications. This approach has the potential to be generalized to a broad range of social marketing dilemmas. The framework integrates multiple ethical philosophies as well as multiple stakeholder groups. (The importance of multiple stakeholders is emphasized in William Smith's model elsewhere in this volume where he argues that social marketers must pay attention to impacts on both intended and unintended audiences.) The framework is called an ethical effects-reasoning matrix or ERM. It has two dimensions: stakeholders and ethical reasoning approach. In a simple analysis, the authors explain that the fear appeals in a commercial advertisement could be assessed by examining the potential benefits and costs that any stakeholder group could reasonably expect to experience from exposure to a commercial ad containing such appeals. Each benefit and detriment is assessed against several ethical reasoning approaches (for a detailed explanation of this process see Duke et al. 1993, 126).

The authors offer the example of an ad for a familiar tire manufacturer (Michelin) that uses babies placed inside a tire for the visual component of the campaign. They indicate that the first issue in conducting an ethical evaluation of the ad is to identify the stakeholders potentially affected by this appeal. One stakeholder is society at-large. Society may perceive that exploiting children in the Michelin ad diverts public attention from important car safety issues and thus the advertisement is ethically questionable. Under an ethical reasoning approach based on Utilitarian principles that focuses on achieving the greatest good for the greatest number, the ad is judged to be ethically weak because it reduces sensitivity to exploitation of children in advertising, and because other (possibly more important) safety issues such as the need for rear safety seats may not be attended to because the ad implies that all one needs to protect the child is Michelin tires! An alternative ethical reasoning approach is the Golden Rule, which views ethical behavior as that which treats others as the ethical actor would expect to be treated. Under the Golden Rule approach, society might view the Michelin ad as unethical because children's safety is being compromised in the advertisement and most social marketers would not want their children treated this way.

A third ethical reasoning approach based on the writings of Emmanuel Kant states that all individuals have basic rights, e.g., to privacy, fair treatment, and so forth. Under this standard, the advertisement might be rated as unethical because it preys upon societal fondness for cute children, thus distracting us from paying attention to diverse issues of child safety. A fourth reasoning approach has been labeled Enlightened Self-Interest and argues that ethical behavior is that which maximizes personal benefits while minimizing the harm to others. In contrast to the other approaches, this standard might view the ad as ethical because the fear appeal is soft, thus there is minimum harm to others, while children may benefit from increased tire safety awareness, a societal benefit.

This analysis only addresses one characteristic of the Michelin advertisement as perceived by one stakeholder group. In the ERM framework, one must list all of the relevant stakeholder groups and the potential significant benefits and detriments for each group. The final step is then to assess how the advertisement would be judged under four ethical reasoning approaches.

The ERM model provides a useful way to examine the ethics of many potential social marketing program decisions. The multiple stakeholder approach certainly suits a marketing mind-set. The listing of benefits and costs for each stakeholder group also fits well into a social marketing philosophy. However, the evaluation of the ethical effects from a range of potential benefits and costs for multiple stakeholders under multiple ethical philosophies may be seen to many practitioners as too cumbersome to be practical. And, as we noted earlier, a major impediment for many social marketers to committing to routine ethical analysis is that they do not have the time. Further, the ERM is designed only for one element of the marketing mix, advertising. Thus, social marketers may reject the approach because it does not consider other elements of the 4 Ps.

To increase the usefulness of the matrix approach, we propose two major revisions. First, we recommend that a Social Marketing Ethical Assessment (SMEA) include benefits and costs for all of the 4 Ps of the marketing mix, as does the American Marketing Association's code of ethics. The second revision is to decrease the number of ethical reasoning approaches in the model. In social marketing, we are concerned with societal good more than individual rights, minimizing the value of the Kantian standard. Further, in our view, the Golden Rule standard (do unto others as you would have them do unto you) encourages idiosyncratic, highly personal standards when we are seeking in this chapter to bring the profession toward the adoption of relatively uniform standards (for example, those that can be publicized across organizations and settings).

This leaves the SMEA model with two major philosophical standards: Utilitarianism ("does the approach to product, price, place, and promotion achieve the greatest good for the greatest number") and Enlightened Self-Interest ("does the approach result in significant benefits for the intended target audience with a minimum harm to others in the unintended audience"). Both standards have the added advantage that they rely on informal calculation of potential impacts and then "rational" judgment of the results of these calculations—procedures that would seem relatively less foreign to social marketing practitioners accustomed to formal evaluations in other parts of their work. This would leave us with a matrix which could be filled in either by subjective estimates by ethics officers, or an ethics committee, or estimated empirically on the basis of nominal group research or focus groups with relevant stakeholders and target audiences.

An Illustration

To illustrate the potential use of the SMEA matrix, let us consider the following situation.

A social marketing program is developing a tobacco prevention program for young women. One of the "price" variables identified during formative research was vanity. Young girls in this country were horrified to see (on a computer imaging system) the effect that tobacco would have on their skin, specifically premature wrinkling and age spots. Other pricing variables were discovered, too. The premature wrinkling "price" was rated the strongest of four prices by this target audience. The program planners hired a creative firm to develop a distribution strategy for a promotional campaign and concepts for the effort. The creative firm is recommending a partnership with two places frequented by women in the targeted age bracket: a cosmetics retailer and a prominent coffee house. They also recommend using *prevention of wrinkles* as a major benefit to smoking cessation, illustrated by way of computer imaging execution in print, posters, and TV ads. They plan to package tobacco cessation information and nicotine patch coupons with a wrinkle cream manufactured under the label of the cosmetics retailer.

The social marketing group is considering the creative firm's recommendation, but feels the need to assess the ethics of the recommended distribution and promotion strategies. The creative ad execution hits a nerve with them. They are a little offended by the blatant in-your-face tone of the ads that stress that having wrinkles makes you undesirable, out-of-touch, and behind the times. They are also concerned about the cross-product packaging of tobacco materials and discount coupons with wrinkle cream. Their ethical dilemmas center on a concern that the campaign will reinforce the country's cultural obsession with youth and beauty, and send an unintended negative message to all women. The execution might drive older and already wrinkled women into plastic surgery—or simply make them feel worse about their own appearance. At the same time, a strong reinforcement of the cultural value of youthful beauty might encourage younger women to try dangerous and unproven methods of retaining their youth.

While this situation may seem a bit exaggerated, one can easily see a scenario like this happening in the near future. Social marketers may feel that strong attacks are needed to attack a serious problem. This predilection may be reinforced when partnering with private sector marketers, like the cosmetics and coffee firms described above, who themselves often employ cutting edge messages and images. The value of a routine ethical assessment using a framework like the SMEA is that it makes it more likely that the social marketers will be protected from moving forward with a campaign that can have serious repercussions to the social marketer's image and its ability to craft future cause-related partnerships (Andreasen 1996).

Conducting an Ethical Assessment Using the SMEA

Table 7-3 presents a form that can be used to conduct a SMEA analysis. In the example just described, those conducting the ethical evaluation should then start by listing their ethical concern in the top left box. Intended and unintended audience segments should be listed in the first column. The second column should identify the parts of the marketing mix that each audience segment affected by. For example, young women who are the primary target audience will be exposed to the advertising, the cross-product packaging, and the in-store promotions. So elements of pricing, product, and distribution come into play for this target audience. (For the sake of brevity, pricing issues are not detailed in the matrix.) Once each marketing element has been briefly described for each segment in the matrix then data on the segment's perceived beliefs about costs and benefits of that marketing element need to be described briefly. These data should ideally come from empirical research with the target audience, including focus groups and key informant interviews. Expert judgment can be substituted for empirical research when the expert has current knowledge of the target audience and when resources are extremely low.

Up to this point the evaluators are merely observing and recording data in a systematic fashion. Ethical reasoning is the next step. The evaluators, possibly with the aid of an ethics consultant, must then assess the poten-

Table 7-3. Social Marketing Ethical Assessment Matrix

Program element description: A proposed advertising campaign aimed at young women will stress that smoking causes wrinkles and that having wrinkles makes a woman undesirable, out-of-touch, and behind the times. Cross-product packaging of tobacco cessation materials with discount coupons for wrinkle cream will reinforce this message

Stake-holder or Target Segment	Marketing Element (4 Ps)	Consequences (Benefit or Cost of marketing element to the target segment)		Ethical Reasoning Approaches and Rating Comments	
		Benefit	Cost	Utilitarian (greatest good for greatest number)	Enlightened Self-Interest (benefits to self and minimal harm to others)
Young women Aged 20–30 (intended audience)	**Product:** cross-product packaging	**Cross-product packaging will provide direct access to quitting materials. Shows that multiple organizations support the idea.**	**Wrinkle cream may increase in price to cover cost of the coupons.**	**A young woman would say:** multiple efforts increase the likelihood that society gains as fewer young women use tobacco and the impact on older women is not great.	**A young woman would say:** multiple efforts increase the likelihood that society gains as fewer young women use tobacco and the impact on older women is not great.
	Promotion: in-your-face ads	**Gives a very personal reason for quitting.**	**Makes growing old and wrinkled a scarier future.**	**A young woman would say:** strong messages are needed to achieve the effect on the most young women.	**A young woman would say:** strong messages are needed to achieve the effect on most young women. They can see that some older women would feel bad.

Table 7-3 (continued). Social Marketing Ethical Assessment Matrix

Stake-holder or Target Segment	Marketing Element (4 Ps)	Consequences (Benefit or Cost of marketing element to the target segment)		Ethical Reasoning Approaches and Rating Comments	
		Benefit	Cost	Utilitarian (greatest good for greatest number)	Enlightened Self-Interest (benefits to self and minimal harm to others)
Middle-aged women Aged 40–55 (unintended audience)	**Product:** cross-product packaging	**All efforts are needed to reduce tobacco use among young women. This will also reduce everyone's healthcare costs.**	**Younger women would feel more pressure to try other unproven and dangerous ways to prevent wrinkles.**	**A middle-aged woman would say:** society gains a major health benefit as fewer young women use tobacco and the implied demeaning of wrinkled women is "only psychological" and minor. So, having multiple supporters is good.	**A middle aged woman would say:** I support the role of multiple organizations in trying to achieve any social change.
	Promotion: in-your-face ads	**All efforts are needed to reduce tobacco use among young women. This will also reduce everyone's healthcare costs.**	**Younger women would feel more pressure to try other unproven and dangerous ways to prevent wrinkles.**	**A middle-aged woman would say:** society gains a major health benefit as fewer young women use tobacco and the implied demeaning of wrinkled women is "only psychological" and minor. So, having a strong message is good.	**A middle-aged woman would say:** strong messages make it most likely that the young women will change and I will get reduced health costs. But, I am disturbed that I am beginning to have wrinkles and the message makes me feel less desirable.

Table 7-3 (continued). Social Marketing Ethical Assessment Matrix

Stakeholder or Target Segment	Marketing Element (4 Ps)	Consequences (Benefit or Cost of marketing element to the target segment)		Ethical Reasoning Approaches and Rating Comments	
		Benefit	Cost	Utilitarian (greatest good for greatest number)	Enlightened Self-Interest (benefits to self and minimal harm to others)
Older women Aged over 55 (unintended audience)	**Product:** cross-product packaging	**All efforts are needed to reduce tobacco use among young women. This will also reduce everyone's healthcare costs**	**Young women will believe older women with wrinkles are less desirable.**	**An older woman would say:** it is good that multiple organizations are trying to get young women to quit smoking. This will reduce my health costs.	**An older woman would say:** I support the role of multiple organizations in trying to achieve any social change.
	Promotion: in-your-face ads	**All efforts are needed to reduce tobacco use among young women. This will also reduce everyone's healthcare costs**	**Women with wrinkles will be seen as inferior and pitiable.**	**An older woman would say:** strong messages are needed to influence the young but the damage to the psyche of wrinkled women is too great.	**An older woman would say:** this is very harmful to me, it makes me feel less desirable, almost a cosmetic burden on society.

tial impact on each audience using as a frame of reference either Utilitarianism or Enlightened Self-Interest. In Table 7-3, we have analyzed the impact of the marketing elements on three female segments using both standards. Within each ethical approach, the evaluators will need to consider how the decision to go forward with the campaign would be judged ethically by the target segment based on a specific view of ethics. The matrix allows the evaluators to see how someone who has a Utilitarian view of ethics might judge the decision to go forward with the marketing plans, and how that might or might not agree with the views of someone who believes that decisions should yield Enlightened Self-Interest. The advantage of analyzing the decision from multiple ethical perspectives is that it allows the social marketer to anticipate different reactions. Thus, if the social marketer opts for a Utilitarian standard that supports the planned campaign but the alternative standard recommends against it, the social marketer can expect criticism. In cases where the criticism might be potentially damaging, the social marketer may wish to add a modest public relations offensive to justify the action and deflect criticism.

In many cases, it may also be desirable to consider the perspectives of partners involved in the proposed campaign. In the example in Table 7-3, it would be important to know the views of the wrinkle-cream maker and retail store about the ethics of the campaign elements. The involvement of collaborators would be especially valuable if the assessment detects possible points of backlash. It is important that all parties present a uniform face to critics in delicate ethical situations.

Finally, it is important to emphasize that program managers must be prepared to act on the changes suggested by the ethical assessment. In the press of campaign time-pressures, managers may be tempted to ignore ethical red-flags or to neglect to prepare needed public relations countermeasures. Such actions could be very injurious to them and their organization. But it would also be damaging to the social marketing profession. If it is to mature and occupy a significant role in future social change programs, our profession cannot afford *not* to conduct ethical assessments and *act on them*. This chapter has presented both a segmentation plan and an ethical analysis framework that should make this outcome more likely.

Note

1. Davidson and Novelli (this volume) argue that private corporations also engage in social marketing.

References

Andreasen, Alan R. 1995. *Marketing Social Change*. San Francisco: Jossey-Bass.

———. 1996. "Profits for Nonprofits: Finding a Corporate Partner." *Harvard Business Review* (November-December): 47–59.

Bandura, Albert. 1992. "Exercise of Personal Agency Through the Self-efficacy Mechanism." In R. Schwarzer (ed.), *Self-Efficacy: Thought Control of Action*. Washington, D.C.: Hemisphere, 3–38.

Duke, Charles R., G. M. Pickett, L. Carlson, and S.J. Grove. 1993. "A Method for Evaluating the Ethics of Fear Appeals." *Journal of Public Policy and Marketing* 12(1): 120–129.

Kotler, Philip, and Alan R. Andreasen. 1996. *Strategic Marketing for Nonprofit Organizations*. 5th ed. Englewood Cliffs, N.J.: Prentice-Hall.

Laczniak, Gene. 1993. "Marketing Ethics: Onward Toward Greater Expectations." *Journal of Public Policy and Marketing* 12(1): 91–96.

Prochaska, J. O., and C. C. DiClemente. 1983. "Stages and Processes of Self-Change of Smoking: Toward and Integrative Model of Change." *Journal of Consulting and Clinical Psychology* 51: 390–395.

———. 1984. *The Transtheoretical Approach: Crossing the Traditional Boundaries of Therapy*. Homewood, IL: Dow Jones-Irwin.

Rothschild, Michael. 1999. "Carrots, Sticks, and Promises: A Conceptual Framework for the Management of Public Health and Social Issue Behaviors." *Journal of Marketing* 63: 24–37.

CHAPTER EIGHT

Teaching and Modeling Ethics in Social Marketing

Michael D. Basil

Concerns about ethical lapses in the 1980s have resulted in the topic of ethics being a large and growing literature within the area of general business (Reidenbach and Robin 1991). The growth of this area can be seen in both the large number of books in most college libraries, as well as in the appearance of a new journal in 1981 titled the *Journal of Business Ethics*. Meanwhile, the discussion of ethics necessarily constitutes a smaller literature in marketing, and an almost non-existent one in the area of social marketing. So if one is trying to find a book or article that specifically focuses on teaching ethics in social marketing, there is little previous work from which to draw. Despite a very small existing literature, there are a number of insights that can be brought to bear from other fields to the teaching of ethics in social marketing.

How do we go about teaching ethics in social marketing? This chapter looks at how people make ethical judgments, whether ethics can be taught, and the principles of ethics instruction in marketing and in other fields. It also includes some definitional issues and other relevant issues for the application of ethics to the field of social marketing, and a discussion of the application and modeling of ethics in the workplace. It can be argued that social marketing organizations ought to be some of the most ethical firms applying marketing techniques. Although doing the right thing and doing it in the right way is an admirable goal, one that we all can and should strive for, it is especially incumbent upon those whose existence implies a public trust.

How People Make Ethical Judgments

Where do people develop their ethical reasoning ability and their ethical standards? To what extent are these standards determined by one's present social environment, and to what extent are they rooted in people's basic value structures such as religion? There has been some previous research tracing the source of people's ethical standards, perhaps the most famous of these being Kohlberg's theory of moral reasoning (Maclagan 1998, 21–23).

In the area of business, Clark proposed that these ethical standards are rooted in religion (1966). He proposed and developed scales to measure what he believed to be the two indicators of religion-based perspectives: personal ethics and social responsibility (toward others). As he predicted, Clark found these two dimensions of ethics to be weakly related to one another. Kassarjian and Kassarjian (1996) then explored Clark's conclusions about religion being a predictor of values in a comparison of U.S. businessmen with MBA students in the U.S., Portugal, Denmark, and Armenia. Not only did they observe the religious differences that Clark had predicted, they also were able to compare trends in the student samples across time, and observed a declining acceptance of ethics and a greater focus on what is legal than what is ethical.

These studies show that ethics is at least partially socially determined. Thus, it would seem to be possible to encourage ethical behavior. But in what venue would this training occur? Clark and others (Shannon and Berl 1997; Stewart, Felicetti, and Kuehn 1996) have noted in a number of studies that the majority of survey respondents support the teaching of ethics in the classroom. So it appears that people believe the best approach to ethics is not mandatory religious training, or a governmental or legal mandate on behavior, but a voluntary call for individuals to develop their own understanding of ethics and hope that this will lead to a conscientious application of these ethical principles. To that end, the systematic teaching of ethics and the voluntary compliance with ethical principles appears to be the preferred strategy to encourage ethical behavior.

Before we recommend the teaching of ethics, though, we should ask whether ethical standards bear any relationship to people's thought processes or actual behavior outside the classroom. There is some evidence that they do. Hunt and Vitell developed a "general theory of marketing ethics" that they believe people apply in their ethical reasoning in marketing situations (1986). According to their theory, ethical judgments involve two separate steps. The first step is when people recognize an ethical dilemma or problem exists. The second step is where people evaluate their behavioral alternatives against some standards of behavior. Research investigating this theory supports the notion that people *do* carry out these steps in everyday situations. Managers, in fact, have been found to reward or punish ethical violations among their sales force (DeConinck and Lewis 1997).

The results of this research suggest that people's behavior does show some relationship with the ethical systems that they bring with them. In addition, managers expect employees to live and work according to ethical standards. Therefore, although people's religious background plays an important role in determining their ethical frames, so do social forces in their everyday life. Perhaps religious backgrounds sensitize people to the ethical issues around them.

Can Ethics Be Taught to Social Marketers?

The association between a person's religion and his or her ethical perspective has recently given way to debate on whether people's ethical principles are amenable to change in these other, more socially mandated means, such as classroom instruction. If religion shapes one's ethical values, can we realistically expect one or two classroom experiences to alter them?

One perspective is that people's ethics are based on values that are established *early* in life by parents and religious training. As a result, these theorists propose that a single ethics class simply *cannot* alter these values (McDonald and Donleavy 1995; Miller and Miller 1976; Parks 1993; Thurow 1987). The evidence they cite is that people's ethical standards are related to their religion (Clark 1966; Kassarjian and Kassarjian 1996). Therefore, they argue, it is not easily alterable. Because these roots are established so early, this perspective reasons that any effort devoted to these ends is bound to fail (Feldman and Thompson 1990).

There is another perspective, however. This perspective is that, despite the difficulty in changing a person's basic values, ethics instruction does offer potential benefits. Like religion, this includes sensitizing people to ethical issues, providing them with a framework to think about ethics, and giving them practice making ethical decisions. It is also hoped that instruction will provide a basis from which people can explore and build their own values systems later in life (Anderson 1997; Cragg 1997; Feldman and Thompson 1990; Oddo 1997). This latter position is consistent with developmental research showing that cognitive development is a necessary but not a sufficient condition for moral development to take place (Maclagan 1998, 22) or for lasting changes to result (Crandall, Parnell, and Shadow 1996).

Previous research tends to suggest that a single classroom experience usually is insufficient to influence people's ethical behavior or values (DeConinck and Lewis 1997). However, theories of cognitive science suggest that increased exposure to ethical issues *can* familiarize people and their thinking with these issues (Anderson 1997). Consistent with those predictions, sensitization to ethical issues does appear to be enhanced by classroom instruction (DeConinck and Lewis 1997). Research also shows that classroom-based consideration of ethics may increase cooperation with others (Cragg 1997).

One may conclude from this research that, although a single ethics class may not result in measurable changes in people's basic values, sensitization to ethical issues can occur. Further, it is possible that exposure to ethics in a number of courses increases the likelihood of instruction having an effect. As Hunt and Vitell's theory of marketing ethics implies, even if ethics training can only increase people's *sensitivity* to ethics, this should increase the likelihood that they will perceive an ethical dilemma or problem to exist in the first place (1986). In addition, however, ethical training should also provide people additional options when they consider their behavioral alternatives.

Teaching Ethics in Schools

The large number of visible ethical lapses in business in the 1980s prompted several studies on the reasons for this behavior. This research demonstrated that ethics was not taught often in business schools in the mid-1980s, thus resulting in calls for more ethics instruction (Murray 1987). These calls were met with an increased frequency of ethical instruction (Schoenfeldt, McDonald, and Youngblood 1991). Despite this increase in ethics instruction as part of today's curriculum, the majority of business students and the general public would like to have more coverage of ethics and ethical issues in college (Shannon and Berl 1997; Stewart, Felicetti, and Kuehn 1996).

But how do we go about teaching ethics in social marketing? The next few pages will outline a summary of the published literature on ethical instruction strategies. In general the literature suggests a three-step approach to ethics instruction. The first step develops a definition of "ethics" and ethical behavior. The second step introduces the student to some of the special ethical issues that arise in the domain of study, in this case, social marketing. Finally, the instructor offers a range of basic strategies from which to choose when faced with specific ethical dilemmas.

Definitional Issues in Ethics

One way to begin ethics instruction is with a definition of "ethical" (Buchholz 1989, Chapter 4). Although there are several approaches to this challenge (Brenkert and Smith, this volume), the two most frequently proposed ways of defining "ethical" are labeled *deontological* and *teleological* (Brady 1999).

Webster's dictionary claims *deontology* is derived from the Greek "deon," which means "obligation." This approach focuses on the *means* that people use. For example, are the means you are using fair and honest? This perspective can also be seen in Kant's categorical imperative—"treat others as you would want to be treated yourself." Clark believes that the roots of deontological ethics can be seen in "Catholic" or Jewish approaches (1966). These religions focus on equity, justice, and fairness. Catholic and Jewish traditions also emphasize a concern for the least able members of society, including the young and mentally disadvantaged (Oddo 1997, 295).

Teleology is the other perspective, the root being the Greek word "*telos*," which means "end." Not surprisingly, this approach focuses on the *ends* that are achieved. Clark (1966) saw the roots of the teleological approach in Weber's "Protestant" ethic that doesn't focus on others, but emphasizes the importance of individualism, the pursuit of profit, and hard work. This approach is closely related to utilitarianism—an approach that strives for the greatest good for the greatest number (Buchholz 1989, Chapter 4). This perspective can be seen whenever anyone applies a cost-benefit analysis or asks the question, "Do the ends justify the means?" Utilitarianism can be seen in the writings of David Hume, Adam Smith, and John Stuart Mill (Rawls 1971, 22–23). The teleological perspective can also be seen in the legal notion of *caveat emptor*—or "let the buyer beware." Instead of a special concern for the least able members of society, it argues that leaving each consumer to take care of him- or herself achieves the most good for the greatest number (i.e., there is no special effort to be "fair" to the disadvantaged).

With regard to contemporary examples, the deontological perspective can be seen when the government or legal system imposes paternalistic rules to protect vulnerable consumers from unethical marketing practices. The teleological approach can be seen whenever government or the legal system keeps its hands off and expects customers to make an "informed choice."

Although there are other ethical perspectives such as social contract theory (Dunfee, Smith, and Ross 1999; Smith, this volume), the two basic perspectives of deontology and teleology are both important and useful in any discussion of ethics (Brady 1999). Starting with this framework provides the ability to draw from philosophers and other theorists, including the classic philosophers. This terminology also makes it easier to shape discussions over whether something is "ethical" or not.

The deontological and teleological perspectives imply that managers, when faced with an ethical dilemma, can take one of two approaches. First, they can decide that only good means can achieve good ends (deontology). Alternatively, they can decide that the ends can justify the means (teleology) and not worry that much about how the ends are achieved. I propose that we use two different terms for these two distinct approaches. In the first case, when good means are used to achieve good ends, let's call this behavior "moral." In the second case, when the more Machiavellian strategy of using bad means to achieve good ends is chosen, let's call this behavior "justifiable."

There is a third possibility, also—the situation when people focus on the means, regardless of the ends that accrue, such as those who follow the dictum that "honesty is the best policy" regardless of the consequences. This case might be labeled "righteous." This approach is shown in Figure 8-1. Although the use of bad means to achieve bad ends fills up

		Ends	
		Good	Bad
Means	Good	*Moral*	*Righteous*
	Bad	*Justifiable*	?

Figure 8-1. Alternative Definitions of "Ethical"

the typology, thankfully I am not aware of any social marketing firms or other movements that advocate this approach.

By breaking down ethical behavior into specific terms, I believe the more specific terms can help reduce the confusion around the issue of ethics, especially in teaching ethics. As soon as you identify that you are "justifying" your behavior, it is easy to conclude that you may be using negative means to achieve positive ends.

Application to Social Marketing

When we first approach the field of social marketing one might think that teleological issues of justification for behavior may occur less frequently because of the lack of a profit motive (Spiller 1964). How can the ends justify the means if we no longer have profits as a justification for our behaviors? The truth is that these ethical concerns remain. Instead of profits, the ends that social marketers are trying to achieve typically are the health or pro-social behavior of people for the greater good. Andreasen has defined such work for the common good as "the application of commercial marketing techniques to the analysis, planning, execution of programs designed to influence the voluntary behavior of target audiences in order to improve their personal welfare and that of society" (Andreasen 1995, 7). So even though the profit motive may be removed, there are still important ends that may move us toward justification. In fact, because we are often personally invested in the ends we are trying to achieve, more weight may be given to these ends. Perhaps as a result, such a justification perspective can lead to a more paternalistic model of health care (Witte 1994). For example, if dollars are limited, as they always are, is it ethical to target a segment of the audience that is easy to change but not particularly vulnerable? If one tries to equalize the rates of incidence of a disease across various racial or socioeconomic segments, how does one justify not spending money on the people who are at lower risk, but still at risk?

As a result of the greater value on social marketing's ends, it is tempting to argue that the means that can be used to achieve those ends can be more questionable than those that can be used to market a commercial product. These means include the use of deception, coercion, and fear appeals. As Witte has rationalized, "one cannot not manipulate when communicating" (1994, 288). Often this manipulation takes the form of a paternalistic and teleological "the ends justify the means" approach. For example, how many people would hesitate at scaring people into a healthy behavior? Scare tactics are used regularly in social marketing. How often is their use questioned? What about deception? Would it be ethical to use a confusing message about the risk of an undesirable behavior if it left the impression with the audience that they were at higher risk, and were therefore more likely to engage in some protective behavior as a result? These situations are good starting points for discussion of ethical issues in the domain of social marketing.

An alternative approach to social marketing is to act morally, i.e., to seek good ends with only good means. It has been argued (Rothschild 1999) that a straight education model would fit this definition. Because education typically relies on teaching and other forms sharing factual information (such as health education campaigns), compliance is entirely a voluntary free choice. So long as the information is factual, there may be no teleological ethical concerns. Witte argues, however, that the facts one chooses to communicate as well as the way one assembles those facts can manipulate an audience (1994). Further, if we generally know that educational programs are limited in effectiveness, yet we knowingly use them, this may raise deontological utilitarian considerations.

When one considers social marketing challenges in developing countries (Brenkert, this volume), important issues of justification arise. Some (generally outside the field of social marketing) argue that social marketing in developing countries exhibits a hegemonistic approach rife with cultural imperialism where a more powerful (or affluent) society imposes its values and beliefs on another. This would raise issues with programs that attempt to "manage" other people or cultures into a Western, industrialized, or perhaps democratic model.

Basic Approaches to Resolving Ethical Dilemmas

There are at least four possible pedagogical strategies that can be used to teach students how to resolve ethical dilemmas. These, however, are not mutually exclusive. One is a principle-based approach that focuses on the teaching of deontological principles of behavior (Reich 1988, 16–19). The second is a dilemma or "quandary-based" approach where people are given exposure to and practice with facing ambiguous situations where there is no clearly ethical solution (Reich 1988, 19). The third is a more reflective approach, where previous situations the person has encountered are discussed (Oddo 1997; Schaupp, Ponzurick, and Schaupp 1992; Smith and VanDoren 1989). The fourth is a modeling approach where students learn how admired individuals faced similar ethical quandaries in the past and how they resolved them (Apostolou and Apostolou 1997).

A possible starting point for the discussion of the principle-based approach to ethics is to make use of professional codes of conduct (Oddo 1997), such as those of the American Marketing Association or the American Advertising Federation. Students can then be asked to discuss "what are the underlying deontological principles here?" Further information on how to examine codes to discover these principles can be found in earlier work (McDonald and Donleavy 1995; Sirgy 1999). Even outside the classroom, discussion of these principles has been seen as a valuable step in the development of guidelines for ethical conduct, both inside and outside the classroom, especially in generating a better understanding of the principles and rules of conduct (Kurtz 1999; Malhotra and Miller 1999).

One of the biggest difficulties with the principles-based approach is deciding what those principles should be (Reich 1988, 16–18). In a Western tradition, we may believe that certain individual rights such as honesty, autonomy, fairness, and the Hippocratic oath to "do no harm" are universal (Rothschild, this volume; Sirgy 1999). This may not be the case in other cultures, however. It may also not always be the case in our culture. For some, the Hippocratic oath requires the physician to do what is in the patient's best interest even if it means deceiving the patient (Reich 1988, 17). Thus, the ends of achieving health may be valued above the means of truth. One exercise that may be useful is to provide students with one or two ethical codes, ask them to identify the underlying deontological principles.

Perhaps the most common approach to teaching ethics in classes and textbooks is through practice in focusing on ambiguous or "quandary" situations (Reich 1988). Our lives are filled with situations where ethical principles are in conflict; for example, when someone asks you whether you like their new purchase or hairstyle. There are, however, two major problems with this approach—the fact that students begin with very different perspectives and the fact that a focus on ambiguous situations tends to transmit the message that one can never know what is right and what is wrong (McDonald and Donleavy 1995, pp. 845–846).

Without clarifying the principles of what is "ethical" (as in the previous discussion), people often fail to understand each other's perspectives. For example, this often occurs in classes mixing business and non-business students. Marketing and other business students tend to approach discussions of ethics from a more teleological (justifiable) and utilitarian perspective. They believe in a rational marketplace and that there are great economic benefits that accompany business activity where profits mean a return for investors (Spiller 1964). This perspective usually leads to an unabashed "let the buyer beware" perspective and an "ends justify the means" *teleological (justifiable)* approach. Meanwhile, health education and communication students often approach ethical questions with a concern for the most vulnerable populations, and a greater level of paternalism, a perspective often echoed in non-business textbooks. The "practice" approach to ethical training, therefore, will be most effective when the discussions move beyond definitions of ethics, especially when the class mixes business and public health students.

A problem with this focus on ethically ambiguous situations, however, is that it tends to result in students often feeling that there is no absolute right or wrong, but that they live in a world of moral relativism. This can perhaps be mitigated by starting with considerations of what is appropriate or inappropriate, which will help students and future social marketers establish primary principles of what is deontologically (morally) good or bad. The discussion could then move on to more ambiguous situations *once those principles are established* (Reich 1988). Therefore, there are good reasons to begin with an attempt to establish a deontological principle-based approach before moving onto discussions of teleological situations (McDonald and Donleavy 1995). Thus, in our classroom scenario, after ethical principles are established students should also try to formulate scenarios in which these basic principles may be challenged by both theoretical and practical ends that individuals may be trying to achieve.

A third approach that could follow the discussion of ethical quandaries is to use more real-world experiential ethics instruction, where people focus on ethical situations and quandaries they have personally faced (Oddo 1997; Schaupp, Ponzurick, and Schaupp 1992; Smith and Van-Doren 1989). There is a theoretical argument in cognitive psychology that personally experienced real-world situations should lead to the most learning (Anderson 1997). For example, students can be asked about ethical issues they have faced in the past. Role playing may also help them take these perspectives, for example by asking them about the promotion of tobacco and then asking whether this fits with the American Marketing Association's code of ethics, and if not, why it is acceptable. In the classroom scenario, this could be best achieved by sharing some real world quandaries that you or others have faced and discuss possible ways to resolve those quandaries. Students with real-world experience could be encouraged to bring in their own experiences.

One final approach to the teaching of ethics involves a discussion of what exemplary people have done. Apostolou and Apostolou propose that one teach ethics by focusing on a discussion of folk "heroes" (1997). My own research on the importance of sports heroes (Basil and Brown 1997) suggests that identification with a hero's decision can be a powerful motivator. Of course, this may require the selection of heroes who have chosen the ethical course. Compiling a list of heroes, their quandaries, and how they resolved them would be very useful in the classroom.

Although the jury may still be out concerning the single *best* approach to teaching ethics, in the interim, perhaps the best strategy is to make use of all four of these approaches or, at least, those with which you are comfortable (Oddo 1997). Whatever strategy is devised, ethics instruction should make sure to help people identify ethical problems and provide them with practice resolving these dilemmas.

Ethics in the Workplace

While the classroom is really an environment in which people can be sensitized to ethics issues, these dilemmas actually occur for social marketers in the workplace. A number of people believe that teaching ethics in the classroom sensitizes people to ethical issues and leads to more ethical decisions in the future (Anderson 1997; Cragg 1997; DeConinck and Lewis 1997; Feldman and Thompson 1990; Maclagan 1998; Oddo 1997). Yet if we do not translate ethics from the classroom to the "real world," we are bound to fail (Malhotra and Miller 1999). For example, how many ethical violations occur by people who were well instructed in ethics, but who observed their colleagues or superiors engaging in less than ethical conduct and copied these examples? Do we believe that the tobacco industry is only staffed with people who did not have an ethics course in college?

There is a considerable body of research that suggests that, although instruction in theories and principles is one way of learning, modeling of behaviors in the real world is often a more powerful tool for shaping behavior (Bandura 1996). But what if real world models represent a standard of ethics *below* that taught in the classroom, what does the person do? In the workplace, paychecks, and concerns about job security can have a coercive power such that people may ignore their ethical concerns rather than risk their livelihood and family well-being. This undoubtedly explains people's employment with the tobacco industry and other industries with questionable ethics. This is also likely a risk for social marketers where one may be tempted to use questionable means to achieve a presumed greater social good. For such individuals, such contradictory demands from interested stakeholders may be the source of considerable stress (Malhotra and Miller 1999).

Codes of Ethics

One strategy that seeks to encourage high standards of ethical conduct in the workplace is for each agency engaging in social marketing to establish a code of ethics that they share with current and future employees in their own organizations (Laczniak and Murphy 1986). Written codes of ethics clearly help to build awareness of the importance of ethics in the workplace (Weaver, Trevino, and Cochran 1999). Because evidence suggests that people's perceptions of their organization's ethical environment is significantly related to the quality of their ethical decisions (Sims and Keon 1999), this is an important foundation for creating an ethical organization.

Procedures for creating a code of ethics have previously been discussed by Lacnzniak and Murphy (1985) and later by Buchholz (1989). Generally, the approach begins with the establishment of a committee to develop real and workable ethical standards. Of course, committee participation increases the likelihood of employee "ownership" of these codes. On completing its work, the committee can then be charged with overseeing the climate and ethical behavior of the organization.

Another approach to the development of ethics codes is to work toward the development of industry-wide standards. This approach has the advantage of reassuring managers that behaving ethically will not put the organization at a disadvantage relative to the competition. An example of such a code is the American Marketing Association's code of ethics.

Encouraging Discussion and Debate

Awareness or even adoption of ethical codes by organizations and their members, though important, does not ensure implementation of these policies (Weaver, Trevino, and Cochran 1999). Thus, in addition to simply developing and communicating ethical codes, social marketing firms should also encourage discussions of ethical issues when they arise. One opportunity for ethical discussions is in the preparation of program strategy and tactics. Whenever these may have ethical connotations, management should encourage skepticism and discussion of alternatives. Both government and non-governmental agencies would likely find more trust in their programs, and perhaps less potential for criticism if, for each project, members of their staffs were routinely encouraged to ask, "Is this the most ethical way to go about promoting this end?"

Another venue for ethics discussions is through occasional—such as monthly—seminars. Providing time for some employees to prepare for these seminars, and for other employees to attend, is a clear message that the organization takes ethics seriously. Instruction in the company's ethical codes is a potential starting point for these seminars. This could be followed by questions and other open-ended discussions of ethical standards and ethical dilemmas faced in the workplace.

Modeling Ethical Behavior

Finally, it is important that employers and leaders *model* high ethical standards and pay close attention to ethical behavior by their employees. Kelman (1961) has shown that the process of identification and internalization is a powerful means of teaching behaviors. Kelman proposed that there are three ways in which behavior change occurs. The first of these, compliance, occurs when someone has power over you. The second form of behavior change, identification, occurs when a person likes or wants to be like someone else. The third process, internalization, occurs when a person adopts basic values of another such as in successful parenting. Kelman notes that, while people may comply with ethical norms in a manager's presence, ethical behaviors will be longer lasting when employees are driven by a desire to be like an ethical manager, or when the person internalizes the value of being ethical. A similar but newer approach is Reidenbach and Robin's proposed model of corporate moral development in which companies move beyond simply giving legalistic lip service to ethics codes, becomes responsive, leading finally to the creation of an ethical organization (1991). They do this through taking issues of ethics to heart and then acting in the appropriate manner with company goals, policy, boards, and discussions.

Conclusions

In the application of ethics into a new realm—social marketing—the basic issues and principles remain the same: how to resolve conflicts about the *ends* and the *means*. Careful review of the literature makes clear that there are varying definitions of "ethical," but that each provides a framework for ethical judgments. To give students and potential social marketers facility in working with these frameworks, a basic understanding of these principles is required. Definitions are a wonderful starting point for ethics instruction. Consideration of the unique circumstances of social marketing is also likely to provide an important sensitization to potential social marketers (see Kirby, this volume). There are four basic approaches that can be followed in teaching ethics in the classroom: teaching principles, presenting quandaries, using personal experiences involving ethical dilemmas, and analyzing the behavior of real exemplars.

Classroom education alone, however, is not enough to ensure ethical behavior in the social marketing workplace. Codes of ethics must be put in place at both the firm and industry level to keep social marketing firms closer to the straight and narrow. In addition, regular discussions of ethical issues and decisions should be encouraged, and high standards of ethical conduct should be modeled by social marketers and other leaders.

References

Anderson, James (1997). What cognitive science tells us about ethics and the teaching of ethics. *Journal of Business Ethics, 16*, 279–291.

Apostolou, Barbara, Apostolou, Nicholas (1997). Viewpoint: Heroes as a context for teaching ethics. *Journal of Education for Business, 73*, 121–122.

Bandura, Albert (1996). *Social Foundations of Thought and Action: A Social-Cognitive Theory.* Englewood Cliffs, NJ: Prentice-Hall.

Basil, Michael D. and Brown, William J. (1997). Marketing AIDS prevention: The differential impact hypothesis versus identification effects. *Journal of Consumer Psychology, 6*, 389–411.

Brady, F. Neil (1999). A systematic approach to teaching business ethics. *Journal of Business Ethics, 19*, 309–318.

Buchholz, Rogene A. (1989). *Fundamental concepts and problems in business ethics.* Englewood Cliffs, NJ: Prentice Hall.

Clark, J. W. (1966). *Religion and the moral standard of American businessmen.* Cincinnati: South-Western Publishing.

Cragg, Wesley (1997). Teaching business ethics: The ethics in business and in business education. *Journal of Business Ethics, 16*, 231–245.

Crandall, William "Rick," Parnell, John A., and Shadow, Susan (1996). Does teaching business ethics really make a difference? A survey of practicing managers. *Central Business Review, 15*(1), 16–20.

DeConinck, James B., and Lewis, William F. (1997). The influence of deontological and teleological considerations and ethical climate on managers' intentions to reward or punish sales force behavior. *Journal of Business Ethics, 16*, 497–503.

Dunfee, Thomas W., Smith, N. Craig., and Ross, William T., Jr. (1999). "Social contracts and marketing ethics." *Journal of Marketing, 63*, 14–32.

Feldman, Howard D., and Thompson, Richard C. (1990). Teaching business ethics: A challenge for business educators in the 1990s. *Journal of Business Ethics, 12*(2), 10–22.

Hunt, S., and Vitell, S. A. (1986). A general theory of ethics. *Journal of Macromarketing, 6*, 5–16.

Kassarjian, H. H., and Kassarjian, T. M. (1996). Values and ethical principles of Portuguese, Armenian, Danish, and American MBA students: A comparative analysis. Paper presented to the Western Marketing Educator's Conference.

Kelman, H. C. (1961). Processes of opinion change. *Public Opinion Quarterly, 25*, 57–78.

Kurtz, D. L. (1999). Commentary on "Social responsibility and the marketing educator: A discussion document. *Journal of Business Ethics, 19*, 207–209.

Laczniak, Gene R., and Murphy, Patrick E. (1986). *Marketing ethics: Guidelines for managers*. Lexington, MA: Lexington Books.

Maclagan, Patrick (1998). *Management and morality: A developmental perspective*. Thousand Oaks, CA: Sage.

Malhotra, Naresh, K., and Miller, Gina L. (1999). Social responsibility and the marketing educator: A focus on stakeholders, ethical theories, and related codes of ethics. *Journal of Business Ethics, 19*, 211–224.

McDonald, Gael M., and Donleavy, Gabriel D. (1995). Objections to the teaching of business ethics. *Journal of Business Ethics, 14*, 839–853.

Miller, Mary S., and Miller, Edward A. (1976). It's too late for ethics courses in business schools. *Business and Society Review*, 40.

Murray, Thomas J. (1987, April). Can business schools teach ethics? *Business Month*, 24–26.

Oddo, Alfonso R. (1997). A framework for teaching business ethics. *Journal of Business Ethics, 16*, 293–297.

Parks, Sharon D. (1993). Is it too late? Young adults and the formation of professional ethics. In T. R. Piper, M. C. Gentile, and S. D. Parks (Eds.) *Can ethics be taught? Perspectives, challenges, and approaches from the Harvard Business School.* Boston: Harvard Business School.

Rawls, John (1971). *A theory of justice*. Boston: Harvard University Press.

Reich, Warren T. (1988). Experiential ethics as a foundation for dialogue between health communication and health-care ethics. *Journal of Applied Communication Research, 16*, 16–28.

Reidenbach, R. Eric, and Robin, Donald P. (1991). A conceptual model of corporate moral development. *Journal of Business Ethics, 10*, 273–284.

Rothschild, Michael. (1999). Carrots, sticks and promises: A conceptual framework for the management of public health an social issue behaviors. *Journal of Marketing, 63*, 24–37.

Schaupp, Dietrich L., Ponzurick, Thomas G., and Schaupp, Frederick W. (1992). The right choice: A case method for teaching ethics in marketing. *Journal of Business Ethics, 14*(1), 1–11.

Schoenfeldt, Lyle F., McDonald, Don M., and Youngblood, Stuart A. (1991). The teaching to business ethics: A survey of AACSB member schools. *Journal of Business Ethics, 10*, 237–241.

Shannon, Richard J., and Berl, Robert L. (1997). Are we teaching ethics in marketing?: A survey of students' attitudes and perceptions. *Journal of Business Ethics, 16*, 1059–1075.

Sims, Randi L., and Keon, Thomas L. (1999). Determinants of ethical decision making. *Journal of Business Ethics, 19*, 393–401.

Sirgy, M. Joseph (1999). Social responsibility and the Marketing Educator: A discussion document. *Journal of Business Ethics, 19*, 193–206.

Smith, Louise W., and VanDoren, Doris C. (1989). Teaching marketing ethics: A personal approach. *Journal of Business Ethics, 11*(2), 3–10.

Spiller, Earl A. Jr. (1964). Profits and ethics: Colleagues or adversaries? In J. W. Towle (Ed.), *Ethics and standards in American business*. Boston: Houghton Mifflin, 50–59.

Stewart, Karen, Felicetti, Linda, and Kuehn, Scott (1996). The attitudes of business majors toward the teaching of business ethics. *Journal of Business Ethics, 15*, 913–918.

Thurow, L. (1987). Ethics doesn't start in business schools. *New York Times*, June 14, Section 4, p. 25.

Weaver, Gary R., Trevino, Linda Klebe, and Cochran, Philip L. (1999). Corporate ethics in the mid-1990's: An empirical study of the Fortune 1000. *Journal of Business Ethics, 18*, 283–294.

Witte, Kim (1994). The manipulative nature of health communication research: Ethical issues and guidelines. *American Behavioral Scientist, 38*, 285–293.

Contributors

Alan R. Andreasen is professor of marketing at The McDonough School of Business at Georgetown University. He is also interim executive director of the Social Marketing Institute.

Michael D. Basil is associate professor of marketing in the Faculty of Management at the University of Lethbridge.

George G. Brenkert is a professor at The McDonough School of Business at Georgetown University and editor-in-chief of *Business Ethics Quarterly.*

D. Kirk Davidson is associate professor and chair of the Department of Business, Accounting, and Economics at Mount Saint Mary's College.

Minette E. Drumwright is assistant professor of advertising in the College of Communications at the University of Texas at Austin.

Susan D. Kirby is senior marketing and communication analyst at the Centers for Disease Control and Prevention.

William D. Novelli is associate executive director of AARP.

Michael L. Rothschild is emeritus professor of marketing at the University of Wisconsin.

N. Craig Smith is associate professor of marketing at the London Business School.

William A. Smith is executive vice president at the Academy for Educational Development.

Index